SEXUAL TEENS, SEXUAL MEDIA

Investigating Media's Influence
on Adolescent Sexuality

LEA's COMMUNICATION SERIES
Jennings Bryant / Dolf Zillmann, General Editors

For a complete list of other titles in LEA's Communication Series, please contact Lawrence Erlbaum Associates, Publishers

SEXUAL TEENS, SEXUAL MEDIA
Investigating Media's Influence on Adolescent Sexuality

Edited by

Jane D. Brown
University of North Carolina–Chapel Hill

Jeanne R. Steele
University of St. Thomas

Kim Walsh-Childers
University of Florida

 LAWRENCE ERLBAUM ASSOCIATES, PUBLISHERS
2002   Mahwah, New Jersey   London

#45505953

Lawrence Erlbaum Associates, Inc., Publishers
10 Industrial Avenue
Mahwah, New Jersey 07430

Cover design by Kathryn Houghtaling Lacey

Library of Congress Cataloging-in-Publication Data

Sexual teens, sexual media : investigating media's influence on adolescent sexuality /
edited by Jane D. Brown, Jeanne R. Steele, Kim Walsh-Childers.
    p.   cm. — (LEA's communication series)
    Includes bibliographical references and index.
    ISBN 0-8058-3489-3 (cloth : alk. paper) — ISBN 0-8058-3490-7 (pbk. : alk. paper)
1. Mass media and teenagers. 2. Mass media and sex. 3. Sex in mass media.
  4. Teenagers—Sexual behavior. I. Brown, Jane D. (Jane Delano), 1950–
  II. Steele, Jeanne R. III. Walsh-Childers, Kim. IV. Series.
  HQ799.2.M35 S49 2002
    302.23′0835—dc21   00-067763
                                                                        CIP

Books published by Lawrence Erlbaum Associates are printed on acid-free paper,
and their bindings are chosen for strength and durability.

Printed in the United States of America
10 9 8 7 6 5 4 3 2 1

Contents

Contributors

Jeffrey Jensen Arnett, PhD, is visiting associate professor in the department of Human Development at the University of Maryland. He is the author of a book about heavy metal fans, *Metalheads: Heavy Metal Music and Adolescent Alienation* (1996, Westview Press), and the textbook *Adolescence and Emerging Adulthood: A Cultural Approach* (2001, Prentice-Hall). Until 1988, he was associate professor in the department of Human Development and Family Studies at the University of Missouri, and has been a visiting scholar at Stanford University and the University of Michigan. Recent research focuses on emerging adulthood, the period between ages 18 and 25, commonly characterized by exploration and instability in industrialized societies.

Jane D. Brown, PhD, is James L. Knight Professor of Journalism and Mass Communication at the University of North Carolina in Chapel Hill. Her research has focused on how adolescents use and are affected by the mass media. She studies a variety of media that adolescents use, including music videos, magazines and televised public service announcements, as well as health-related issues, including adolescent aggressive behavior, cigarette smoking, alcohol use, and sexuality. Along with this volume, Brown co-edited the books *The Media, Social Science and Social Policy for Children*, and *Media, Sex and the Adolescent*.

Kirstie M. Cope-Farrar is a doctoral candidate in communication at the University of California, Santa Barbara. Her primary research interest is in the area of mass media and adolescent socialization. She is especially interested in the effects of televised depictions of risky health behaviors (e.g., "unsafe sex," alcohol abuse) on adolescent risk taking.

Adena Cytron-Walker graduated with a bachelor's degree in psychology from the University of Michigan in 1998. She received her masters' degree in Social Justice Education from the University of Massachusetts–Amherst in 2001.

Alyse Gotthoffer, PhD, is an assistant professor of Advertising and Public Relations in the School of Communication at the University of Miami, Coral Gables, Florida. Her research centers on health communication.

Benjamin Gorvine is a doctoral student in developmental and clinical psychology at the University of Michigan. His research interests span the impact of fathers on young children's socioemotional development, infant–parent attachment, and the role of television in children's and adolescents' emerging understandings of sexuality.

Bradley S. Greenberg, PhD, is University Distinguished Professor of Communication and Telecommunication at Michigan State University, where he teaches the social influences of the mass media. Current research focuses on media portrayals of male and female body images, and parenting practices regarding young people's access to mass media. Greenberg's seminal work on analyzing sexual content in movies and on television and effects of the content have been widely emulated.

Linda Hofschire is a doctoral student in the Mass Media program at Michigan State University. Her research interests include the effects of traditional and new media on adolescents, particularly in the areas of sexuality and body image.

L. Monique Ward, PhD, is an assistant professor of Developmental Psychology at the University of Michigan. Her research examines the dynamics of gender role development and sexual socialization, focusing on how children and adolescents interpret, use, and are affected by the messages they receive about male–female relationships from their parents, peers, and the media. Much of her current work examines contributions of television, in particular, to the sexual socialization of American youth.

Carol J. Pardun, PhD, is an associate professor in the School of Journalism and Mass Communication at the University of North Carolina, Chapel Hill. She is editor of *Mass Communication and Society*.

Carolyn Ringer Lepre, PhD, is an assistant professor in the department of Journalism at California State University, Chicago, where she teaches courses on newspaper and magazine writing and editing. Her research interests are health communication, journalism education, and media effects. Professional experience includes work on the editorial staff of *Martha Stewart Living* and *Modern Bride* magazines, and freelance writing.

Sandi W. Smith, PhD, is a professor in the department of Communication at Michigan State University where she teaches courses in interpersonal communication, relational persuasion in the health context, memorable messages as guides to behavior, and interpersonal communication on talk shows. She and Bradley Greenberg have published articles on talk shows in *Communication Studies* and the *Journal of Broadcasting and Electronic Media*, among others.

Jeanne Steele, PhD, began her research on teens and the media as a doctoral student at the University of North Carolina, Chapel Hill. She continued her work at Ohio University where she and Wray teamed up to research zines. Now she shares what she has learned about adolescents' media practices with journalism students at the University of St. Thomas. Steele is interested in cross-cultural communications and public health, and next plans to explore where media fits into the lives of immigrant teens and their families.

Susannah Stern, PhD, is a visiting assistant professor in the Communications Department at Boston College. Her research interests include gender, electronic media uses and effects, and media literacy.

Debbie Treise, PhD, is an associate professor in the department of Advertising, College of Journalism and Communications, University of Florida. Her research centers on health and science communication. She has served as principle investigator on a National Aeronautics and Space Administration (NASA) grant for the past five years investigating science communication.

Kim Walsh-Childers, PhD, is an associate professor of journalism at the University of Florida. She teaches journalism and mass communication ethics classes and a seminar on mass media and health. Her research focuses on health news coverage and mass media effects on health and health policy.

Jennifer Wray graduated cum laude from Ohio University's Honors Tutorial College with a bachelor's degree in magazine journalism in June 2000. Her work has been published in *All-States Sports*, a magazine devoted to high school athletes. An avid zine reader, Wray hopes to publish her own zine someday.

Preface

Young people today are faced with often conflicting and confusing messages about how they are supposed to behave sexually. Adults and socializing institutions in the culture are not in agreement about when, what, or where youth should learn about sexuality. Although we might hope that parents would be the primary source of sexual guidance for their children, parents often find it difficult to present timely and clear expectations, or even accurate information. Many parents want schools to provide sexuality education, but schools are increasingly reluctant to do more than say "Wait until marriage." And many religious institutions still maintain that sex outside heterosexual marriage is a sin. In contrast, the mass media—television, movies, magazines, music, the Internet—are not at all reticent, frequently portraying sexual behavior as riveting, central in everyday life, and emotionally and physically risk free.

Many adults haven't liked what they've seen about sex in the media, but they don't agree about what should be done about it, either. Religious leaders, parents, and some politicians, claiming that the media encourage youth to be sexually active before they are ready and without the sanction of marriage, want the media to clean up their acts. Health advocates argue that if we're going to have sex in the media, at the least we should show the risks and responsibilities too. Politicians threaten further regulation if program ratings and content blocking devices such as the V-chip aren't sufficient. But media producers say, "Leave us alone; we're exercising our constitutional rights." Advertising executives believe that sex sells and don't want to give up their potential advantage in a highly competitive marketplace.

Remarkably, despite the consternation in many quarters, relatively little scientific research exists on how sexual content in the media affects teens (Huston, Wartella, & Donnerstein, 1998). One reason is that many schools, the places where adolescents are easiest to find, are reluctant to let researchers in. Federal and state agencies have been leery, too, afraid that conservative legislators will cut off funding if they sponsor research that requires talking with youth about sex. As a consequence, nonprofit, nongovernmental organizations have had to take on most of the work.

The Henry J. Kaiser Family Foundation has been one of the most active, commissioning a number of studies on both sexual content in the media and youths' response to that content. Since 1995, the foundation has worked with a number of researchers to conduct national surveys, focus groups, and several content analyses in an effort to find out what kinds of sexual messages children and teenagers are being exposed to through the media—especially on television and in magazines—and how they are reacting. The results of the Kaiser studies have been disseminated through their active media relations and reprint program (see their Web site: www.kff. org), but they have never been pulled together in one place before.

For this book, we asked a number of the authors of the Kaiser studies and others who have been doing innovative research on the media's sexual content and adolescents to put together their most interesting results. We asked them to think about sexuality broadly, to include evidence not only about physical sex acts, but also evidence about the role the media play in the development of gender roles, sexual orientations, standards of beauty, and courtship and relationship norms.

Each of the chapters in this book contributes an intriguing look at what's currently in the media that teens are most likely attending to, or some insight into how teens are understanding and applying what the media present about sex and sexuality. The studies take a number of different methodological approaches, include a diversity of adolescent audiences, and deal with a wide variety of media content ranging from teens' favorite TV programs (section 1), to magazines (section 2), and movies, music, and teen girls' web pages (section 3). Taken as a whole, the chapters paint a picture that suggests we should be paying attention to the media as important players in adolescents' sexual lives.

We encouraged the authors to write as accessibly as possible so audiences not familiar with some of the research methods could understand and use these findings. We are interested in having our culture's ongoing debate about what is appropriate sexual media content informed by what these studies show. We believe it is preferable that public policy and interventions designed to help youth be based on systematically gathered and analyzed evidence. Too often, conclusions about the effects of the media seem to be based on conjecture or on what someone may have seen once when he walked by his son or daughter watching an especially outrageous music video.

We are motivated, too, by our hope that all children may live sexually healthy lives in the future. We hope that our children will not have to be as confused as we were by our sexual feelings and the media that said "Yes," our parents who said "No, wait until marriage," and our friends who said "Yes, but watch your reputation!" We hope that our children will not be pressured by the media or anyone else to have sex before they are ready and that they may grow up with a less narrowly defined set of sexual expectations, which will allow them to explore the pleasures of their sexuality safely within loving relationships when they are ready.

We embrace the approach that the National Commission on Adolescent Sexual Health took in its consensus statement, which has been endorsed by 48 national organizations. The commission, assuming that a majority of adolescents will become involved in sexual relationships, argued that adolescents should receive support and education for developing the skills they need to evaluate their readiness for sexual relationships. The commission also defined the characteristics of "responsible adolescent intimate relationships," saying that such relationships, "like those of adults, should be based on shared personal values, and be: consensual, nonexploitative, honest, pleasurable, and protected against unintended pregnancies and sexually transmitted diseases, if any type of intercourse occurs" (Haffner, 1995, p. 4).

ACKNOWLEDGMENTS

We'd like to thank the Kaiser Family Foundation for their interest in and support of research in this area. We appreciate that most of these studies would not have been done if the Kaiser Foundation had not made the entertainment media and reproductive health a high priority. We are grateful to each of the authors who generously agreed to take another look at their data and write chapters that might make a difference in the sexual lives of adolescents in the future.

Jane Brown thanks her weekly writing group—inspiring women who insist on clear, meaningful writing—her husband, Jim, who's been willing to listen about adolescent sexuality for 20 years; her son Alex, who told her what was really going on while he was an adolescent; and her daughter Lily, who at 7 years old wanted to know what "sexy" was after seeing the Spice Girls' movie.

Jeanne Steele says thank you to Jane for introducing her to the rewards of doing research on adolescent sexuality; her daughters, Missy, now 23, Katie, 21, and Kristin, 17, for understanding why their mother would give up "a good-paying job" to teach and do research on teens and sex; and her students and study teenagers from whom she has learned so much.

Kim Walsh-Childers thanks her husband Hoyt for all the extra hours of solo parenting he did so she could work on this book, and her sons, Ian, 3, and Aidan, $1\frac{1}{2}$, for constantly reminding her that play is important work too.

—*Jane D. Brown*
—*Jeanne R. Steele*
—*Kim Walsh-Childers*

REFERENCES

Haffner, D. (Ed.). (1995). *Facing facts: Sexual health for America's adolescents*. New York: SIECUS.
Huston, A. C., Wartella, E., & Donnerstein, E. (1998). *Measuring the effects of sexual content in the media: A report to the Kaiser Family Foundation*. Menlo Park, CA: The Henry J. Kaiser Family Foundation.

1

Introduction and Overview

Jane D. Brown
University of North Carolina–Chapell Hill

Jeanne R. Steele
University of St. Thomas

Kim Walsh-Childers
University of Florida

ZITS

Reprinted with special permission King Features Syndicate

The idea of adolescence is a relatively recent phenomenon and to some extent peculiarly American. In some cultures this transitional stage between childhood and adulthood is brief—a child's physical "coming of age" is acknowledged as readiness to assume the adult roles of reproduction, parenting, and work. But in the United States, adolescence has become a relatively long life stage—generally marked at the beginning by both biological changes (a growth spurt and development of secondary sexual characteristics, e.g., breast, penis, and pubic hair growth) and by social factors (increasing independence from parents and increasing influence of peers). As one commentator put it: "America invented a space between the child's ties to family and the adult's re-creation of family. Within this space, America's teenagers are supposed to innovate, to improvise, to rebel, to turn around three times before they harden into adults" (Rodriguez, 1999, p. 91).

WHAT IS ADOLESCENCE?

Developmental psychologists typically divide the life stage of adolescence into three overlapping periods: *early* (8 to 13 years old for girls, 11 to 15 for boys), *middle* (13 to 16 for girls, 14 to 17 for boys), and *late* (16 and older for girls and 17 and older for boys (Haffner, 1995). The stages are marked by physical, cognitive, social, and psychological development. An *early adolescent*, just beginning to adjust to the physical changes of puberty, may be especially concerned about his or her body image and will begin to concentrate on relationships with peers. The average age of first menarche has been dropping, so that today the average age for girls is $12\frac{1}{2}$ years old; in 1900, the average age was 15 (Herman-Giddens et al., 1997). Some marketers have divided this early stage even further, focusing on what they call "tweens"—youth who are between childhood and adolescence, typically 8- to 11-year-olds who are beginning biological development and may be enticed by the allures of adolescence (Kantrowitz & Wingert, 1999).

Middle adolescents typically are attaining increased independence from their families, paying more attention to their peers, and experimenting with relationships and sexual behaviors. *Late adolescents,* in general, are becoming more secure about their bodies, gender roles, and sexual orientation and have developed greater intimacy skills as they begin to define and make the transition to adulthood.

Not all adolescents, however, mature at the same rate. Some 15-year-olds may be ready to assert themselves in sexual relationships but others may still be disgusted by kissing scenes in TV shows (Brown, White, & Nikopoulou, 1993). "Adulthood," as traditionally understood, may not be entered until well into the 20s as educations are pursued and the establishment of new families and partnerships is postponed. The median age for first marriage in the United States today is older than it ever has been; in 1996, more than half the men who were getting married for the first time were 27 years old or older and half the women were 25 years old or older (U.S. Bureau of the Census, 1997). So, in the United States, young people may spend 9 to 17 years being considered adolescents.

SEXUAL TEENS

And therein lies one of the current paradoxes of teen sexuality. Is it fair or reasonable to expect adolescents to wait so long between sexual maturity and sexual activity? Adherents of what some would call the "old morality," based primarily on Christian religious asceticism, would say yes, sexual activity should be reserved for heterosexual marriage. In contrast, advocates of what might be called the "new morality" argue no, sexual pleasure is an important part of human behavior and should not be repressed or forced into a narrow set of restrictive norms (Hyde, 1994). Others take more of a middle ground.

In some European countries, the Netherlands, France, and Germany, for example, where adolescence is not considered such a specific life stage as it is in the United States, the prevailing understanding is that sexuality is a normal part of human development. Rather than asking youth to abstain from intercourse until marriage, health advocates promote values of respect and responsibility and encourage communication in relationships. Sex education is integrated throughout many school subjects and grade levels, and young people have access to both birth control pills and condoms if they have sexual intercourse. Does this openness result in early sexual intercourse and promiscuity? No; on the contrary, youth in these European countries begin having sexual relations more than one year later than American teens and have fewer sexual partners during their teen years (Kelly & McGee, 1999).

Unfortunately, in the United States today, cultural norms of appropriate adolescent sexual behavior are not easy to figure out. From some adult quarters teens will hear that you should be abstinent until married because otherwise you will have sinned. From others they will hear that it would be best if you wait until you are mature, but if you choose not to, use protection so you won't get pregnant, a disease, or even die.

Girls may learn on the street and in the school yard that if they express their sexual desires they will be "bad girls." If they choose to be "good girls" instead, they will sense it isn't as much fun and may find themselves vulnerable to aggressive boys who don't believe that "no" means "no" (Tolman & Higgins, 1996).

Boys are subject to a more consistent message, which is basically that the more women a man has sex with, the more of a man he is because a "real" man would never say no to the opportunity to have sex with a woman. This expectation is problematic for those boys who do not aspire to stud status.

To most teens, sexuality is not just about having intercourse, it's also about attractiveness, reputation, relationships, and finding love and intimacy. The dominant adult discourse, however, tends to focus on sexual intercourse, too often leaving out the other concerns many teens find equally, if not more, important. We saw this in sharp relief when U.S. Surgeon General Jocelyn Elders was forced to resign because she had dared discuss the possible benefits of masturbation. While the adults battle, teens are provided an inadequate, often confusing, and potentially harmful picture of sexual expectations.

Fortunately, an emerging body of research has begun to examine some of the other aspects of teens' sexuality and may help stimulate a healthier dialogue about teen sexuality. As a whole, these studies show that most young people live through adolescence in good physical and mental health, coming into adulthood capable of living fulfilling sexual lives. Most teens who have intercourse do so responsibly (Haffner, 1995). Some adolescents, however, have a tougher time sorting out who they are and how they want to be sexually, and some are at significant risk for negative outcomes—surrounded by a culture that at best provides mixed messages, and at worst promotes unhealthy sexual attitudes and behaviors.

Here's a brief profile of American adolescents' sexual activity, defined broadly to include the precursors to as well as outcomes of sexual intercourse.

Sexual Attractiveness

Getting comfortable in a changing body is a daily concern of most teenagers. Girls and boys can spend hours in front of the mirror getting their hair, makeup, and clothes "just right." A large survey of adolescents in Minnesota found that one out of three girls and one out of nine boys said they were "highly concerned" about their physical appearance (Blum, 1997). In a national survey, half of the adolescent girls said they had been on a diet; three fourths of these said because they wanted to look better (Commonwealth Fund, 1999). But "looking good" can become a dangerous preoccupation. Girls not yet finished growing are having cosmetic surgery to reshape their noses and eyelids, and to reduce or enlarge the size of their breasts (Kalb, 1999).

For some girls, getting thin enough becomes an obsession; dangerous eating patterns such as self-starvation and binging and purging are not uncommon, especially among White middle-class girls. In one national survey, 13% of early adolescent girls and 18% of middle and late adolescent girls reported having binged and purged (Commonwealth Fund, 1999). Anorexia nervosa affects 1% of girls ages 16 to 18, and bulimia affects 15%. These are serious illnesses that can result in damage to the body's organ systems and even death (Palla & Litt, 1988).

Dating, Kissing, and Sexual Touching

A majority of American teenagers date; 85% say they have had a boyfriend or girlfriend and have kissed someone romantically. By the age of 14, more than half of all boys have touched a girl's breasts, and a quarter have touched a girl's vulva. One fourth to one half of young people report experience with fellatio and cunnilingus (Newcomer & Udry, 1985; Roper Starch Worldwide, 1994).

Sexual Orientation

Males' and females' sexual orientation often emerges during adolescence. Two to five percent of teenagers report some type of same-gender sexual experience (Coles & Stokes, 1985). In one study of middle and late adolescents, 88% described themselves as predominantly heterosexual, 1% as bisexual or predominantly homosexual, and 11% were "unsure" of their sexual orientation. Older adolescents were more likely than the younger to be sure (Remafedi, Farrow, & Deisher, 1991). Gay males report developing a gay identity between the ages of 15 and 17, whereas lesbians report knowing their sexual orientation between the ages of 18 and 20 (Downey, 1994).

Homosexual feelings can be difficult for teens in a culture that continues to stigmatize and ostracize nonheterosexuals. Recent studies have found that lesbian, gay, and transgender youth are 2 to 6 times more likely to attempt suicide than other youth; and they may account for 30% of all completed suicides among teens, although they are only 10% or less of the teen population (Gibson, 1989; Savin-Williams, 1994).

First Sexual Intercourse

More than 80% of Americans first have sexual intercourse as teenagers, although the majority wait until middle and late adolescence. The average age of first intercourse is 16 for males and 17 for females. Typically, teenage men and women who have sexual intercourse do so less than once a month (Haffner, 1995).

The majority of teenagers say they do not feel peer or partner pressure to have sexual intercourse, and a majority of those who have had intercourse say it was with someone they love or "seriously date" (Roper Starch Worldwide, 1994). But one fourth of women aged 15 to 24 who described their first intercourse as voluntary still gave it low ratings on a scale of how much they wanted it to happen (Abma, Driscoll, & Moore, 1997).

Sexual Coercion

In a national survey of sexually experienced teenagers, 55% of females and 40% of males said they had done something sexually or felt pressure to do something sexually that they felt unready to do (Kaiser Family Foundation and *YM* Magazine, 1998). In another national survey, 8% of high school girls and 5% of boys said they had been forced by a date to have sex against their will. Rape myths are prevalent: One study found that almost two thirds (62%) of high school students surveyed believed that a male is not at fault if he rapes a girl who dresses "provocatively" on a date; one fourth said that it would not be rape for a male to get his date drunk and have sex with her after she said "no" to sexual intercourse (Telljohann et al., 1995).

At least one fourth of all rapes are of women 11 to 17 years of age (National Center for Victims of Crime, 1992). About half of the sexual assaults on children and teens are committed by family members (Abma et al., 1997). Gay, lesbian, and bisexual teens face an additional form of abuse related to their sexuality. A study in New York City found that half of the homosexual and bisexual teens reporting an assault said the assault was related to their sexual orientation, and for two thirds the assault occurred within their families (Hunter, 1990).

Girls who have unwanted sexual experiences are more likely than those who don't to have many sexual partners and greater vulnerability to STDs and early pregnancy (Abma et al., 1997).

Sexually Transmitted Diseases

Condom use has increased dramatically since the discovery of the HIV virus, so that today adolescents use condoms and birth control as frequently as most adults. But still, fewer than half of teenaged boys and only about one third of girls use contraceptives every time they have intercourse, and not all of these use condoms. One in five never use contraceptives (Kaiser Family Foundation and *YM* Magazine, 1998).

Three million teenagers every year—about one of every four sexually active teens—contract an STD. Some STDs, including gonorrhea and chlamydia, are more common among teenagers than among older men and women. Since the early 1990s, AIDS has been one of the leading causes of death among 15- to 24-year-olds in the United States. Although HIV incidence rates have been declining overall, there has been no comparable decline in new HIV cases in young people. The Centers for Disease Control (1998) estimates that half of all new HIV infections occur among people younger than 25, and many of these young adults likely were infected as teenagers through sexual contact.

Girls are at special risk from STDs. For both biological and social reasons, girls are more likely than boys to contract an STD from an infected partner, are less likely to notice symptoms, and more likely to suffer long-term health consequences, including infertility, tubal pregnancies, and cervical cancer (American Social Health Association, 1996). In the 1990s, girls also continued to have more sexual partners than they had had in the past, which also put them at increasing risk for acquiring STDs. A teenaged girl who has unprotected sex with an infected partner just one time has a 1% chance of contracting HIV, a 30% chance of contracting genital herpes, and a 50% chance of contracting gonorrhea (Alan Guttmacher Institute, 1996).

Unintended Pregnancy

Early and unprotected sexual activity also puts girls at increased risk for unintended pregnancy. Although teen pregnancy rates are declining in the United States, the country continues to have one of the highest rates of teen pregnancy of any Westernized country in the world (Piot & Islam, 1994). By the end of the 1990s, about 97 of every 1,000 young women (15 to 19 years old) in the United States got pregnant each year—about half of those gave birth and one third had abortions. These rates are in dramatic contrast to other countries such as the Netherlands and France where only 7 to 9 teen girls per 1,000 give birth each year and abortion rates are half what they are in the United States (World Bank, 1999).

Native American girls have the highest birth rates, and Asian American girls the lowest. Although the birth rate for unmarried Black girls has been declining, the birth rate for Black and Hispanic teenage girls is twice that for White girls (Commonwealth Fund, 1999).

Teen pregnancy is seen both as a moral and as a health problem in this country. The moral argument today is grounded in concern that most teen mothers are not married. In the early 1960s, only 17% of teens giving birth were not married, primarily because girls who got pregnant often were compelled to get married in so-called "shotgun" weddings. By the late 1990s, however, the stigma of out-of-wedlock pregnancy was significantly diminished, and three fourths of the teens who gave birth were not married (Children's Defense Fund, 1997).

Public health advocates are concerned because pregnancy during adolescence can result in short- and long-term health problems for both mother and child; and children in single-parent households are more likely to live in poverty than children in two-parent households. Girls who are mothers before age 18 are less likely to continue in school, achieve higher income levels, or maintain marital relationships (Commonwealth Fund, 1999).

SEXUAL MEDIA

A recent study tour of European countries (the Netherlands, France, and Germany) concluded that a large part of the disparity between U.S. and European patterns of adolescent sexual behavior could be attributed to a different outlook on youth and youth's sexuality:

> In the countries studied, adolescents are valued, respected, and expected to act responsibly. Equally important, most adults trust adolescents to make responsible choices because they see young people as assets, rather than problems. That message is conveyed in the media, in school texts, and in health care settings. (Kelly & McGee, 1999, p. 11)

We might hope the climate would be similar in the United States, but, unfortunately, it looks more like schools are talking about sex as little as possible, health care providers receive little training or incentive to work with youth, and youth are newsworthy only when they have committed crimes. Other sources of information teens might turn to for advice, such as their parents or religious advisers, are still reluctant to say more than "Just say no." (See Sutton et al., chap. 2, this volume, for an overview of the role parents and schools play in sex education.)

And that, to some extent, leaves entertainment media to fill the breach. Entertainment media may be important sex educators for at least three reasons: (1) teens have limited access to countervailing information or ideas, (2) much of the content teens attend to is designed for adults and depicts sexual roles and relationships, and (3) media messages about sexuality are relatively consistent (Roberts, 1982).

A Model of How Teens Choose and Use Media

Over the past decade, we have conducted a series of ethnographic studies designed to explore how adolescents choose and use sexual messages in the mass media in their daily lives. Out of this research we have developed the Media Practice Model (Steele, 1999) to illustrate the process of media use exhibited by teens (see Fig. 1.1).

The model has three features that distinguish it from more traditional approaches to studies of the effects of the mass media. First, the model is a seamless circuit because we assume that most media use is active in a number of ways: through selection of which medium and genre to attend to; through interacting and making sense of what is seen and/or heard; and by applying some or all of what is attended to. This circularity also represents the idea of the interactive nature of media practice; rather than there being a linear process of the mass media simply affecting the passive receiver—we assume that individuals are both affected by and affect the media they use.

Second, the Media Practice Model assumes that an adolescent's current and emerging sense of self, or identity, is a compelling component as decisions are made about what media will be selected, interacted with, and ap-

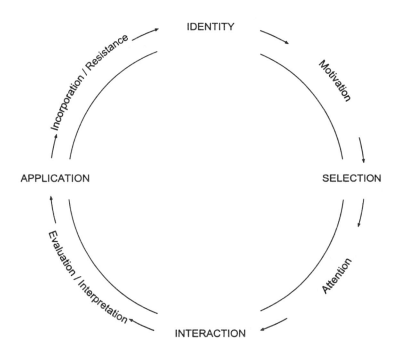

FIG. 1.1. Adolescents' media practice model. © J. R. Steele (1999).

plied in everyday life. Typically, studies of the effects of the mass media assume similarity in selection of, exposure to, and interpretation of media content. This model assumes that adolescents (and probably others, as well) choose media and interact with media based on who they are or who they want to be at the moment. This is similar to the assumptions of media uses and gratifications theory, which suggests that media consumers come to the media with different needs and motives and that what they take away from the media will depend on why they came to it (Rubin, 1994). Uses and gratifications theory would predict, for example, that an adolescent who watches talk shows to learn more about relationships would learn something about relationships; another who watches to be entertained would be more likely amused than edified.

Importantly, the Media Practice Model goes beyond uses and gratifications theory to assert that what is learned will also vary according to the adolescent's sense of self (identity) and "lived experience." Lived experience is a sociogenetic construct that accounts for the complex ways in which race, class, gender, developmental stage, and many other factors differentiate one person's experience of day-to-day occurrences from another person's.

Teens' Access to and Selection of Sexual Media Content

One of the most dramatic differences in the media today, compared to when the parents of today's adolescents were growing up, is the access youth have to many more media channels. Developments in media technology, such as satellite transmission, digital information recording and transmission, and the Internet have expanded enormously the number of media materials available. The videocassette recorder (VCR), the remote control, and portable compact disc players also have given today's teens much more control over when and where the media will be used. Almost all teens have their own source of music, many subscribe to at least one magazine, and more than two thirds have their own television, frequently hooked up to cable and a VCR, in their bedroom (Roberts, 2000).

Teens spend up to half the time they are awake with some form of media. Some even sleep with their radios or televisions on, many use more than one medium simultaneously; for example, a boy will watch a football game on TV with the sound off while listening to the radio play-by-play on his headphones, while flipping through the swimsuit issue of *Sports Illustrated*. A summary of the amount of time spent with media and the attractive attributes of the media adolescents are exposed to most frequently is presented in Table 1.1. Although television remains the dominant medium, at least in terms of time spent with it, it is important to note that television use tends to decline in middle adolescence in favor of more portable and more teen-oriented media, especially music, movies, and magazines.

All the media available to youth today are becoming increasingly specialized, offering different audiences different kinds of content. In the late 1990s, for example, teen girls knew that the WB Network was their TV channel because its prime-time lineup featured such shows as *Dawson's Creek*, *Buffy, the Vampire Slayer*, and *Felicity*, designed especially to lure teen girls back to television. Part of the push for these specialized media has come from advertisers who have begun to realize how lucrative the teen market segment can be. They have begun to demand more media vehicles in which to put their products in front of teens. American teens directly influence the spending of billions of dollars each year (up to $300 billion by the year 2000) on things—from food to cars—their families buy. As the teen population swells over the coming decade, marketers will focus even more closely on how to persuade teens to buy their products and be loyal to their brands, and they are likely to continue to use sexual appeals to attract teens' attention (Zollo, 1995).

TABLE 1.1
Availability, Frequency of Use, and Attractive Attributes of Mass Media
Used by Adolescents (8–18 Years Old)

Medium	Availability and Average Use[a]	Attractive Attributes
Overall	Girls: 7:41 hrs./day; Boys: 8:10; White: 7:16; Hispanic: 9:02; Black: 9:52	Girls > music than boys; boys > TV/video/video games; Blacks, Hispanics > TV/video than Whites; Whites, Blacks > print media than Hispanics
Television[b]	Two thirds (65%) have TV in bedroom; $3\frac{1}{2}$ hrs./day; 20+ hrs./week	Favorite shows familiar, relaxing, funny; Teen-oriented shows relevant
Music[c]	Almost all (74–94%) have radio, tape player, and/or CD player in bedroom; 2–3 hrs./day; 20+ hrs./week	Highly specialized; portable; arousing
Movies	About one third (28–38%) have VCR, cable TV, and/or satellite hookup in bedroom; $\frac{1}{2}$ hr./day[d]; 1/mo. in theaters	Favorite media stars; relevant; arousing
Magazines	15 min./day	Show trends, set standards; portable
Computer/ Internet	About half (in 1999) are computer users; average use $\frac{1}{2}$–1 hr./day	For schoolwork, games (boys primarily), recreational Web sites, chat rooms, e-mail
Advertising	In all media; estimated 20 ads/hr.[e]	Signal trends, what's cool

Note. [a]Source: Roberts (2000); [b]Includes broadcast and cable television, taped TV shows, and commercial videos; [c]Includes radio, CDs, and tapes; [d]Includes commercial videos, movies on TV and in theaters; [e]Source: Potter (1998).

Teens' Media Diets

Given the vast array of media material available today, teens must make choices about which media and content they will pay attention to. In Fig. 1.2 we use the familiar USDA food group pyramid to illustrate some possible dimensions of what we call adolescents' "media diets." At the bottom of the triangle is what Willis (1990) called "the common culture"—the images, styles, ideas that most youth will attend to in the media. It is not clear anymore that this is a significant part of a young person's daily media fare. Because media are now so specialized, there are only a few media vehicles that attract a majority of the teen audience. When television first became a family staple, for example, the "bread and grains" category was a larger part of a teen's media diet than it is today. In 1958, the three networks (ABC, CBS, and NBC) attracted in the evening, on average, nearly two thirds (61%) of American households owning televisions; but in 1998, only one fourth (26%) of TV households could be counted on to be watching one of the three networks when their TV set was on (Roberts, 1999).

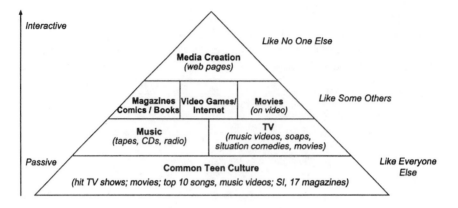

FIG. 1.2. Adolescents' media diet pyramid.

In 1958, teen girls had no choice but *Seventeen* magazine, while today at least 10 magazines vie specifically for the teen girl audience segment (e.g., *Teen, YM*), and increasing numbers of magazines are published for Black and Hispanic teen girls and boys (e.g., *Latina; XXL: Hip Hop at a Higher Level*). Recorded music has been highly specialized for some time, so that many large markets have a number of stations programming for different segments of the youth audience (e.g., alternative rock, Hot 100 [or Top 40], rap, country western). With the advent of streaming audio and webcasting, teens no longer need to be geographically within reach of their favorite stations. They can simply tune them in on their computers. More than 4,000 radio stations could be accessed on the World Wide Web in Spring 2000.

In such a differentiated media market there may be relatively little that is as common as french fries for a majority of teens. Today, it may be only the biggest hits, movies such as *Titanic* and television shows such as *Dawson's Creek*, that most teens will consume. What we see today is a smorgasbord of media from which teens may choose idiosyncratic diets. Taste for the increasingly specialized media "food groups," we speculate, is governed primarily by the teen's developing sense of self, or identity. The development of a firm sense of identity is a central task of adolescence. Exploring personal values and beliefs about sexuality and interpersonal relationships is a core piece of this identity work.

Some adolescent development theorists have suggested that each teen is learning in what ways he or she is like all other people, like some others, and like no others (Gallatin, 1975). The media may be used as virtual tool kits of identity possibilities. At the common culture level, a teen is (or yearns to be) like all other people. At the next level, though, the teen is like only some others—e.g., "skaters" who read *Thrasher* magazine, rent skateboarding videos, and listen to a particular kind of rap music; or "popular girls" who, if White, read *Elle* and *Vogue* and watch the *Young and the Restless* soap opera, or, if Black, read *Ebony* and watch *Oprah Winfrey* in the afternoons.

We know teens' media diets differ dramatically by gender and race. In one national survey of teens' magazine use, for example, *Sports Illustrated* was at the head of the boys' and the bottom of the girls' list of top 15 magazines. *Seventeen*, the magazine most read by girls (46%) wasn't even on the boys' list. The magazine boys and girls had most in common was *TV Guide*; 36% of the girls and 30% of the boys said they read a typical issue (Zollo, 1995).

Blacks and Whites choose dramatically different television diets, especially since the early 1990s when a number of cable channels began providing more shows with Black characters. In 1999, only four TV shows were in the top-10 lists of both Black and White viewers. The highest-rated show in Black households was *The Steve Harvey Show* on the WB network, but that situation comedy ranked 154th among White TV viewers (*Jet*, "Gap between black and white," May 17, 1999).

Living Single, the top-ranked show in Black households in 1995, revolved around four Black 20-something Brooklyn women and two Black men who shared their thoughts about life, love, and careers. At the same time, one of the top shows among young Whites was *Friends*, which featured six White 20-somethings, three men and three women, doing pretty much the same thing, but in Manhattan. One young Black viewer said he preferred watching *Living Single* "because I can relate better to its themes, the clothes the characters wear, their lingo and the situations they go through. I think that's why most Black people watch 'Black' shows" (Dean, 1995, p. 30). This selection of a show based on identification with characters the viewer sees as similar is exactly what the Media Practice Model predicts.

At the top of the pyramid is where youth can express their desires to be like no one else. Computer technology gives teens today the opportunity to express their uniqueness in semipublic ways, such as on personally designed web pages and in zines (privately produced, limited circulation magazines) that they can distribute to their friends or post on the Internet. Two chapters in this book (chaps. 9 and 13) provide a close analysis of teen girls' personal web pages and zines. Apparently some girls, most at present from affluent families, are using these new media forms as ways of expressing their developing sense of themselves, which frequently include questions and revelations about their sexuality and erotic relationships.

Sexual Media Content

Five chapters in this volume provide current pictures of what sexual content looks like in the media from which adolescents choose their daily media diets. These content analyses show that although sexual content is frequent, it is not uniformly depicted across media, so some teens may be exposed to more and different kinds of sexual content than other teens are.

Television Prime-Time. The television shows teens watch most frequently during prime-time (8 p.m. to 11 p.m. EST) are full of talk about and depictions of sexual activity. In 45 episodes of the top prime-time television shows that teens watched most frequently in 1996 (including *Friends, Seinfeld, Married with Children*), the primarily late teen and young adult characters talked about sex and engaged in sexual behavior in two thirds of the shows. However, most of the sexual content on television still is talk—characters discussing their own or others' current or future sexual activity. The idea of sexual risks or responsibility, however, is almost never talked about or shown; talk about or depictions of needing to wait or taking precautions occurred in only 5% of scenes portraying sexual behaviors (see Cope-Farrar & Kunkel, chap. 3).

Television Talk Shows. Talk shows that frequently feature dysfunctional couples publicly disclosing their troubles and infidelities are another favorite television genre of teen audiences. These shows also talk about rather than explicitly depict sexual behavior. Recent studies have found that parent–child relations, marital relations and infidelity, other sexual relations, and sexual orientation are the most commonly talked about topics. Sexual themes are more frequent on the shows teens most prefer (e.g., *Geraldo Rivera, Jenny Jones, Rolonda Watts,* and *Jerry Springer*) rather than on others that attract older audiences (e.g., *Oprah Winfrey*). A number of the talk shows include professional therapists who are supposed to comment on how the problems might be solved; but these "experts" get less air time than anyone else on the set, including the audience (see chap. 4, Greenberg & Smith).

Teen Girls' and Women's Magazines. Magazines are an important part of most teen girls' daily media diets. Analyses of teen girl magazines such as *Seventeen* and *'Teen* reveal that they are designed primarily to tell girls that their most important function in life is to get sexually attractive enough to catch a desirable male (Peirce, 1995). The message (e.g., "What's your lovemaking profile?" or "Perfect pickup lines: Never again let a guy get away because you can't think of anything to say") is repeated more explicitly in the women's magazines, such as *Cosmopolitan, Glamour,* and *Mademoiselle,* which many middle and late teen girls read. One of the most comprehensive studies of teen girls' and women's magazines ever done (chap. 7) shows that these magazines are indeed full of information about sexuality.

Movies. Although teens are one of the primary audiences for Hollywood movies in theaters and for at-home movies on cable and videocassettes, few studies have systematically examined the sexual content in them. We do know that more than two thirds of the movies produced and rated each year in the United States are R-rated, frequently because of the sexual content. Although only teens older than 16 are supposed to see R-rated movies without an adult present, most children today have seen R-rated movies long before that (Greenberg et al., 1993).

An analysis of R-rated movies popular with teens in the early 1980s found an average of 17.5 sexual portrayals per movie (Greenberg et al., 1993). In this book (chap. 10), Pardun finds that in the top-grossing movies of 1995, romantic and sexual relationships are present even in action adventure movies such as *Apollo 13*. Although Greenberg's analysis suggested that teens' movies are more sexually explicit than their television shows, in the movies Pardun analyzed there's more talk than action. Much of the talk is third-party discussions—two people talking about the relationships of other people. Underlying these discussions are some basic ideas that romantic relationships are mysterious, difficult to sort out, and primarily for the young.

Music and Music Videos. As Arnett discusses in chapter 12, music and music videos popular with teens continue to be primarily about sex and sexuality. Music becomes an especially important part of older teens' media diets as they use the sounds and images to enhance their moods and learn more about themselves and youth culture.

Interaction With Sexual Media Content

The second major step in adolescents' media practice is interaction: Once content is selected, how is it understood? What aspects of the content are attended to, engaged with? A few previous studies of teens' interpretation of media content, and a large body of work on the concept of selective perception, suggest that not all members of an audience will see or interpret the same message in the same way (Livingstone, 1989; Zillmann & Bryant, 1985).

In earlier studies, Brown and Shulze (1990), for example, found striking differences in how males and females and Blacks and Whites interpreted Madonna's music video *Papa Don't Preach*. Although most White females thought the video was about a teen girl deciding to keep her unborn baby, Black males were more likely to think the girl in the video was singing about wanting to keep her boyfriend "baby."

The few studies that have looked more closely at how teens process sexual media content have shown that their interpretations differ not only by gender and race but also by developmental level, prior sexual experience, and parental involvement (Brown et al., 1993; Huston, Wartella, & Donnerstein, 1998; Steele, 1999).

Social Learning and Cultivation Theory

Two theories of how we might learn from the media have dominated the study of media's effects on youth. Gerbner's Cultivation Theory, focused primarily on television as the dominant cultural storyteller of the age, predicts that viewers who watch a great deal of television are more likely than those who watch less often to accept the worldview most frequently depicted on TV (Gerbner, Gross, Morgan, & Signorielli, 1994). Bandura's Social Learning Theory and its successor, Social Cognitive Theory (Bandura, 1994), predicted further that viewers will be more likely to assimilate and perhaps imitate behaviors they see frequently depicted by attractive models who are rewarded and/or not punished. Social Learning Theory also predicts that imitation is more likely if the media consumer thinks the portrayal is realistic and identifies with or desires to be like the media character.

A number of the studies in this book either explicitly or implicitly work from the predictions and explanations offered by these theories. Basically, these studies are built on the premise that the more frequently a sexual value or behavior occurs in the media, and the more frequently it is presented as positive rather than negative, the more likely viewers, readers, and listeners will be to adopt that value or engage in that behavior.

Although the analyses of content alone can only speculate about what the effects on the viewer might be, the studies are on firmer ground when they take into account not only how frequently sexual content occurs, but also who the characters are, how realistic the depictions are, and the negative or positive outcomes of the depicted talk or portrayal.

Studies that take us beyond content to the audience find that the content is more likely assimilated if the situation is considered realistic and if the characters are seen as attractive and worthy of emulation. Ward, Gorvine, and Cytron-Walker (chap. 5), for example, find significant gender differences in how college students perceived portrayals of jealousy and competition, male lust, and miscommunication in clips from popular situation comedies such as *Roseanne* and *Martin*. They find that young women were more likely than young men to think the sexual scenes they saw were realistic, and the women were more approving than the men of behaviors that are relationship maintaining (e.g., jealous husband protecting wife) and less approving of relationship threats (e.g., a man contemplating cheating).

Through their focus group interviews with teenagers, Treise and Gotthoffer (chap. 8) found that many teens use magazines not only for sexual health information but also as a guide to forming their own beliefs and attitudes about how sexuality fits into their relationships. However, a number of the teens also resisted the manner in which information is presented in the magazines, expressing concerns about the depth and accuracy of articles and about how advertisers influenced the content.

Steele, in chapter 11, reveals significant gender and racial differences in how the movie *Higher Learning* is interpreted by high school students.

Application of Sexual Media Content

As teens attend to and interpret sexual media content, they also evaluate and may or may not incorporate what they are seeing into their own developing sense of sexuality. This is the step that we traditionally have thought of as media effects. We ask, does the sexual content in the media influence how adolescents think about sexuality or how they behave sexually?

Only a few studies in the past have investigated the link between exposure to sexual media content and teens' sexual attitudes and behaviors. These have documented relationships between teens' viewing of music videos and permissive attitudes about premarital sex (Strouse, Buerkel-Rothfuss, & Long, 1995). And frequent viewers of soap operas have been found more likely than those who watch less often to believe that single mothers have relatively easy lives and male friends who will be important in their children's lives (Larson, 1996). Marriage has not been as pleasantly perceived. Heavy television viewers have been more likely than lighter viewers to be ambivalent about the possibility that marriage is a happy way of life (Signorielli, 1991). Two studies suggest that heavier exposure to sexual content on television is related to earlier initiation of sexual intercourse (Brown & Newcomer, 1991; Peterson, Moore, & Furstenberg, 1991).

Three chapters in this volume examine how teens incorporate and sometimes resist the sexual content they attend to in the media. Hofschire and Greenberg (chap. 6) find that the slim and muscular standards of beauty prevalent in both magazines and television do have an impact on both male and female high school students' perceptions of what their own bodies should look like. Television viewing, magazine reading, and identification with thin models in the media are related to body dissatisfaction, belief in ideal body stereotypes (e.g., slim for females, muscular for males), and dieting and exercising.

On the other hand, two qualitative studies of how girls use the Internet (chap. 9, Wray & Steele; chap. 13, Stern) show that girls also can be remarkably astute media critics and producers. These two chapters illustrate what is meant by "resistance" in the Media Practice Model: opposition to the dominant ideas of attractiveness and the female's role in heterosexual relationships. The zines and Web sites produced by teen girls show that teens can be oppositional readers of mainstream media, and teens can be active audience members when they are also producers.

In short, adolescents have some control over media's influence on them and, thanks to new media technologies, they have it within their power to produce sexual media content. In addition, as audience members and as consumers they have considerable influence over what more mainstream media producers offer. Some are choosing less nutritious sexual media diets than others. Some are able to resist the temptations of the mainstream culture that says that women should be thin and beautiful, men strong, and both should be engaged in sexual activity, consequences be damned. Others are seduced, and model their developing sexual lives on the frequently unhealthy sexual media content they consume.

AN AGENDA FOR FUTURE RESEARCH

Although the studies included in this book provide a comprehensive look at the role the media play in teens' sexual socialization, we still have much to learn. In fall 1998, the Kaiser Family Foundation sponsored a symposium of key researchers in the field to discuss how best to proceed on understanding the impact of sexual content in the media on young people in the United States. In the final report based on the discussions at that symposium, the report authors noted that future research should be: (a) interdisciplinary; (b) use a variety of methods; (c) be guided by the results of smaller-scale studies designed to refine research questions and measures; and (d) be able to account for variations by gender, ethnicity, and sexual development level (Huston et al., 1998).

Future research should build on this foundation of research and continue to address such questions as:

1. *Patterns of selection:* How do sexual media diets differ among teens of different pubertal stages, races, genders, sexual experience levels? When are teens, and which ones, most likely to be seeking sexual information in the media?

2. *Media portrayals:* How do different media and different genres within those media vary in their portrayals of sexuality? Which media or genres are more likely to include healthy versus unhealthy presentations of sexual behavior? How do the media portray sexual negotiation and other communication about sex? What are the media's messages about sexual power and vulnerability, about safe sex, about the role sex plays in relationships?

3. *Application/resistance or media effects:* How does the use of sexual content in media influence cognitive factors such as knowledge and beliefs about sexuality, sexual health, normal versus deviant behavior, and sexual schemas and scripts? How does the use of sexual content influence teenagers' sexual attitudes, such as the positive or negative feelings they associate

with safe sex practices, contraception, and the number and types of sexual partners they might have? Can the media promote healthier sexuality than they do now?

IMPLICATIONS FOR MEDIA PRODUCERS, PARENTS, AND EDUCATORS

Given what we know about how teens use and are affected by sexual content in the media, is there anything media producers, parents, and educators should or could do now? Can anything be done to help young people select a more nutritious sexual media diet? We think there are a number of promising strategies for the industry as well as for parents and teachers and others interested in youth living healthier sexual lives.

Edutainment

One of the most promising approaches is what has been called "edutainment"—the practice of imbedding socially desirable messages within entertainment programming. The technique, building on the principles of social learning theory and role modeling—which was first applied to sexuality issues in Mexico and then other Latin American countries—has been successful in promoting family planning and contraceptive use (Westoff, Rodriguez, & Bankole, 1996). In the United States, a number of organizations now have experts available to Hollywood writers and directors to help them develop more sexually responsible scripts.

In one effort, the Kaiser Family Foundation worked with writers and producers of the prime-time medical drama *ER* to imbed information about emergency contraception in one of the story lines. Although it was mentioned for only 10 seconds in one episode, before and after surveys of the audience showed a 17% increase in viewers' awareness of the contraceptive method immediately after the show (Folb, 2000).

Lobbyists have found that writers and producers are hungry for good story ideas and often appreciate accurate information about sexual issues. The primary limitation to this approach is that some topics, such as abortion, are still taboo, and producers are reluctant to "spoil the mood" with technical information or discussion/depiction of contraceptives or negative outcomes. The bottom line of attracting and maintaining audiences in an increasingly competitive media market is still paramount.

Content Ratings, Screening Devices

The television networks in the mid-1990s reluctantly agreed, after extensive Congressional pressure, to provide ratings on all non-news shows. These ratings, based primarily on the rating system in place since the 1950s for

Hollywood-produced movies, allow viewers to screen programs for content and age appropriateness. If the television set also is equipped with the V-chip, an electronic screening device originally conceived of as a tool for blocking violent content (hence the acronym), viewers also can block content with undesirable sexual content ratings from being shown. The problem with ratings is that they rarely give enough information for making reasonable decisions about whether to view shows, and some teens are drawn to content that is not age appropriate (Cantor, 2000). Screening devices for the Internet tend to block potentially valuable sexuality information as well as more problematic content. We should work to make sure that advances in technology and increased consumer awareness increase the value of these tools in the future.

Guidelines for Media Depictions

Another possibility is to encourage media producers voluntarily to create and distribute sexual content that better serves young media consumers. The National Commission on Adolescent Sexual Health endorsed an excellent set of guidelines that, if followed, could lead to a healthier and better-balanced image of sexuality in the media (Haffner, 1995). These guidelines are as important for American teens as they are for young people in other countries as American media expand their reach around the globe. American prime-time series such as *Baywatch*, music videos, and movies are now available and consumed by millions of young people all over the world (Bryant, 2000). *Seventeen* and *Cosmopolitan* have international editions in many languages but with basically the same content whether published in Greek or Dutch.

The guidelines call for writers, producers, programming executives, reporters, and others in the media to:

- Provide diverse and positive views of a range of body types.
- Eliminate stereotypes that only beautiful people have sexual relationships.
- Eliminate the stereotype that all adolescents have sexual intercourse.
- Show that the majority of sexual encounters are planned, not spur-of-the-moment responses in the heat of passion.
- Model interpersonal communication about an upcoming sexual encounter.
- Include use of contraceptives in descriptions and portrayals of sexual encounters.
- Discuss or portray possible short- and long-term negative consequences of portrayals of unprotected intercourse.
- Portray typical interactions between men and women and boys and girls as respectful and nonexploitative.

- Include information about or portrayal of effective parent–child communication about sexuality and relationships.
- Provide ways for young people to obtain additional information about sexuality.

Media Literacy

Another promising strategy that is just taking foothold in the United States is called "media literacy" "the ability to access, analyze, evaluate and communicate messages in a variety of forms" (Hobbs, 1997, p. 7). Across the country, local groups are working in schools and community centers teaching youth and parents to be more critical media consumers by showing them that media messages are constructed and can be deconstructed to uncover their assumptions and hidden values; messages are produced within economic, social, and political contexts; and that they can create media themselves (Thoman, 1998).

So far, although more research is needed, evaluation studies have shown that children who are taught such concepts are less susceptible to the negative effects of subsequent media use (e.g., Austin & Johnson, 1997). Other countries around the world, such as Canada and Australia, have incorporated extensive media literacy curricula in their schools, and a number of states in the United States now include media literacy in their state-wide educational goals. The American Academy of Pediatricians (AAP, 1991) issued policy statements on media effects, including sexuality and contraception, and has embraced media literacy as an important strategy for decreasing the negative effects of the media on youth. Their "Media Matters" campaign includes a media-use inventory, which pediatricians are encouraged to have their young patients fill out and discuss with their parents.

Increasing media literacy among parents and children will require significant resources to ensure that all who need it get it. Teachers will need to be trained, curricula developed, school systems persuaded that this is another important topic they should add to already overloaded school days. The most crucial part may be educating parents to think of media as an important source of influence in their children's lives, and to help more children become even more active users of the media that surround them. Ultimately, a more media-literate populace should result in a more responsive and responsible media industry and a culture that nurtures healthy sexuality.

CONCLUSION

If we are genuinely concerned about the sexual well-being of American adolescents, we would do well to break free from our disciplinary harnesses and personal beliefs to consider adolescence as holistically as possible. Adolescent sexuality is not something to be feared. Rather, we should view adolescents' sexuality as a naturally occurring part of development that holds the potential of a sexual self that is self-affirming and sustaining. Simon (1996, p. 143) cautions that sexuality is a complex aspect of the human experience, and even when sexuality is reduced to "gender and species reproduction" or "some kind of heterosexual intercourse," its experience inevitably will be different for each individual.

Thus, it is important, even as we research the influence of sexual media on teens, that we do so with our eyes open to the array of possibilities available to adolescents as they move toward adulthood. Rather than worrying too much about what teens should not do, we might more productively follow the lead of some of the European countries. Letting teens know that they are valued, respected members of their communities, who are expected to act responsibly—not just sexually but in all aspects of their daily lives—and giving them the education, tools, and services to accomplish that, would be a good way to begin.

REFERENCES

Abma, J., Driscoll, A., & Moore, K. (1997). *Differing degrees of control over first intercourse and young women's first partners: Data from Cycle 5 of the National Survey of Family Growth.* Paper presented at the annual meeting of the Population Association of America, Washington, DC.

Alan Guttmacher Institute (1996, June 24). *Teenage sexual and reproductive behavior in the United States.* Fact sheet prepared for a briefing "The entertainment media as 'sex educators?' " Washington, DC.

American Academy of Pediatricians (1995). Sexuality, contraception and the media (RE9505). *Policy statement, 95*(2), 298–300. [Online]. Available: *www.aap.org.*

American Social Health Association (1996). *Gallup study: Teenagers know more than adults about STDs.* Durham, NC: Author.

Austin, E., & Johnson, K. (1997). Immediate and delayed effects of media literacy training on third graders' decision making for alcohol. *Health Communication, 94,* 323–349.

Bandura, A. (1994). Social cognitive theory of mass communication. In J. Bryant & D. Zillmann (Eds.), *Media effects: Advances in theory and research* (pp. 61–90). Hillsdale, NJ: Lawrence Erlbaum Associates.

Blum, R. W. (1997, December). *Adolescent females: Vulnerabilities and risk reduction.* Paper presented at the National Campaign to Prevent Teen Pregnancy and the Family Impact Seminar, Washington, DC.

Brown, J. D., & Newcomer, S. (1991). Television viewing and adolescents' sexual behavior. *Journal of Homosexuality, 21*(1/2), 77–91.

Brown, J. D., & Schulze, L. (1990). The effects of race, gender, and fandom on audience interpretation of Madonna's music videos. *Journal of Communication, 40*(2), 88–102.

Brown, J. D., White, A. B., & Nikopoulou, L. (1993). Disinterest, intrigue, resistance: Early adolescent girls' use of sexual media content. In B. S. Greenberg, J. D. Brown, & N. L. Buerkel-Rothfuss (Eds.), *Media, sex and the adolescent* (pp. 177–195). Cresskill, NJ: Hampton Press.

Bryant, W. (2000, February 17). "Baywatch" by the numbers. *USA Today,* p. D1.

Cantor, J. (2000). Media violence. *Journal of Adolescent Health, 27*(2), 30–34.

Centers for Disease Control and Prevention, National Center for HIV, STD, TB Prevention, Division of HIV/AIDS Prevention, Surveillance Branch data: Retrieved July 3, 2000: cdc.gov/nchstp/hiv_aids/graphics/adolesnt.htm.

Children's Defense Fund (1997). *The state of America's children: Yearbook 1997.* Washington, DC: Author.

Coles, R., & Stokes, F. (1985). *Sex and the American teenager.* New York: Harper & Row.

Commonwealth Fund (1999, January). *Improving the health of adolescent girls: Policy report of the Commonwealth Fund Commission on Women's Health.* New York: Author.

Dean, M. (1995, June 26). For many holding a remote, choices are in black and white: TV viewers watch programs with characters of their own race. *Insight on the News, 11*(25), 30.

Downey, J. I. (1994). Sexual orientation issues in adolescent girls. *Women's Health Issues, 4,* 117–121.

Folb, K. (2000). "Don't touch that dial!" TV as a—what!?—positive influence. *SIECUS Report, 28*(5), 16–18.

Gallatin, J. E. (1975). *Adolescence and individuality.* New York: Harper & Row.

Gap between black and white TV viewing habits narrows. (1999, May 17). *Jet, 95*(24), 65.

Gerbner, G., Gross, L., Morgan, M., & Signorielli, N. (1994). Growing up with television: The cultivation perspective. In J. Bryant & D. Zillmann (Eds.), *Media effects: Advances in theory and research* (pp. 17–41). Hillsdale, NJ: Lawrence Erlbaum Associates.

Gibson, P. (1989). *Gay male and lesbian youth suicide. Report of the Secretary's Task Force on Youth Suicide, Vol. 3: Prevention and interventions in youth suicide.* Rockville, MD: U.S. Department of Health and Human Services.

Greenberg, B. S., Siemicki, M., Dorfman, S., Heeter, C., Stanley, C., Soderman, A., & Linsangan, R. (1993). Sex content in R-rated films viewed by adolescents. In B. S. Greenberg, J. D. Brown, & N. L. Buerkel-Rothfuss (Eds.), *Media, sex, and the adolescent* (pp. 45–58). Cresskill, NJ: Hampton Press.

Haffner, D. W. (Ed.). (1995). *Facing facts: Sexual health for America's adolescents.* New York: SIECUS.

Herman-Giddens, M., Slora, E., Wasserman, R., Bordony, M. V., Bhapkar, G., Koch, G., & Hasemeier, C. (1997). Secondary sexual characteristics and menses in young girls seen in office practice: A study from the Pediatric Research in Office Settings Network. *Pediatrics, 99*(4), 505–514.

Hobbs, R. (1997). Literacy for the information age. In J. Flood, S. B. Heath, & D. Lapp (Eds.), *Handbook of research on teaching literacy through the communicative and visual arts* (pp. 7–14). New York: Simon Schuster Macmillan.

Hunter, J. (1990). Violence against lesbian and gay male youths. *Journal of Interpersonal Violence, 5,* 295–300.

Huston, A. C., Wartella, E., & Donnerstein, E. (1998). *Measuring the effects of sexual content in the media: A report to the Kaiser Family Foundation.* Menlo Park, CA: The Henry J. Kaiser Family Foundation.

Hyde, J. (1994). *Understanding human sexuality* (5th ed.). New York: McGraw-Hill.

Kaiser Family Foundation and *YM* Magazine (1998). *National survey of teens: Teens talk about dating, intimacy, and their sexual experiences.* Menlo Park, CA: The Henry J. Kaiser Family Foundation.

Kalb, C. (1999, August 9). Our quest to be perfect. *Newsweek,* 52–59.

Kantrowitz, B., & Wingert, P. (1999, October 18). The truth about tweens. *Newsweek,* pp. 62–72.

Kelly, M. A., & McGee, M. (1999, December/January). Report from a study tour: Teen sexuality education in the Netherlands, France, and Germany. *SIECUS Report, 27*(2), 11–14.

Larson, M. (1996). Sex roles and soap operas: What adolescents learn about single motherhood. *Sex Roles: A Journal of Research, 35*(1/2), 97–121.

Livingstone, S. M. (1989). Interpretive viewers and structured programs. *Communication Research, 16*(1), 25–57.

National Center for Victims of Crime (1992). *Rape in America*. Arlington, VA: Author.

Newcomer, S., & Udry, R. (1985). Oral sex in an adolescent population. *Archives of Sexual Behavior, 14*, 41–46.

Palla, B., & Litt, I. F. (1988). Medical complications of eating disorders in adolescents. *Pediatrics, 81*, 613–623.

Peirce, K. (1995). Socialization messages in *Seventeen* and *'Teen* magazines. In C. M. Lont (Ed.), *Women and media: Content, careers, and criticism* (pp. 79–85). Belmont, CA: Wadsworth.

Peterson, J. L., Moore, K. A., & Furstenberg, F. F. (1991). Television viewing and early initiation of sexual intercourse: Is there a link? *Journal of Homosexuality, 21*(1/2), 93–118.

Piot, P., & Islam, M. Q. (1994). Sexually transmitted diseases in the 1990s: Global epidemiology and challenges for control. *Sexually Transmitted Diseases, 21*(2, Suppl.), S7–S13.

Potter, W. J. (1998). *Media literacy*. Thousand Oaks, CA: Sage.

Remafedi, G., Farrow, J. A., & Deisher, R. W. (1991). Risk factors for attempted suicide in gay and bisexual youth. *Pediatrics, 87*, 869–875.

Roberts, D. (2000). Media and youth: Access, exposure, and privatization. *Journal of Adolescent Health, 27*(2), 8–14.

Roberts, E. J. (1982). Television and sexual learning in childhood. In D. Pearl (Ed.), *Television and behavior: Ten years of scientific progress and implications for the 80s* (pp. 209–223). Washington, DC: U.S. Government Printing Office.

Roberts, J. L. (1999, April 26). Out of the box. *Newsweek*, 42–45.

Rodriguez, R. (1999, September). Points to ponder. *Reader's Digest*, 91.

Roper Starch Worldwide. (1994). *Teens talk about sex: Adolescent sexuality in the 90's*. New York: Sexuality Information and Education Council of the United States.

Rubin, A. (1994). Media uses and effects: A uses-and-gratifications perspective. In J. Bryant & D. Zillmann (Eds.), *Media effects: Advances in theory and research* (pp. 417–436). Hillsdale, NJ: Lawrence Erlbaum Associates.

Savin-Williams, R. C. (1994). Verbal and physcial abuse as stressors in the lives of lesbian, gay male, and bisexual youths: Associations with school problems, running away, substance abuse, prostitution and suicide. *Journal of Consulting Clinical Psychology, 62*, 261–269.

Signorielli, N. (1991). Adolescents and ambivalence toward marriage: A cultivation analysis. *Youth and Society, 23*, 121–149.

Simon, W. (1996). *Postmodern sexualities*. New York: Routledge.

Steele, J. (1999). Adolescent sexuality: Factoring in the influences of family, friends and school. *The Journal of Sex Research, 36*(4), 331–341.

Strouse, J., Buerkel-Rothfuss, N., & Long, E. (1995). Gender and family as mediators of the relationship between music video exposure and adolescent sexual permissiveness. *Adolescence, 30*, 505–521.

Telljohann, S. K., Price, J. H., Summers, J., Everett, S. A., & Casler, S. (1995). High school students' perceptions of nonconsensual sexual activity. *Journal of School Health, 65*, 107–112.

Thoman, E. (1998). *Skills and strategies for media education*. Los Angeles: Center for Media Literacy.

Tolman, D. L., & Higgins, T. E. (1996). How being a good girl can be bad for girls. In N. B. Maglin & D. Perry (Eds.), *Women, sex, and power in the nineties* (pp. 205–225). New Brunswick, NJ: Rutgers University Press.

U.S. Bureau of the Census (1997, March). *Current Population Reports, Series P20-509, Household and Family Characteristics*. Washington, DC.

Westoff, C., Rodriguez, G., & Bankole, A. (1996). *Family planning and mass media effects*. The Carolina Population Center, Chapel Hill, NC: The Evaluation Project.

Willis, P. (1990). *Common culture*. Boulder, CO: Westview.

World Bank (1999). *1999 world development indicators*. Washington, DC: Author.

Zillmann, D., & Bryant, J. (1985). *Selective exposure to communication*. Hillsdale, NJ: Lawrence Erlbaum Associates.

Zollo, P. (1995). *Wise up to teens: Insights into marketing and advertising to teenagers*. Ithaca, NY: New Strategist.

2

Shaking the Tree of Knowledge for Forbidden Fruit: Where Adolescents Learn About Sexuality and Contraception

Michael J. Sutton
Jane D. Brown
University of North Carolina, Chapel Hill

Karen M. Wilson
Jonathan D. Klein
University of Rochester

It is paradoxically the Holy Grail and forbidden fruit of adolescence. Few other combinations of three letters are so cloaked in mystery, so freighted with developmental and health implications as the word *sex.*

American teenagers find themselves faced with a confusing array of contradictory messages and sources of sexual and contraceptive information. Unable to extricate sexuality from the moral stances and medical issues that have become entangled with it (Koch, 1993), socializing forces ranging from parents to peers, from doctors to actors, and from television to the Internet present sex alternately as something forbidden and dangerous yet irresistibly desirable and pleasurable. Sex is showcased as a rite of passage that promises entry into the adult world. However, it is a journey rife with potential perils such as unwanted pregnancies and sexually transmitted diseases (STDs), and the road maps provided by one source of information may influence how other sources are received: whether they are followed, questioned, or rejected.

With menarche occurring at a younger age—and marriage put off until a later one—today's adolescents are sexually at risk for a longer period of time than any previous generation. Although America has experienced an 11% drop in adolescent sexual intercourse since 1991 (Centers for Disease Control, 1998), the nation nonetheless continues to have the highest adolescent rates of STDs and adolescent birth rates of any industrialized country on Earth (Piot & Islam, 1994). The number of adolescent AIDS cases in the United States increased more than sevenfold over a 10-year period (Centers for Disease Control, 1998).

Teens can learn about sex from the mass media. They've grown up as neighbors to the residents of *Melrose Place* on television, watching preening fictional characters swap sexual partners as casually as baseball cards. Whether through the glossy pages of magazines, the surreal images of music videos, or the pulsing beat of songs piped through headphones, media-borne images of sexuality and potential sexual behaviors swirl around today's American adolescents just when they are working to define themselves as sexual beings (Hendren & Strasburger, 1993) and are especially receptive and vulnerable to the "sexual scripts" (Simon & Gagnon, 1984) they encounter.

And yet, in one of the great ironies for a popular culture that drenches its adolescents in wave after wave of sexual information, some of the most important knowledge related to sexual activity apparently has been lost. One example: According to survey data, nearly half of all teenagers do not know where to seek confidential health care services should they need them. Birth control ranked among the top three services they were least likely to be able to locate (Klein, McNulty, & Flatau, 1998). The average American teenager will hear nearly 14,000 sexual references, innuendos, and jokes on television per year. But a mere 165 of the references will deal with topics such as birth control, self-control, abstinence, or STDs (Committee on Communications, American Academy of Pediatrics, 1995). This has created a popular culture that frames sex in terms of the "invisible" three Cs: no commitment, no contraception, no consequences.

But despite the media's noisy sexual maelstrom—felt by adolescents both directly and through interactions with peers who are media consumers themselves—our survey data reveal that today's adolescents most frequently turn to a comparatively quiet and previously unheralded source for responsible sexual information: school. The classroom has today become the principal setting where adolescents learn about safe sex in the nation; although controversy remains about what form school-based sexual education should take, STDs have joined the ABCs on the blackboard.

THE COMMONWEALTH FUND SURVEY OF THE HEALTH OF ADOLESCENTS

In this chapter, we use the 1997 Commonwealth Fund Survey of the Health of Adolescents to look more closely at what sources American adolescents use for contraceptive information, and we focus on how the effects of these various sources may interact, reinforcing or undermining each other.

PRIOR RESEARCH

The ascendancy of school-based sex education programs as the top-ranked source of contraceptive and birth control knowledge demonstrates a notable reshuffling of sources of sexual and contraceptive information over the past 25 years. Although both print and electronic media typically have been lumped into the amorphous category "mass media" (Amonker, 1980; Inman, 1974; Yankelovich Partners, Inc., 1993), when a distinction has been made, print media such as magazines have ranked high among sources of sexual information (Davis & Harris, 1982; Thornburg, 1981). However, prior to the Commonwealth Fund Study television had not been noted individually as such a powerful agent of contraceptive information. Because of these shifting categorizations, making comparisons to past research can be tricky; prior investigations also frequently have examined not just contraceptive information but adolescents' acquisition of sexual knowledge in general. It is instructive, however, to examine how these trends in sexual information gathering have changed.

Research since 1974 has repeatedly indicated the same top four sources of sexual information for adolescents—peers, parents, school health classes, and various mass media—but in shifting order (Table 2.1). Although in

TABLE 2.1

Historical Rank of Sources of Sexual Information Among Adolescents

	1974 (Inman, 1974[a])	1980 (Amonker, 1980[b])	1981 (Thornburg, 1981[c])	1982 (Davis & Harris, 1982[d])	1993 (Yankelovich Partners, Inc., 1993[e])		1998 (Kaiser Family Foundation, 1998[f])
					Ages 13–15	Ages 16–17	
Rank order, from most commonly used sources to less-used sources:							
1	Families	Friends	Peers	Friends	Parents	Friends	Friends/siblings
2	Friends	Mass media	Literature	Schools	Friends	Parents	Schools
3	Schools	Parents	Mother	Books/magazines	Schools	Mass media	TV/movies
4			Schools	Parents	Mass media	Schools	Magazines
5			Experience	Movies			Parent
6			Fathers	Television			Book/brochure
7			Physicians	Siblings			Religious leader
8			Ministers	Doctors/nurses			MTV
9				Church			Counselor/therapist
Sample size:	417	372	1,152	288	500		650
Scope:	9th–12th graders, Phoenix and Yuma, AZ	Teens 13–19 visiting Planned Parenthood, Springfield, MO	Students at single, unidentified Midwestern H.S.	Students 11–18 at five public schools, NM	National telephone poll of teens 13–17		National telephone poll of teens 13–18

Question asked: [a]What is your major source of sex information?

[b]What is your main source of information about sex, birth control, pregnancy, or human sexuality?

[c]From whom did you first learn about each of the following concepts: abortion, conception, ejaculation, homosexuality, intercourse, masturbation, petting, prostitution, seminal emissions, and venereal disease?

[d]How much sexual information have you received (a lot/a little/none) from the following sources? (See list above.)

[e]Where have you learned the most about sex?

[f]Have you ever gotten any good ideas about talking with girls/boys about sexual issues from . . . ? (See list above.)

28

1974, adolescents ranked family first and friends second (Inman, 1974), peers have most consistently been named by adolescents as their primary source of sexual knowledge, topping the list in studies published in 1980, 1981, 1982, and even almost two decades later, in 1998 (Amonker, 1980; Davis & Harris, 1982; Henry J. Kaiser Family Foundation, 1998; Thornburg, 1981).

Perhaps, given the increasingly conservative social tenor of the times, early 1980s researchers looked for explanations as to why the family—and parents in particular—had diminished in prominence as sexual educators since the early 1970s. A 1983 evaluation of the role of parents and family as sources of sexual information indicated that a societal swing toward a more conservative social milieu—which included a more repressed approach to sexuality—may have been one obstacle to effective parental–child communication about sex. "Our best evidence suggests that parents who engender fear and guilt about sex in their children have children who are least prepared for sexual encounters," wrote researchers Walters and Walters (1983, p. 14).

But the dominance of parents or peers as sexual educators may depend more on the age of the adolescents surveyed than the decade. The Yankelovich Partners, Inc. (1993) survey split adolescents into younger and older age groups; among teenagers aged 13 to 15, parents ranked first and peers second. However, for teens aged 16 to 17, peers are the source of information from whom they have learned the most about sex. This shift from the social orbit of parents to that of peers supports sociocognitive developmental theories that describe such a change in orientation as a normal and crucial part of adolescence (Brown, 1990).

In terms of gender, prior studies also found more females than males receiving sexual information from parents (Davis & Harris, 1982; Henry J. Kaiser Family Foundation, 1998). In the Kaiser study, almost 40% of teen girls reported getting sexual information from a parent; only 25% of teen boys did. Although the drop of parents from their first- and second-place rankings in the 1993 poll to fifth place in the 1998 Kaiser study (fourth, if mass media are grouped as one category) is noteworthy, data from our Commonwealth Fund survey paints a rosier picture of parent–child communication: Although parents rank third, more than 56% of the high school girls surveyed indicated that a parent or parents had been a source of information about contraception, and more than 48% of boys did as well. It is important to note that the Kaiser researchers asked teens about their sources of ideas for discussing sexual information rather than about where they learned contraceptive information; nonetheless, a parent–child conversation about contraception is likely indicative of a conversation about sex as well. It is difficult to imagine talking about contraception without also talking about sex.

Medical professionals such as physicians and nurses ranked either very low or were not included as possible sources of sexual information in previous surveys; they ranked a distant sixth in our Commonwealth Fund data.

The caveats that need to be attached to previous studies, especially those conducted in the 1970s and early 1980s, are numerous. Small samples ranging from just over 200 adolescents (Davis & Harris, 1982) to slightly more than 400 (Inman, 1974) raise questions about the statistical validity of the research conclusions. Even the far more sophisticated Yankelovich (1993) and Kaiser (1998) surveys featured samples of only 500 and 650, respectively. The one study (Thornburg, 1981) with a sizable sample, 1,152, culled all of its respondents from a single Midwestern high school. Additional problems with geographic and demographic representativeness further muddy the conclusions of the earlier studies. All of the respondents to the Inman study (1974) were drawn from the Phoenix and Yuma, Arizona, areas. In addition, the ratio of White to Black students was 11 to 1 in Inman's sample. Nine out of 10 respondents in Amonker's sample (1980) were female, and more than 97% of the teens were White; less than 3% were Black.

THE COMMONWEALTH FUND SURVEY SAMPLE

Stratified samples of students at 297 public, private, and parochial schools—drawn from a database of about 80,000 schools provided by the National Center for Educational Statistics—were selected to complete a questionnaire administered by Lou Harris and Associates. The responses of the 6,748 adolescents in grades 5 to 12 who completed the survey were weighted to reflect national demographics in terms of gender, race, geographic region (rural, suburban, and urban), and grade enrollment. Four differing versions of the survey were administered, targeting boys in grades 5 to 8, girls in grades 5 to 8, boys in grades 9 to 12, and girls in grades 9 to 12. Some questions regarding contraception and sexuality were asked only of 9th through 12th graders, and gender-specific questions about topics such as menstruation and pelvic examinations were asked only of girls. Wilson and Klein conducted statistical analyses of the Commonwealth Fund Survey data set at the University of Rochester, based on research questions and hypotheses generated by Sutton and Brown, who framed the purpose of this chapter and interpreted the survey results, drawing the conclusions and placing them in the context of prior research.

OVERVIEW OF CONTRACEPTIVE INFORMATION SOURCES

The ranking of sources of contraceptive knowledge among American adolescents demonstrated by the Commonwealth Fund study (Table 2.2) shows a shift in the informational power structure from previous surveys. For the

TABLE 2.2

Percentage Who Have "Learned About Birth Control, Contraception, or Preventing Pregnancy" From Different Sources[a]

Sources of Contraceptive Information	Gender		Race		Parental Education[b]		Income		Total
	Male (N) = 1,253	Female 1,691	White 1,799	Non-White 947	Only High School or Some College 1,362	College Degree or More 1,274	Hard Times or Just Getting By 585	Few or No Problems 2,143	
Health class, pamphlets, or videos at school	60.9	69.1**	66.8	62.1	62.8	69.0*	67.5	64.9	65.1
Friends	52.2	68.5**	62.6	58.1*	62.5	60.1	60.2	61.7	60.7
Parents	48.4	56.3**	53.0	51.9	54.2	51.6	46.8	54.0*	52.5
Magazines	39.7	63.4**	52.5	51.9	51.7	54.2	55.6	51.6	52.0
Television	50.0	51.6	50.5	51.7	51.4	51.6	53.9	50.4	50.9
Health professionals (Doctor/nurse)	31.5	47.4**	37.2	44.9*	38.3	40.4	42.5	38.6	39.8
Other adults	25.5	33.3**	26.7	34.6**	32.0	26.8*	31.8	28.5	29.6
Siblings	21.0	21.6	20.1	24.6*	22.9	19.7	23.8	20.7	21.3
Boy/girlfriend	22.1	20.1	20.6	22.6	23.9	18.3*	20.9	21.0	21.1
Don't know	8.3	1.6**	4.5	5.7	4.5	3.6	4.7	4.7	4.9
Internet	5.0	1.5**	3.0	3.9	2.3	4.2*	3.7	3.2	3.2
Nobody	1.0	0**	.2	1.2	.6	.3	.5	.5	.5
Church	.2	.2	.2	.2	0	.4*	0	.2*	.2

Note. [a]This question was asked of boys and girls grades 9–12 only. [b]Parental education was based on one or both parents.

*p ≤ .05 **p ≤ .001

first time, 9th- to 12th-grade adolescents cited school-based sexual education—such as health classes, pamphlets, or videos—as their source for information about birth control more frequently (65.1%) than they did peers—
who ranked second (60.7%).

Gender Differences Among Adolescents

As Table 2.2 illustrates, the most significant overall differences in sources of
contraceptive information occur along gender lines. A higher proportion of
high school girls reported learning about birth control from most of these
sources than did boys—with the exceptions of siblings, television, boy-
friend/girlfriends, and church, from which an equal proportion of girls and
boys acquired knowledge. About one half of boys and girls learned about
contraception from TV, about one fifth from siblings and boyfriends/girl-
friends, and very few from church. This complements data from the 1998 Kaiser study, which also indicates that teenage girls are more likely to seek sexual information from a wider variety of sources than are boys (Henry J.
Kaiser Family Foundation, 1998). The possibility of getting pregnant—which
obviously does not have as life-altering consequences for boys as for girls—
may well lead girls to garner contraceptive information from a wider spectrum of sources in order to learn as much as possible and therefore protect
themselves. Another reason for girls to cast a wider net for knowledge may
relate to STDs; apart from HIV and AIDS, the symptoms of many STDs are
more severe for women than for men, even leading to sterility in some cases
(Henry J. Kaiser Family Foundation, 1998). However, the fear of getting pregnant or contracting STDs may not be the central motivating force for all girls,
and this point of view may to some degree reflect societal gender stereotyping; interest in contraception may arise from pleasure seeking or curiosity as
well—motives more traditionally associated with males.

The differing importance of various forms of media to each gender is
also apparent. Males were more likely than females to get sexual information from the media in the early 1980s (Davis & Harris, 1982). However, our
new data suggest that adolescent girls have pulled even with boys in getting contraceptive information from television, and that they learn about
contraception from magazines about one and one half times as often as
their male counterparts.

Television ranks third as a source of contraceptive information—above
parents for boys, but below parents for girls. This is not due to greater acquisition of birth control knowledge from TV among males—about half of
both genders cite it as a source—but rather to the fact that girls learn such
information from parents in greater numbers (56.3% as opposed to 48.4% for
their male counterparts). Boys are more than three times as likely as girls
to use the Internet as a source of knowledge, but this number must be put
in perspective: Only slightly more than 3% of all the adolescents surveyed

named the Internet as a way they had learned about birth control and contraception. A significantly higher percentage of girls have learned about contraception from magazines than boys (63.4% to 39.7%). Among girls, magazines rank higher than parents as a source of such information; among boys, magazines rank lower than parents or television.

Racial Factors in Learning Patterns

The most significant difference between White and non-White high school students is non-Whites' greater use of "other adults" (i.e., other than parents) as sources of contraceptive information. About half of both White and non-White adolescents have learned about birth control from their parents. However, although more than one fourth of White teens consult with other adults about contraception, more than one third of their non-White counterparts do. Clearly, the cultural norms for discussing birth control with adults outside the immediate family differ for these groups. Other sources that show statistically significant differences include siblings, friends, and medical professionals. White adolescents are less likely to have learned about contraception from siblings (about one fifth as compared to almost one fourth for non-Whites), but learn from friends more often. Non-White adolescents are more likely to gain contraceptive knowledge from doctors or nurses than are White teens.

The Effects of Parental Socioeconomic Status

A parent's level of education also has an impact on the sources of contraceptive information reported by adolescents. Teens with parents who have only a high school degree or some college are less likely to name health classes in school as a source of information (62.8%) than are students with at least one parent who has a college degree or more (69%). This may reflect a greater emphasis on the value of education in highly educated households. Yet paradoxically, about the same number of teens with parents in the less educated category (about 54%) as teens whose parents had at least a college degree (almost 52%) say that their parents were a source of birth control information. Apparently, being well-educated does not necessarily provide significant advantages when a parent finds herself or himself cast into the role of sex educator. Adolescents with highly educated parents are less likely to have learned about contraception from boyfriends/girlfriends and other adults, but—not surprisingly—are nearly twice as likely to have acquired such information on the Internet. One caveat to these observations is that the Commonwealth Fund Survey did not draw distinctions about the quality of the sexual information that respondents said their parents had provided.

The most striking difference among higher- and lower-level income families is that adolescents whose families have few or no problems getting by economically report that parents were a source of birth control knowledge more frequently (54%) than those in families that are facing hard times or just getting by (47%). Presumably, coping with severe economic pressure to put food on the table and a roof over their family's heads makes at-home sexual and contraceptive education less of a priority for such parents.

Helping to Define Agendas for Contraceptive Education

By identifying where America's adolescents are most frequently acquiring their knowledge about contraception and birth control, we can provide a road map of the most commonly traveled channels of communication, helping public health officials and educators discern where they might best focus their efforts to encourage a more responsible approach toward sexual activity among adolescents. We also draw on previous research to offer methods that may help make adolescents' trips along these informational highways as smooth as possible, especially given the bumpy roads facing them as they travel through the crucial and central task of identity development in this and other areas of their lives.

From Classroom to Bedroom: Do School Sexual Curricula Make the Grade in the Real World?

In our data, school-based health classes, including teaching aids such as pamphlets and videos, consistently rank as the primary source of contraceptive, birth control, and pregnancy prevention information among adolescents—across all gender, race, parental education, and income categories. The effectiveness of in-school curricula varies most significantly with the gender of the adolescent and the educational level of her or his parents. (See Table 2.2.)

Nationally, surveys show that 79% of American adults support sexuality education in schools, with 62% strongly in favor of such programs (Lake Research, 1996); however, fewer than half of the states—22 plus Washington, D.C., and Puerto Rico—mandate a sex education curriculum (Gambrell & Patierno, 1995).

Because our data indicate that in-school programs have now assumed a central role in educating adolescents about responsible sexual behaviors, key questions asked repeatedly by educators have become more important than ever: Do these programs work? Do they achieve their stated goals?

The answers to both questions depend on the program being examined. At the moment, sexuality education programs may be divided into two principal categories: abstinence-only and abstinence-plus. Abstinence-only (sometimes called chastity) programs teach students that refraining from sex until marriage is the only acceptable form of behavior. Contraceptive information is either absent or discussed only in the context of deriding the type of student who lacks the willpower to meet this standard. Abstinence-plus programs—also known as comprehensive sexuality education—promote abstinence as the most surefire method to prevent pregnancy and disease, but also acknowledge that some sexual activity among adolescents is likely. Such programs include contraceptive information and cover other sexuality issues, in addition to teaching skill building to resist peer and other social pressures to have sex (Kirby, 1997).

Because students begin attending school well before they initiate sexual behavior, the classroom is seen as having immense potential for addressing and reducing the probability of unhealthy sexual activity. Schools not only have a ready made organizational structure that can broadly implement sexual education programs, but they also provide a primary forum for the social interactions of adolescents and their friends, and "thus have the potential for affecting peer pressures and norms" (Kirby, Korpi, Adivi, & Weissman, 1997, p. 45).

The dependence of such a large percentage of high school-age adolescents—almost two thirds in our data—on school sex education programs for information on contraception raises concerns about the inevitable intersections between moral stances and effective education. A World Health Organization (WHO) review of 35 sex education programs around the globe found that abstinence-only programs were not as effective in promoting less risky adolescent sexual behaviors as abstinence-plus programs (Baldo, Aggleton, & Slutkin, 1993). Domestically, reviews of six evaluations of the abstinence-only programs Living Smart, ENABL, Project Taking Charge, Stay SMART, and Success Express found no evidence that any effectively delayed first intercourse (Kirby, 1997). Five other studies conducted on the abstinence-only programs Sex Respect, Success Express, and AANCHOR (An Alternative National Curriculum on Responsibility) showed similar results (Berns & Huberman, 1995). Nonetheless, from 1998 to 2000, the federal government earmarked a $50 million appropriation to be divided among states that teach that physical and emotional harm results from premarital sex (Daley, 1997).

However, even abstinence-plus programs, as widely taught now, do not appear to reduce adolescent sexual activity. Although no evaluation of an abstinence-plus program has indicated that teaching about contraception either hastened the start of adolescent sexual activity, such as intercourse, or increased its frequency, one recent study concluded that pregnancy prevention programs have no impact on adolescent sexual activity—although many do positively influence contraceptive use and reduce pregnancy rates (Corcoran, Miller, & Bultman, 1997). Panels assembled by the Centers for Disease Control (CDC) and the Program Archive on Sexuality, Health, and Adolescence (PASHA) also concluded that several comprehensive sexuality education programs were effective in reducing sexual risk taking, such as

Be Proud! Be Responsible! and Teen Talk (Card, Niego, Mallari, & Farrell, 1996; Kirby, 1997). An evaluation of the abstinence-plus program Reducing the Risk found a 40% reduction in unprotected intercourse for adolescents who were inexperienced at pretest compared with a control group (Kirby, Barth, Leland, & Fetro, 1991).

Yet some of Kirby's more recent investigations have yielded less positive results. A 1997 study identified only four sex education programs nation-wide—all aimed at high school students—that actually delayed intercourse or increased use of condoms or other forms of contraception (Kirby, Korpi, et al., 1997).

But even this may be a case of locking the barn door after the horse has been stolen: Few adolescents are likely to become abstinent once they have initiated intercourse. Therefore, sex education programs may need to place more emphasis on targeting middle school students; by the time they reach 9th grade, 38% of American adolescents already will be sexually active (Kirby, Korpi, et al., 1997). Yet Kirby's group of researchers concludes that "there currently does not exist any sex or HIV education program designed for middle-school youth for which there is good evidence that it delays intercourse or otherwise reduces sexual risk-taking behavior" (Kirby, Korpi, et al., 1997, p. 45).

An evaluation of Project SNAPP (Skills and kNowledge for AIDS and Pregnancy Prevention)—an attempt to create and evaluate an effective sex education curriculum for 7th-grade students at six middle schools in southern California—also yielded disappointing results. Although knowledge about sexual topics increased, subsequent questionnaires administered 5 months and 17 months after the program began showed no statistically significant differences between the SNAPP group and the control group in the number of times they had sex, number of sexual partners, or use of condoms or birth control pills (Kirby, Korpi, et al., 1997). The researchers concluded that the program had been too brief to have a lasting impact and that the theoretical framework upon which such sexual education programs are built—social learning theory and the health belief model—is insufficient to the tasks of delaying intercourse or teaching contraceptive use (Kirby, Korpi, et al., 1997). Another review of the effectiveness of sexual education in Western countries examined 22 studies, 15 of which evaluated American programs (Visser & van Bilsen, 1994). The conclusions again were less than encouraging: No educational program could demonstrate an appreciable impact on communication skills, or contraceptive use, or on sexual behavior such as intercourse (Visser & van Bilsen, 1994).

The Achilles heel of such sex education programs may well be their failure to take into account the popular culture outside the school and the resulting discontinuity between what students see and hear inside the classroom and what they experience elsewhere: "Teenagers never see people on television who use contraception while having sex, or women who refuse to have sex if no contraception method is used. Social norms are also a major factor in the shaping of adolescents' behavior" (Visser & van Bilsen, 1994, p. 154).

But it is important for educators to note that these social norms extend beyond the media. In general, learning from one source of contraceptive information seems to stimulate learning from others. In a regression analysis of our data that examined the interaction between learning contraceptive information from multiple media sources and from other sources, adolescents with a wide breadth of media learning were significantly more likely to say that they had also learned from health classes, age-mates (friends, siblings, and boyfriends/girlfriends), and parents.

The difficulty of carrying the lessons of sex education from school into nonschool situations may arise largely from the way it is typically taught. Groups of male and female middle school students ages 11 to 15 found it challenging to apply dire statistics about issues like pregnancy and AIDS to concrete, recognizable, and personal situations—even hypothetical ones—in a series of focus groups (Palmer, Boardman, & Bauchner, 1996). All the young adolescents saw AIDS as "a disease of adults," and participants in one boys' group could not envision using a condom until they were 17 or 20 or "had been dating for 12 months" (Palmer et al., 1996, p. 299). Boys indicated they were more likely to ask about a potential lover's past partners than offer to wear a condom. Girls, on the other hand, indicated that condom use was a sign of "true affection" because "if he really loved her, he would use condoms" (Palmer et al., 1996, p. 299). All students mentioned peer pressure as one reason they might have sex or not use a condom (Palmer et al., 1996).

The socialization effects and sexual scripts created by mass media both fail to reinforce and often actively contradict the educational lessons taught through the schools. Perhaps the answer lies in a greater emphasis on role playing among middle school students that would simulate real-world situations where an adolescent may feel pressured to have unprotected sex. Such classes could provide a set of sexual scripts for real-life scenarios that reinforce responsible sexual behaviors.

Getting by With a Little Help From Their Friends: Peers as Contraceptive-Information Sources

The influence of peers becomes more pervasive as adolescents grow older and seek to form a sense of identity. Traditional psychoanalytic theory views the central task of adolescence as establishing autonomy from parents, and assumes that parent–child conflict and rebellious behavior are necessary parts of accomplishing that task (Christensen & Roberts, 1998). High school students typically spend twice as much of their time with peers

(29%) as with parents or other adults (15%); by 6th grade, adults besides parents account for only one fourth of most early adolescents' social networks. The shift away from adults is accompanied by movement toward peer groups that are increasingly independent of adult guidance, include more members of the opposite sex, and grow beyond dyads and cliques to form larger social collectives—which become the basis for normative peer "cultures" distinct from the cultural traits that mark adult groups (Brown, 1990).

This shift is apparent in the 1993 Time/CNN poll on adolescents' sources of sexual information, in which parents and peers reverse as the number one and two sources of knowledge as adolescents grow older (Yankelovich Partners, Inc., 1993). (See Table 2.1.)

With this in mind, the importance of friends as providers of contraceptive and pregnancy prevention information across all gender, racial, and socioeconomic categories, as demonstrated in our data, is hardly surprising. Some groups of adolescents depend more heavily on their friends for contraceptive information than others do, however.

High school girls (68.5%) are significantly more likely than boys (52.2%) to have learned about contraception from friends. White teens (62.6%) are more likely than non-White teens (58.1%) to have acquired birth control knowledge from friends. These findings are supported by previous research that has shown a gender bias in initiating communication about sexual topics. Focus groups show female middle school students ages 11 to 15 are better able than their male counterparts to envision themselves discussing sexual issues—such as condom use—with a prospective intimate partner (Palmer et al., 1996). Although our data indicate that equal proportions (about one fifth) of male and female adolescents have learned about contraception from boyfriends or girlfriends, prior studies indicate that females are the more frequent initiators of such conversations. Among those in late adolescence who are already involved in heterosexual relationships, communication and information gathering about sexual risks such as STDs and HIV are usually started by women. Once the woman has started safe-sex talk, however, men are willing to discuss it. For both partners, a prerequisite to frank discussions about sexual risks was being involved in a caring relationship and a building of trust (Lock, Ferguson, & Wise, 1998). If, as some research indicates, mothers typically are expected to assume a greater part of the burden than fathers in initiating sexual discussions with children, it's possible that adolescents are replicating a pattern in which women are expected to take the first step in such conversations (Simanski, 1998).

At least one school system has turned adolescents' reliance on peers (and their sometimes dubious sexual information) to its advantage. The Dade County School System in Florida has created a program using adolescents as trained peer counselor/educators (PCEs) for other dropout-prevention-program students who generally are disengaged from school and thus unlikely to learn much from sex education classes. Pre- and postintervention questionnaire results indicated an increase in AIDS awareness and discussion among at-risk students and an increase in condom use (O'Hara, Messick, Fichtner, & Parris, 1996).

This approach's strength is its de facto acknowledgment of peers as a major source of sexual information—rather than trying to substitute adult authority figures, which conventional adolescent psychosocial development theory would say runs counter to adolescents' natural and expected tendency to reject parents and other adults in favor of friends (Brown, 1990). At the core of this approach is the simple but effective idea that if adolescents are going to inform other adolescents about sex anyway, those spreading the information might as well have accurate and risk-reducing facts as they do so. It is, as the authors point out, "a promising health education strategy" (O'Hara et al., 1996, p. 176).

Parental Communication: Potential Contributions, Powerful Inhibitions

Parents are still an important source of contraceptive information for adolescents, cited by about half in our survey (Table 2.3). A significantly higher percentage of girls than boys have learned about birth control information from parents (56.3%, compared to 48.8%, respectively). But race and the educational level of parents don't appear to affect the use of this source. However, adolescents in families facing tougher economic times are less likely to have learned about contraception from parents (46.8%), compared to adolescents in families on firmer economic footing (54%).

The division along gender lines observed in Table 2.3 has been noted in previous studies, and attributed in part to an American cultural pattern that allows the role of parental sexual educator to fall to the mother by default. A 10-city study indicated that mothers (74%) were more likely than fathers (49%) to discuss AIDS with their children (Centers for Disease Control, 1991). Other research has indicated that adolescent girls are more likely to have discussed pregnancy, conception, and abstinence with their parents than are boys (Leland & Barth, 1992). Mother–daughter communication also is more likely to include information on sexual health issues than father–son or even mother–son communication (Nolin & Peterson, 1992).

Another study examined 26 how-to articles about discussing sex with one's children, published between 1984 and 1993 in magazines that specifically target mothers and families, such as *Working Mother*, and in more general-interest publications, such as *Readers Digest*. The conclusion: This is an area in which the media could have a positive effect, with the popular press acting as a viable parent education tool. One principal suggestion to improve the way magazines in particular have approached this is to draw fa-

TABLE 2.3

Proportions Who Have Discussed Different Kinds of Sexual Information With Parents or Guardians

Topics Discussed With Parents Guardians	Gender		Race		Parental Education		Income		Grade		Total
	Male	Female	White	Non-White	Only High School or Some College	College Degree or Further	Hard Times or Just Getting By	Few or No Problems	5th–8th	9th–12th	
(N) questions asked of grades 5–12 =	2,539–	3,157–	3,336–	2,011–	2,394–	2,411–	1,232–	4,014–	2,591–	3,105–	
	2,579[a]	3,192	3,367	2,044	2,427	2,439	1,251	4,065	2,618	3,146	
(N) questions asked of grades 9–12 only =	1,351–	1,739–	1,872–	985–	1,407–	1,321–	608–	1,232–	—	3,079–	
	1,380	1,762	1,885	1,014	1,428	1,333	620	1,251		3,146	3,146
Having sex[b]	67.6	72.8*	69.8	72.1	70.9	70.9	69.8	70.7	—	70.2	70.2
How women become pregnant	54.8	68.0**	62.8	59.8	62.2	63.0	59.4	62.2	61.2	61.9	61.6
How to prevent pregnancy	49.4	61.2**	54.7	56.8	58.4	54.6*	54.1	55.8	52.6	58.4*	55.5
Use of condoms	49.6	53.2*	49.5	54.4*	54.7	48.8**	50.7	51.1	52.3	50.6	51.4
Sexually transmitted diseases (STDs)[b]	49.6	52.2	49.0	55.6*	52.7	50.0	51.0	51.1	—	50.9	50.9
AIDS	53.7	55.7	53.6	57.2*	55.3	56.1	51.3	55.7*	54.5	54.9	54.7
Sexual abuse of children by adults[b]	35.0	43.3**	38.0	41.6	41.9	37.3	44.2	37.9*	—	39.2	39.2

Note. [a]Ranges due to missing data in survey responses. [b]These topics asked of only grades 9–12.
*p ≤ .05 **p ≤ .001

thers more into the process. The majority of the articles appeared in women's and family-focused magazines, which typically also target female readers. Greater inclusion of fathers in how-to articles on sexual discussion will create a stronger sense of shared responsibility for sexual education among parents and may broaden teenagers' perspective about sexuality by better representing the male role (Simanski, 1998).

Many of these gender-based differences are borne out in our own data on the sexuality topics that adolescents most frequently report discussing with their parents or guardians. (See Table 2.3.) The six top-ranked topics are "having sex," "how women become pregnant," "how to prevent pregnancy," "use of condoms," "sexually transmitted diseases," and "AIDS." The most-cited topic was "having sex," with more than 70% of the adolescents surveyed reporting such a discussion with parents. Although more girls than boys reported such a discussion with their parents (72.8%, compared to 67.6%, respectively), the more significant gender differences come in the areas of pregnancy explanation and prevention. Although 68% of girls reported discussing with parents how women get pregnant, only 54.8% of boys did. Similarly, 61.2% of girls said they had talked about pregnancy prevention with parents; 49.4% of boys did. Even in the area of condom use, a less dramatic but still significant gender difference in parental communication was noted: 53.2% of girls had discussed condom use with parents, versus 49.6% of boys. Collectively, these data point to a cultural norm for parents to view pregnancy prevention and avoiding sexually risky behavior as primarily a female responsibility. Even in the area of "sexual abuse of children by adults," a significantly higher proportion of girls (43.3%) reported discussing the topic with parents than did boys (35%).

A significantly greater proportion of non-White adolescents discussed STDs, AIDS, and the use of condoms with parents than did White adolescents. This may be indicative of the greater impact—in terms of the proportion of the population affected—that such diseases have had in non-White communities.

Education was no predictor of the breadth of parental communication about sexuality. Essentially equal proportions of students with more highly educated and those with less-educated parents reported conversations about "having sex," "how women become pregnant," "sexually transmitted diseases," and "AIDS"; but highly educated parents were significantly less likely to tackle topics such as "how to prevent pregnancy" and the "use of condoms." This result is counterintuitive, given the emphasis that parents with advanced degrees are likely to place on education and teaching.

Acting as a sex educator is probably not a task that comes easily to most parents, regardless of their educational background. Many are uncomfortable with having this role thrust on them and may inadvertently send out nonverbal messages that discourage open communication—such as giving the impression that sex is something "dirty" (Simanski, 1998). Stunted parent–child discussion of sexual topics may have ramifications as well for the ability of adolescents to communicate with sexual partners about topics such as condom use and AIDS. A study of 80 male and female heterosexual adolescents indicated that "communication with one's sexual partner is positively associated with having discussed sexual matters with parents," suggesting that "adolescent–adult sexual discussion may help adolescents feel competent about discussing comparably sensitive matters with sexual partners" (Shoop & Davidson, 1994, p. 146).

Although simple embarrassment may be a significant factor that inhibits low-communication parents from talking about sex with their children, Fisher (1986) suggested that some parents' lack of knowledge about sexual and reproductive functioning also may keep them from discussing sexuality with their children. When 90 adolescents and 73 mothers were asked in a recent study to define the following terms related to sexual development—ejaculation, hormones, menstruation, ovulation, puberty, semen, and wet dreams—mothers were more likely to provide correct definitions than adolescent boys or girls, but still were not able to adequately define most of the terms. The authors of the study concluded: "These results raise the concern that mothers are ill-prepared to teach their children about sex or reinforce information that adolescents learn in school. . . . The reluctance of parents to provide information to their children may be due to their own uncertainty" (Hockenbury-Eaton, Richman, DiIorio, Rivero, & Maibach, 1996, p. 46). One suggestion to remedy the situation: development of continuing adult sex education curricula to teach parents how to communicate better about sexual topics with their adolescents (Hockenbury-Eaton et al., 1996).

One form of sex education that has a beneficial effect on parent–child communication about sexuality and contraception already exists, however: in-school health classes. The fact that school-based sexuality education has become the primary source of such knowledge for adolescents apparently has beneficial ripple effects in the home, despite questions raised about such programs' general efficacy. One study found that prior to a sexuality education program, about half of the students surveyed had discussed abstinence with their parents, and 37% had talked about contraception. After the program, the level of parent–child communication about abstinence had increased to 66%, with 52% now discussing contraception as well (Barth, Fetro, Leland, & Volkan, 1992). Another investigation indicated that an HIV education program not only improved students' knowledge of HIV, but also their ability to discuss it with parents (Levy et al., 1995).

Discussion and education don't necessarily translate into the desired sexually responsible behaviors, however. For instance, one study of 12- to 14-year-olds and their parents investigated the differences in sexual knowledge, sexual attitudes, and contraceptive choices between young adolescents whose parents frequently discussed sexual topics with them and

those whose parents rarely discussed sex. The findings surprised researchers by indicating no differences in knowledge, attitudes, and contraceptive
choices between the adolescents, based on whether they came from high-
communication or low-communication families (Fisher, 1986). Responses indicated that "the primary effect of parent–child discussions about sexuality
was in the area of sexual attitudes, not sexual knowledge or contraceptive
choice" (Fisher, 1986, p. 524). Thus, high-communication, conservative parents ended up transmitting, intentionally or otherwise, their beliefs about
the proper role of sex in their childrens' lives; liberal, more sexually permissive, high-communication parents did the same, but with different attitudes
conveyed. Therefore, the extent of parent–child sexual communication may
not always be a good indicator of whether or not adolescents will be inhib-
ited from sexual activity or knowledgable about protection—although such
communication may affect activity through the transmission of attitudes
(Fisher, 1986).

Medium, Not Well Done: Mass Media's Skewed Presentation of Sexuality

However, none of the aforementioned sources of contraceptive and sexual
information operates in a vacuum, and one source may influence the effectiveness of others.

Media messages have the potential to significantly undermine the impact
of school-based sexual education (Visser & van Bilsen, 1994). The perceived
need to create dramatic conflict to attract and stimulate viewers and listeners means that in the minds of programmers, risky behavior makes for
good television, movies, and music videos. The bottom line: An adolescent
who watches 3 to 5 hours of television each day witnesses about 2,000 sex
acts per year. A typical R-rated film presents 14 to 21 sex acts, most of
which are visually explicit (Brown, Greenberg, & Buerkel-Rothfuss, 1993).
About 75% of concept videos (those containing narrative story lines as opposed to concert footage) on Music Television (MTV) involve sexual imagery, and 80% combine sex and violence (Committee on Communications,
American Academy of Pediatrics, 1995).

Dawson's Creek may not sell itself as educational television, but it is. As
in its trend-setting predecessors, *Melrose Place* and *Beverly Hills, 90210*,
beautiful adolescents are locked in an elaborate waltz of ever-changing intimate relationships, spiced with sex that rarely has dire consequences. Such
shows provide "American adolescents with one of many tantalizing impressions of teen social life" where, "needless to say, infection with *Chlamydia
trachomatis* has not been a recurring storyline" (Clark, Cohall, Joffe, & Starr,
1997, p. 102).

Even apparently well-intentioned media efforts to provide sexual information to adolescents may be undercut by their desire to be entertaining,

such as MTV's *Loveline*, a late-night, hour-long program to which pseudonymous adolescent callers can phone in, describe their sexual issues, and get answers over the air. A panel consisting of celebrity guest stars (such as actresses from the hit television show *Felicity*), comedian Adam Carolla, and Dr. Drew Pinsky (described by MTV Online as a "board-certified internist and addictionalogist") discusses sexual concerns with teens and 20-somethings, but the callers chosen tend to be ones with unusual, sensationalistic sexual problems rather than everyday concerns. One wonders whether Carolla's nonstop barrage of jokey patter and the rapid-fire MTV-style pacing interfere with the relatively reserved Pinsky's ability to get his advice across. The program is billed as talk-health-comedy by MTV Online, and emphasis frequently falls on the last of these three descriptors.

The media rarely promote medically accurate and health-enhancing images (Brown & Steele, 1996) and often present an influential and consequence-free portrait of sexuality in which abstinence among adolescents is rarely presented in a positive light (Committee on Communications, American Academy of Pediatrics, 1995). This tendency to focus on stimulation rather than education becomes a cause for concern in light of the Commonwealth Fund Survey data.

More than half of the adolescents surveyed cited magazines and television as sources of information about birth control, contraception, or preventing pregnancy—placing both these media less than two percentage points below parents (52.5%) in popularity among teens and far above the next most popular source, physicians (39.8%). No significant variations in the use of media for contraceptive information were observed among different racial and socioeconomic groups, but age and gender appear to play a major role in adolescents' choices of media.

Across all categories, age was a consistent predictor of use of media sources. Middle school-aged adolescents (5th to 8th grade) were significantly more likely than high school students to name multiple media as sources of contraceptive information. The heavier use of media as learning sources among this age-group lends weight to research indicating that school-based sex education needs to begin in middle school, earlier than it generally does now (Kirby, Korpi, et al., 1997); the sooner such intervention takes place, the sooner a counterbalance to media messages about sexual behavior is made available to the group most drawn to media presentations of sexuality.

Although high school boys and girls are equally likely to have learned about contraception from television (50% and 51.6%, respectively), girls are far more likely to have acquired information from magazines (63.4% of girls named magazines; 39.7% of boys did). For females, magazines ranked above parents as a source of knowledge about birth control, and television ranked below. Among males, the opposite was true: Television was named more commonly than parents, but magazines were identified less frequently. The dramatic difference between the proportion of boys and girls who say they have learned contraceptive information from magazines may be largely attributed to the dramatic difference in the content of magazines that target male and female adolescent audiences. Boys' publications tend to focus on activities such skateboarding and sports. Popular girls' periodicals such as *Seventeen* continue to promote an ideology drawn heavily from their cosmetics and other fashion advertisers' agendas (Steiner, 1995): The overriding priority of adolescent girls should be concern with their appearance, and "they should concentrate their efforts on finding a boy—a 'guy' in teen magazine speak" (Peirce, 1995). Magazines like *Cosmopolitan* and *Vogue* direct articles on sexual activity and heterosexual relationships at female readers. The teen magazine *YM* has included a self-test on kissing proficiency, and *Seventeen* has offered cover stories such as "Sex: How much DON'T you know?" (Brown et al., 1993). The emphasis in girls' magazines on how to be sexually attractive to men and their articles on sexual activity generally make these publications more prolific providers of information on topics relating to contraception—and of articles on birth control itself—than their male-oriented counterparts (see chaps. 7 and 8 in this book).

Another media source from which adolescents can gather sexual information lies at their fingertips: the Internet. According to the U.S. Department of Education, Internet access in public schools increased from 35% to 78% between 1993 and 1997. As of 1999, more than 89% of secondary schools in the country reported being connected to the World Wide Web (Little, 1998). Library and home access to the Internet also were expanding rapidly (Tenopir, 1998; Cravatta, 1997). Internet usage among children and adolescents aged 2 to 17 (who have online access at home) is expected to grow from 6.5% in 1996 to 31.4% by 2002 (Cravatta, 1997).

However, our Commonwealth Fund Survey data demonstrate that this projected online explosion of information access as of 1999 had only a relatively small impact on where adolescents learn about contraception, birth control, or pregnancy prevention: Only 3.5% of adolescents named the Internet as a source of such knowledge, ranking it 11th in popularity—above "nobody" and "church." The level of usage also appeared to be closely related to gender. High school boys were more than three times as likely as girls to say they learned about contraception through the World Wide Web. Although no significant differences emerged along racial or family income lines, parental education level seemed to play a significant role. Almost twice as many teens whose parents had a college degree or more (4.2%) named the Internet as a source of birth control or pregnancy prevention information, versus 2.3% of adolescents whose parent had only a high school education and perhaps some college.

Despite these low numbers, the Internet eventually may prove to be a valuable resource for adolescents seeking sexual information in a proactive way. New educational sites are appearing every day. Helpful sites on the World Wide Web can be divided into two categories: information providers and Q&A forums. The Planned Parenthood web page (www.ppfa.org/ppfa) is an online resource for information about sexual and reproductive heath, contraception, birth control, family planning, pregnancy, STDs, sexuality education, and abortion and reproduction rights. It includes links to other Web sites and access to the Planned Parenthood Federation Library. The Campaign for Our Children has a Web site geared just toward adolescents (www.cfoc.org/3_teen/3_index.cfm) to complement its Internet site for parents.

Another approach, which has been highly successful with adults (and perhaps more than a few adolescents, surreptitiously) is the cyberspace Q&A Web site, such as the pioneering "Go Ask Alice," a simple, text-based health-advice site run by Columbia University. This site is frank and informative, with a section on sexual health that offers valuable information (and links to other Web sites) about topics such as birth control and STDs (Shattuck, 1998).

Of course, the individual educational value of sites varies widely, and some adult-oriented versions carry links to pornographic Web sites or even ads from pornographic sponsors. Again, if Q&A Internet sites of genuine educational value are to be made available to adolescents, the technology must exist to block out their shadier siblings; otherwise, blanket—and perhaps politically motivated—opposition to providing teens access to any Internet-based sexual material may inhibit development of this potentially fruitful educational resource. Although some Internet browser services, such as America Online, Compuserv, and Prodigy come equipped with programs that can be used to lock out undesirable adult segments (Mossberg, 1994), often such services restrict access based on keywords—thus blocking out innocent and helpful information on topics such as breast cancer, simply because the word *breast* is present.

An interactive web page involving discussion of sexual issues of concern to adolescents could be employed in conjunction with school-based sex education among middle school and high school students, who might even be able to post questions and receive responses from counselors anonymously. Access to the page could be limited by a special password or code. Tying the underutilized power of the Internet to the most popular source of contraceptive information among teens—school health classes—could ultimately enhance the effectiveness of both.

Health Care Professionals: An Underprescribed Resource for Sexual Information

Medical professionals such as physicians and nurses have perenially ranked low (or not at all) on the adolescent informational totem pole as sources of knowledge about sex, birth control, and pregnancy prevention (see Table 2.1). But both our survey data and past studies indicate that this is not due to adolescents' lack of desire to talk about these topics with doctors; it is instead often attributable to the failure of many physicians to initiate such discussions. Our findings reflect past researchers' conclusions: Even if they're not sexually active, many adolescents are hungry for more information about sexual issues, but they are frequently too embarrassed or afraid to take the first step in beginning such conversations.

Across all gender, racial, parental education, family income, and age levels studied in the Commonwealth Fund Survey, adolescents were about two to four times as likely to say that doctors or health care professionals should talk with them about sexual health topics—such as STDs, pregnancy prevention, and physical/sexual abuse—as they were to say that health professionals did talk about these issues with them. Overall, more than twice as many adolescents say that health care professionals should discuss STDs and pregnancy prevention with them (61.4% and 49.9%, respectively) as those who say physicians and nurses have discussed these topics (26% and 20.6%). And more than three times as many adolescents believe that health care professionals should discuss physical and sexual abuse with them (42%) as the percentage who report that health care providers have done so (12.4%).

Differences are also apparent in both the desire for and the receipt of information on STDs, pregnancy prevention, and physical/sexual abuse among varying gender, racial, and age categories.

Table 2.4 shows that a significantly higher percentage of female adolescents than males noted that physicians and other health professionals should be discussing these topics; a significantly higher percentage of girls than boys also noted that medical professionals had discussed sexual issues such as STDs and pregnancy prevention with them. In fact, almost twice as many adolescent women as men said that physicians or other health care professionals had discussed pregnancy prevention with them (26.3% of girls as opposed to 14.6% of boys). This disparity suggests a continuing societal view that pregnancy prevention is still primarily a woman's responsibility.

Even so, the level of adolescent–physician discussion of sexual topics reported by girls still falls far short of what women want: Two thirds of adolescent girls want to discuss STDs with their doctors or a health care professional (65.4%), but only one fourth have had such a discussion (27.7%). The same pattern holds true for pregnancy prevention (58.2% want to, 26.3% have done so) and physical/sexual abuse (47.3% want to, but only 12.5% have). A similar discrepancy emerges among figures for boys: more than half say medical professionals should discuss STDs (57.5%); less than one fourth (24.3%) have had such discussions. Although 41.4% of males favor discussing pregnancy prevention and 36.3% support talking about physi-

TABLE 2.4

Percentage Who Say a Doctor or Health Professional Should Discuss/Has Discussed Selected Sexual Topics With Adolescents

Topics a Doctor or Health Professional Should Discuss/Has Discussed:	Gender		Race		Parental Education		Income		Grade		Total
	Male	Female	White	Non-White	Only High School or Some College	College Degree or More	Hard Times or Just Getting By	Few or No Problems	5th–8th	9th–12th	
(N) Should discuss =	3,001	3,525	3,532	2,192	2,564	2,565	1,356	4,284	3,090	3,436	
(N) Has discussed[a] =	2,341	2,934	2,833	1,720	2,098	2,079	1,107	3,449	2,479	2,796	
STDs											
Should discuss	57.5	65.4**	61.1	62.1	64.6	60.8*	60.6	61.7	51.4	72.7**	61.4
Has discussed	24.3	27.6*	23.2	30.6**	27.9	25.1	28.5	25.0	20.0	32.8**	26.0
Preventing pregnancy											
Should discuss	41.4	58.2**	51.2	49.0	54.4	50.2*	49.7	50.7	36.5	65**	49.9
Has discussed	14.6	26.3**	18.5	24.4**	22.9	19.6*	23.2	19.8*	14.1	27.8**	20.6
Physical/sexual abuse											
Should discuss	36.3	47.8**	41.5	43.2	43.2	41.3	43.8	41.6	39.8	44.5*	42.0
Has discussed	12.3	12.5	10.3	16.1**	12.9	11.3	14.8	11.5*	14.0	10.6*	12.4

Note. [a]Adolescents who said a topic has been discussed were significantly more likely to have regular sick care and to have had a recent checkup.
*$p \leq .05$ **$p \leq .001$

cal/sexual abuse, only 14.6% reported discussing the former with a medical professional and 12.3% said they had communicated about the latter.

Overall, our new figures support past research that consistently has found that adolescents would like to learn more about contraceptive and sexual topics from doctors and nurses (Clark et al., 1997; Schuster, Bell, Peterson, & Kanouse, 1996).

CONCLUSIONS

Adolescents are hungry for sexual information. This is a time in their lives when the formation of a healthy sexual identity is vital to their mental health (Brown, 1990), and developing a sense of efficacy in dealing with sexual matters will have profound, long-lasting effects (Koch, 1993). Identifying sources from which American adolescents are most likely to acquire such information is crucial; it provides a guide for public health officials and educators as they seek to inject a message of responsible and healthy sexual behavior into those sources that are most influential among adolescents. The 1997 Commonwealth Fund Survey of the Health of Adolescents is a valuable resource in assessing where adolescents are learning about contraception, the breadth of what they are learning about sexuality and health issues, and why some sources are not as effective as they might be. A survey of prior research suggests that messages from one source may interact with information from other sources to reinforce or to weaken their respective messages.

The emergence of school-based health classes as the highest ranking source of contraceptive information among adolescents—cited by almost two thirds of respondents—makes evaluation of these programs more critical than ever before. This is an area in which the collision of conservative moral stances and educational needs may have tragic results for some adolescents. Despite the lack of evidence that any abstinence-only program has successfully reduced the rate of intercourse among adolescents, the federal government has given states more than $50 million to promote the idea that premarital sex causes physical and emotional harm (Daley, 1997). Although no evidence exists that abstinence-plus programs reduce (or encourage) the rate of adolescent sexual intercourse, studies have shown that many such programs do have a positive effect on condom use and pregnancy reduction (Corcoran et al., 1997). Although no direct cause and effect conclusion can be drawn, condom use among sexually active high school students has increased by 23% since 1991, and more than half (57%) of high school students reported in 1997 that they had used condoms the last time they had intercourse (Centers for Disease Control, 1998).

Yet HIV increased seven-fold among adolescents over the same time period (Centers for Disease Control, 1998), and 38% of adolescents will be sexually active by the time they even reach high school (Kirby, Korpi, et al., 1997); perhaps more emphasis needs to be placed on health classes for middle school students: in short, earlier intervention and education.

School-based sex education programs also should acknowledge that their messages frequently may be weakened by factors outside the classroom (Visser & van Bilsen, 1994), such as a discontinuity of messages between sex education curricula and the sexual knowledge (or lack of it) possessed by parents (Fisher, 1986; Hockenberry-Eaton et al., 1996); this leads to a failure to reinforce school-based sexual knowledge. Other key factors include distorted representations of what constitutes normative or healthy sexual behavior in the media (Brown et al., 1993), and too much emphasis in school curricula on providing scientific information about topics such as pregnancy and STDs. School sex education classes that include a media literacy component specifically addressing the misrepresentation of sex in the media could be helpful, especially because media literacy may be a topic that schools can address more comfortably with younger children. More effective school programs also might place greater emphasis on practicing practical, concrete behavioral responses to perceived pressure among adolescents to have sex, such as role playing in familiar, recognizable, relevant, hypothetical situations (Palmer et al., 1996). Such programs would draw an explicit connection between what is being taught in school and real-life, on-the-spot decision making about sex elsewhere. Employing the Internet as a means of providing an anonymous Q&A resource in the classroom may further enhance channels of communication between sex educators and adolescents. In addition, this would be an opportunity for area physicians to help their adolescent patients (and nonpatients) by offering to serve as the online "ask-the-doctor" sources, perhaps rotating with other physicians and health professionals in the community.

This leads to several other recommendations drawn from both our Commonwealth Fund Survey data and prior research:

• *Start sex education earlier.* Not only school programs, but parents and health professionals as well should initiate discussions about sexuality, responsible sexual behavior, and contraception with their children earlier than they do now. For example, although half (51.4%) of 5th- to 8th-grade students in our survey responded that physicians or other health care professionals should discuss STDs with them, only one fourth of these students had discussed STDs with such professionals. Similarly, more than half said doctors and their colleagues should discuss pregnancy prevention with middle schoolers; fewer than one-fifth of these adolescents said that they had.

• *Put peer influence to educators' advantage*: Due to the natural developmental shift from parents to friends as adolescents grow older (Brown, 1990), teens are more likely to listen to their peers than adult authority figures; this is why friends have consistently ranked first or second as sources of sexual information for the past two decades (see Table 2.1), and have placed second only to schools as sources of contraceptive information in the Commonwealth Fund Survey (see Table 2.2). Peer sexual-health counselors have proved effective in some school settings and may provide a way to bridge this transition.

• *Provide support for parents that eases their roles as sexual educators*: Researchers and organizations such as The National Campaign to Prevent Teen Pregnancy are increasingly recognizing that many parents need more sexual knowledge themselves and techniques for discussing sex with their adolescent children. One suggestion has been to send the parents themselves back to school, through continuing sex education classes tailored to bolster their competence in their often uncomfortable role as impromptu sex educators (Hockenberry-Eaton et al., 1996).

A pamphlet aimed at parents from The National Campaign to Prevent Teen Pregnancy offers concrete advice on how to guide adolescents through the sometimes treacherous currents of their emerging sexuality—such as taking a stand against allowing a daughter to date a boy significantly older than she is (The National Campaign to Prevent Teen Pregnancy, 1998). The brochure also provides a list of resources for strengthening parents' ability to talk with adolescents about love, sex, and relationships. These include publications from organizations such as the American Social Health Association and the Bureau for At-Risk Youth, and Web sites on the Internet—which typically provide links to other helpful World Wide Web home pages. For example, The National Parenting Center offers more than 100 online chat rooms for parents to discuss challenges such as communicating with their adolescent children (http://www.tnpc.com; The National Campaign to Prevent Teen Pregnancy, 1998).

Organizations such as Advocates for Youth and Planned Parenthood provide informative brochures, videos, and even Web sites that offer strategies to parents nervous about raising the much-feared topic of sex with their adolescent children.

• *Stop viewing pregnancy prevention as primarily a female responsibility*: Parents in our survey were significantly more likely to discuss having sex, how women become pregnant, pregnancy prevention, and the use of condoms with their adolescent daughters than with their sons. (See Table 2.3). Physicians were significantly more likely to talk about pregnancy prevention with female adolescent patients than with male patients. (See Table 2.4.) However, no female adolescent becomes pregnant without a male's participation. Therefore, both genders should be equally educated about this topic. And fathers especially should shoulder a more equal share of the educational burden (Simanski, 1998).

• *Physicians should initiate discussions about sexual-health issues with adolescents*: Our survey results confirm prior research that embarrassment frequently prevents adolescents from starting conversations with health care providers about sexuality and contraception. Doctors and nurses should be aware that embarrassment is more likely to keep adolescent female and middle school patients from voicing concerns or questions than other groups; therefore, medical professionals should raise these subjects as soon as possible. Physicians also need to do more than just spit out facts. They need to try to grasp the social context in which the adolescent is operating. For example, a teenager may be feeling tremendous peer pressure to have sex, and doctors should discuss in general the reasons why adolescents might feel they want to have sex at this point in their lives (Clark et al., 1997).

• *Work with media such as magazines and television to cocreate messages that promote more responsible sexual behavior.* Groups such as the National Campaign to Prevent Teen Pregnancy and Advocates for Youth, in partnership with the Kaiser Family Foundation, already are working to inject messages into mass media that encourage less risky sexual activity. However, a lack of coordination among such groups—combined with the sometimes self-serving agendas of broadcasters—often leads to a confusing array of messages for adolescents (Huston, Wartella, & Donnerstein, 1998).

Nonetheless, because the Commonwealth Fund Survey shows that adolescents draw almost as much contraceptive information from magazines and television as from parents, the sexual scripts (Simon & Gagnon, 1984) provided by these media have considerable potential to shape emerging adolescent identity (Steele & Brown, 1995). An alternative is for schools and parents to attempt to mediate media messages by promoting greater media literacy (Potter, 1998)—an understanding of how to deconstruct and analyze media messages—among adolescent consumers.

These are only some of the possible ways to focus sexual health education efforts where they will reach the adolescent audience. But these steps may help ensure that an adolescent's first bite of the "forbidden fruit" of sexuality won't have dire consequences.

ACKNOWLEDGMENTS

This study was supported by a grant from the Commonwealth Fund of New York, and by the Centers for Disease Control. Dr. Klein is also supported by a Generalist Faculty Scholar's Award from the Robert Wood Johnson Foundation.

REFERENCES

Amonker, R. G. (1980). What do teens know about the facts of life? *Journal of School Health, 50*(9), 527–530.

Baldo, M., Aggleton, P., & Slutkin, G. (1993). *Does sex education lead to earlier or increased sexual activity in youth?* Presented at the IXth International Conference on AIDS, Berlin, June 6–10, World Health Organization, Geneva, Switzerland.

Barth, R. P., Fetro, J. V., Leland, N., & Volkan, K. (1992). Preventing adolescent pregnancy with social and cognitive skills. *Journal of Adolescent Research, 7,* 208–232.

Berns, L. A., & Huberman, B. K. (1995). Sexuality education: Sorting fact from fiction. *Phi Delta Kappan, 77,* 229–232.

Brown, B. B. (1990). Peer groups and peer cultures. In S. S. Feldman & G. R. Elliott (Eds.), *At the threshold: The developing adolescent* (pp. 171–196). Cambridge, MA: Harvard University Press.

Brown, J. D., Greenberg, B. S., & Buerkel-Rothfuss, N. L. (1993). Mass media, sex and sexuality. In V. C. Strasburger & G. A. Comstock (Eds.), *Adolescent medicine: State of the art reviews, Vol. 4, No. 3* (pp. 511–525). Philadelphia: Hanley & Belfus.

Brown, J. D., & Steele, J. R. (1996). Sexuality and the mass media: An overview. *SIECUS Report, 24*(4), 3–9.

Card, J. J., Niego, S., Mallari, A., & Farrell, W. S. (1996). The program archive on sexuality, health, and adolescence: Promising "prevention programs in a box." *Family Planning Perspectives, 28*(5), 210–220.

Centers for Disease Control and Prevention (1991). Characteristics of parents who discuss AIDS with their children—United States, 1989. *Morbidity and Mortality Weekly Report, 40*(46), 789–791.

Centers for Disease Control and Prevention (1997). AIDS rates. *Morbidity and Mortality Weekly Report, 46*(15), 333–334.

Centers for Disease Control and Prevention (1998). *CDC Facts: Adolescents and HIV/AIDS.* Washington, DC: Author.

Christensen, P. G., & Roberts, D. F. (1998). *It's not only rock & roll: Popular music in the lives of adolescents.* Cresskill, NJ: Hampton Press.

Clark, L. R., Cohall, A. T., Joffe, A., & Starr, C. (1997). Beyond the birds and the bees: Talking to teens about sex. *Patient Care, 31*(7), 102–116.

Committee on Communications, American Academy of Pediatrics (1995). Sexuality, contraception and the media. *Pediatrics, 95*(2), 298–300.

Corcoran, J., Miller, P. O., & Bultman, L. (1997). Effectiveness of prevention programs for adolescent pregnancy: A meta-analysis. *Journal of Marriage and the Family, 59*(3), 551–557.

Cravatta, M. (1997). Online adolescents. *American Demographics, 19*(8), 29.

Daley, D. (1997). Exclusive purpose: Abstinence-only proponents create federal entitlement in welfare reform. *SIECUS Report, 25*(4), 3–7.

Davis, S. M., & Harris, M. B. (1982). Sexual knowledge, sexual interests, and sources of sexual information of rural and urban adolescents from three cultures. *Adolescence, 17*(66), 471–492.

Fisher, T. D. (1986). Parent–child communication about sex and young adolescents' sexual knowledge and attitudes. *Adolescence, 21*(83), 519–527.

Gambrell, A. E., & Patierno, C. (1995). *SIECUS review of State Education Agency HIV/AIDS prevention and sexuality education programs.* New York: SIECUS.

Hendren, R. L., & Strasburger, V. C. (1993). Rock music and music videos. In V. C. Strasburger & G. A. Comstock (Eds.), *Adolescent medicine: State of the art reviews, Vol. 4, No. 3* (pp. 577–587). Philadelphia: Hanley & Belfus.

The Henry J. Kaiser Family Foundation (1998). *Kaiser Family Foundation and YM Magazine national survey of teens: Teens talk about dating, intimacy, and their sexual experiences.* Menlo Park, CA: The Henry J. Kaiser Family Foundation.

Hockenberry-Eaton, M., Richman, M. J., Dilorio, C., Rivero, T., & Maibach, E. (1996). Mother and adolescent knowledge of sexual development: The effects of gender, age, and sexual experience. *Adolescence, 31*(121), 35–47.

Huston, A. C., Wartella, E., & Donnerstein, E. (1998). *Measuring the effects of sexual content in the media: A report to the Kaiser Family Foundation*. Menlo Park, CA: The Henry J. Kaiser Family Foundation.

Inman, M. (1974). What teenagers want in sex education. *American Journal of Nursing, 74*(10), 1866–1867.

Kirby, D. (1997). *No easy answers: Research findings on programs to reduce teen pregnancy*. Washington, DC: The National Campaign to Prevent Teen Pregnancy.

Kirby, D., Barth, R. P., Leland, N., & Fetro, J. V. (1991). Reducing the risk: Impact of a new curriculum on sexual risk-taking. *Family Planning Perspectives, 23*(6), 253–263.

Kirby, D., Korpi, M., Adivi, C., & Weissman, J. (1997). An impact evaluation of Project SNAPP: An AIDS and pregnancy prevention middle school program. *AIDS Education and Prevention, 9*(1, Suppl.), 44–61.

Klein, J. D., McNulty, M., & Flatau, C. N. (1998). Adolescents' access to care: Teenagers' self-reported use of services and perceived access to confidential care. *Archives of Pediatrics & Adolescent Medicine, 152*(7), 676–682.

Koch, P. B. (1993). Promoting healthy sexual development during early adolescence. In R. Lerner, (Ed.), *Early adolescence* (pp. 293–307). Hillsdale, NJ: Lawrence Erlbaum Associates.

Lake Research (1996). *New poll shows family services are overwhelmingly popular*. Washington, DC: Author.

Leland, N. L., & Barth, G. P. (1992). Gender differences in knowledge, intentions, and behaviors concerning pregnancy and sexually transmitted disease prevention among adolescents. *Journal of Adolescent Health, 13*, 589–599.

Levy, S. R., Weeks, K., Handler, A., Perhats, C., Franck, J. A., Hedecker, D., Zhu, C., & Flay, B. R. (1995). A longitudinal comparison of the AIDS-related attitudes and knowledge of parents and their children. *Family Planning Perspectives, 27*(1), 4–10.

Little, A. (1998, September 23). Expose kids to technology early. *The Daily Tar Heel*, p. 12.

Lock, S. E., Ferguson, S. L., & Wise, C. (1998). Communication of sexual risk behavior among late adolescents. *Western Journal of Nursing Research, 20*(3), 273–294.

Mossberg, W. S. (1994, June 30). Keeping your kids away from creeps as they play online. *The Wall Street Journal*, p. B1.

The National Campaign to Prevent Teen Pregnancy (1998). *Ten tips for parents to help their children avoid teen pregnancy* (pp. 1–6). Washington, DC: Author.

Nolin, M. J., & Peterson, K. K. (1992). Gender differences in parent–child communication about sexuality: An exploratory study. *Journal of Adolescent Research, 7*, 59–79.

O'Hara, P., Messick, B. J., Fichtner, R. R., & Parris, D. (1996). A peer-led AIDS prevention program for students in an alternative school. *Journal of School Health, 66*(5), 176–182.

Palmer, D. A., Boardman, B., & Bauchner, H. (1996). Sixth and eighth graders and Acquired Immunodeficiency Syndrome: The results of focus group analysis. *Journal of Adolescent Health, 19*(4), 297–302.

Peirce, K. (1995). Socialization and messages in *Seventeen* and *'Teen* magazines. In C. M. Lont (Ed.), *Women and media: Content, careers, and criticism* (pp. 79–85). Belmont, CA: Wadsworth.

Piot, P., & Islam, M. Q. (1994). Sexually transmitted diseases in the 1990s: Global epidemiology and challenges for control. *Sexually Transmitted Diseases, 21*(2, Suppl.), S7–S13.

Potter, W. J. (1998). *Media literacy*. Thousand Oaks, CA: Sage.

Schuster, M. A., Bell, R. M., Peterson, L. P., & Kanouse, D. E. (1996). Communication between adolescents and physicians about sexual behavior and risk prevention. *Archives of Pediatrics & Adolescent Medicine, 150*(9), 906–913.

Shattuck, J. (1998). Let's talk about sex. *Computer Life, 5*(3), 164–167.

Shoop, D. M., & Davidson, P. M. (1994). AIDS and adolescents: The relation of parent and partner communication to adolescent condom use. *Journal of Adolescence, 17*(2), 137–148.

Simanski, J. W. (1998). The birds and the bees: An analysis of advice given to parents through the popular press. *Adolescence, 33*(129), 33–45.

Simon, W., & Gagnon, J. (1984, November–December). Sexual scripts. *Society, 22,* 53–60.

Steele, J. R., & Brown, J. D. (1995). Adolescent room culture: Studying media in the context of everyday life. *Journal of Youth and Adolescence, 24*(5), 551–576.

Steiner, L. (1995). Would the real women's magazine please stand up . . . for women. In C. M. Lont (Ed.), *Women and media: Content, careers, and criticism* (pp. 99–108). Belmont, CA: Wadsworth.

Tenopir, C. (1998). The digital reference of world. *Online, 22*(4), 22–30.

Thornburg, H. D. (1981). Adolescent sources of information on s

ex. *Journal of School Health, 51*(4), 272–277.

Visser, A. P., & van Bilsen, P. (1994). Effectiveness of sex education provided to adolescents. *Patient Education and Counseling, 23*(3), 147–160.

Walters, J., & Walters, L. H. (1983). The role of the family in sex education. *Journal of Research and Development in Education, 16*(2), 8–15.

Yankelovich Partners, Inc. (1993, May 24). Sidebar to Cole, W., Emery, M., Horowitz, J., Towle, L., Hequet, M., How should we teach our children about sex? *Time,* 60–66.

TELEVISION

3

Sexual Messages in Teens' Favorite Prime-Time Television Programs

Kirstie M. Cope-Farrar
Dale Kunkel
University of California, Santa Barbara

SIGNE WILKINSON, Philadelphia Daily News

Media images contribute to the socialization of young people across a broad range of areas, particularly those in which the viewer has relatively limited real-world experience (Huston et al., 1992). By the onset of adolescence, most young people develop interest in learning about sexual matters, although they tend to lack much direct experience in this realm (Hyde & Delameter, 1997). Consequently, the media provide important learning opportunities for adolescents to observe sexual norms and behaviors in action.

Research indicates that adolescents may obtain sexual scripts and norms from media examples (Brown, Childers, & Waszak, 1990), with as many as one in five teenagers reporting that television is their most important source of sexual information (Brown & Steele, 1995). Given the strong potential for media influence in this realm, it is important to consider the nature and extent of messages about sexuality that are conveyed by television, which despite increasing competition still remains the medium most heavily used by young people (Nielsen Media Research, 1998).

In the research reported in this chapter, we consider one of the most significant sources of sexual messages that may influence America's youth: the prime-time television programs most frequently viewed by teenagers. While many previous studies have examined the sexual content presented on television, very few have devoted attention to the programs most popular with teens. In this chapter, we consider the nature and extent of sexual messages that are presented in these programs, placing particular emphasis on their treatment of sexual risk and responsibility concerns.

Sexual Content on Television

Previous studies have found that sexually related talk and behavior occurs from 8 to 10 times per hour in prime-time programming (Kunkel, Cope, & Colvin, 1996; Lowry & Shidler, 1993), with two thirds (67%) of all network prime-time shows including some sexual material (Kunkel et al., 1999). The most frequent behaviors portrayed involve kissing and physical flirting, although intercourse is sometimes depicted or implied (Franzblau, Sprafkin, & Rubinstein, 1977; Kunkel et al., 1996; Kunkel et al., 1999; Sapolsky & Tabarlet, 1991). Studies have documented that intercourse occurs most often between partners who are not married to each other (Greenberg & Busselle, 1994; Greenberg & D'Alessio, 1985).

The few studies examining programming favored by teens have also reported that sexual messages are common. Greenberg et al. (1993) identified a substantial numbers of "sex acts," including talk about sex as well as sexually related behavior, in teens' favorite programs aired in 1985–1986. More recently, Ward (1995) found that more than one in four of all verbal interactions between primary characters in the prime-time shows watched by young viewers contained comments related to sexuality.

Because teens are at particular risk for transmission of AIDS and other STDs, and unplanned pregnancy, it is especially important to examine the messages that television conveys about the risks and responsibilities associated with human sexual activity. The few available studies examining these concerns indicate that risk and responsibility issues (e.g., use of condoms) have rarely been engaged by television (Kunkel et al., 1996; Lowry & Shidler, 1993; Sapolsky & Tabarlet, 1991).

Theoretical Approaches to Understanding Effects

Several theoretical approaches address the potential effects of televised portrayals on young audiences. Cultivation theory (Gerbner, Gross, Morgan, & Signorielli, 1994) predicts that heavy television viewers will, over time, come to perceive the world as portrayed on television as an accurate reflection of reality. For example, if unmarried couples are frequently depicted as engaging in sexual intercourse, cultivation theory would predict that adolescents who watch a lot of television would come to see unmarried intercourse as a cultural norm. Evidence suggests that the media contribute to social perceptions of human sexuality in exactly the way cultivation predicts (Buerkel-Rothfuss & Strouse, 1993; Courtright & Baran, 1980).

Social cognitive theory (Bandura, 1994) asserts that young people may adopt the behavior of others through observational learning. The theory predicts that people are more likely to emulate the behavior of others when those models are attractive, successful in achieving goals valued by the observer, or otherwise rewarded for their behavior. Applying this perspective, Brown and Steele (1995) predict that teens who spend more time watching television programming with attractive characters who enjoy having sexual intercourse and who rarely suffer any negative consequences for their actions will be likely to imitate the behavior.

Consistent with these expectations, several studies have reported correlations between the amount of exposure to sexual portrayals on television and early initiation of sexual intercourse by adolescents (Brown & Newcomer, 1991; Peterson, Moore, & Furstenberg, 1991); another study found heavy viewing of "sexy" television to be predictive of negative attitudes toward remaining a virgin (Courtright & Baran, 1980). Additionally, an experiment by Bryant and Rockwell (1994) indicated that teens who were exposed to prime-time television programming with sexual content rated descriptions of casual sexual encounters less negatively than teens who did not view any sexual content. Thus, although the direct evidence of effects is still somewhat limited, all the available evidence is consistent with our theoretical expectations about the media's contribution to sexual socialization.

Focus on Adolescents

Although numerous studies have documented the prevalence of sex on television, most have focused on programs targeting general audiences, for example those looking at soap operas or all prime-time network shows. Certainly, adolescents watch such content, but these programs do not necessarily represent the shows that these young people see most frequently. Indeed, according to a recent analysis by the *Washington Post* (Farhi, 1998), the 15 most popular programs for teen audiences (aged 12 to 17) included only 3 from the list of the 15 most popular programs among all viewers. Although the numerous studies of sexual content on television tell us much about the overall program environment, we still know relatively little about the sexual messages contained in the programs most popular with teenagers.

In order to address this gap in knowledge, the present study focuses solely on the shows viewed most frequently by adolescents. It offers a comprehensive analysis of the sexual messages they contain, including careful assessment of their treatment of sexual risk and responsibility concerns. More specifically, the following research questions are addressed:

How often do adolescents' favorite shows portray sexually related talk and behavior?

What types of talk about sex and/or sexual behaviors are portrayed and in what context?

What positive and/or negative consequences, if any, do the characters involved in sexually related behavior experience?

How often are messages about sexual risk (e.g., AIDS, STDs, or unplanned pregnancies) or responsibility (e.g., waiting until a relationship matures to have sex; practicing safe sex) portrayed in these shows?

METHOD

This study examined the top 15 television shows watched by young people between the ages of 12 and 17 in the United States, according to 1996 Nielsen data (see Table 3.1). Three episodes of each show were recorded between January and November 1996, for a total of 45 programs and 28.5 hours of content. Three fourths (73%) of the sample were situation comedies and the rest were dramas.

TABLE 3.1
Top 15 Shows Most Frequently Viewed by Adolescents (Spring 1996)

Program Title	Episode 1	Episode 2	Episode 3	Rating*
1. *The Simpsons*	2/4/96	2/18/96	3/10/96	10.8%
2. *Friends*	2/1/96	2/15/96	3/7/96	10.6%
3. *Boy Meets World*	2/2/96	2/16/96	10/25/96	10.5%
4. *In the House*	2/12/96	10/28/96	11/11/96	10.4%
5. *Home Improvement*	10/29/96	11/12/96	11/19/96	10.3%
6. *Lois and Clark*	2/11/96	2/18/96	3/10/96	9.7%
7. *Fresh Prince of Bel Aire*	2/12/96	3/29/96	3/29/96	9.7%
8. *Seinfeld*	10/17/96	10/31/96	11/7/96	9.5%
9. *E.R.*	10/31/96	11/7/96	11/14/96	9.0%
10. *Family Matters*	2/2/96	2/16/96	3/8/96	8.9%
11. *Married with Children*	3/10/96	10/13/96	10/20/96	8.8%
12. *Beverly Hills, 90210*	1/31/96	2/14/96	3/13/96	8.6%
13. *Caroline in the City*	11/12/96	11/19/96	11/26/96	7.5%
14. *New York Undercover*	10/31/96	11/7/96	11/14/96	7.4%
15. *3rd Rock From the Sun*	1/30/96	2/13/96	3/5/96	7.0%

Note. *Nielsen ratings reflect the percent of audience members (in this case adolescents) tuned in to a particular program during the average minute. Ratings reported here indicate an average between two independent audience ratings for teens 12–14 and 15–17.

Definition of Sexual Content

For this study, sex was defined as any depiction of talk or behavior that involves sexuality, sexual suggestiveness, or sexual activities/relationships. Sexual behavior and talk about sex were measured separately, with the caveat that dialogue categorized as talk toward sex that occurred concurrently with any sexual behavior was not recorded, in order to avoid double coding. To be considered sexual behavior, physical actions must imply potential or likely sexual intimacy between the participants. Thus, actual sexual relations (e.g., intercourse) need not occur to fit the definition. Indeed, some precursory behaviors such as physical flirting or passionate kissing were included, depending on the context in which they were presented.

Units of Analysis

To capture the context surrounding sexually related talk or behavior, three distinct units of analysis were employed: (a) interactions, (b) scenes, and (c) overall program level measures. The most basic unit of measurement was the interaction. An *interaction* was defined as a verbal or physical exchange between two or more individuals. The exchange may involve talk, physical actions, or elements of both. Reciprocal communication or sexual behavior by the receiver was considered part of the original interaction. An interaction encompassed all of the exchange involving sex or sexuality between the same characters within the same scene.

A *scene* was defined as a sequence in which the place and time held constant in the ongoing narrative flow of the program. Characters might come and go; they did not define a scene. A substantial shift in time and/or place typically signaled a new scene, as did any break for a commercial or other program interruption.

Interaction Level Measures

There were two basic types of interactions: talk about sex, and sexual behaviors.

Talk about sex included the following categories: talk directly promoting sexual activity (talk toward sex); comments about one's past sexual activity; comments about one's interest in future sexual activity; comments about others' sexual interests/activities; and seeking/giving of advice about sex.

Sexual behavior encompassed actions as modest as physical flirting (actions meant to arouse or likely to arouse sexual interest), romantic touches or embraces, and kissing; and more intimate types of behaviors such as heavy petting or fondling and sexual intercourse implied (coded to the extent that the program portrays one or more scenes immediately adjacent to an act of sexual intercourse, which is clearly inferred by narrative device), or sexual intercourse depicted (some portion of the physical act is shown, such as a couple that is understood to be nude climbing on top of one another under the covers).

For sexual behaviors, several contextual features that are important message factors also were measured. The marital status of participants in behavioral interactions was coded as either married to one another, not married to each other, or can't tell/not applicable. Participants' relationships with one another was coded as: characters involved have an established sexual/romantic relationship with each other (the characters have previously shared a sexual or romantic activity and they have established some degree of commitment involving responsibility or expectations about future behavior); characters involved have no established relationship with each other; characters involved have no established relationship with each other and have just met for the first time; characters involved have no established relationship with each other and are on a first date; and can't tell/not applicable.

Participants' relationship with others outside of the interaction being coded also was noted. The categories were: none of the characters involved have an established sexual/romantic relationship with another person; characters involved have an established sexual/romantic relationship with another person; and can't tell/not applicable.

Scene Level Measures

All scenes with sexual behavior were coded for degree of explicitness, which indicated the physical appearance of the characters involved in the behavior. The categories were: provocative/suggestive dress or appearance (attire alone indicates a strong effort to flaunt one's sexuality); characters begin disrobing; discreet nudity (characters are known to be nude but no private parts of the body are shown); and nudity (baring of normally private parts of the body).

Each scene with any sexual content was examined for a strong focus on one of the three primary types of risk and responsibility themes:

1. sexual patience (saying no/protecting virginity/waiting until a relationship matures to have sex)
2. sexual precaution (taking precautions when sexual behavior is pursued, or discussion of the importance of taking precautions when sexual behavior is contemplated)
3. depiction of risks (clear depiction of risks and/or negative consequences of unplanned/promiscuous sexual behavior)

Program Level Measures

In addition to character information, two additional measures were gathered: consequences of sexual behavior experienced, and overall risk and responsibility themes. Coders were instructed to evaluate an entire program when making these judgments.

Consequences of sexual behavior were judged as positive, negative, or none shown. Examples of positive outcomes included obtaining personal satisfaction, enhancing peer status or popularity, or establishing a desired relationship. Possible negative outcomes included damage to a relationship, a loss in peer status or popularity, or experiencing personal guilt or remorse.

Programs also were evaluated for any overall risk and responsibility themes involving sexual behavior. This variable was coded to the extent that the program as a whole emphasized one of the themes as a strong focus throughout the overall narrative. The same three categories that were used to measure this construct at the scene level (sexual patience, sexual precaution, or depiction of risks) were employed to evaluate the overall message at the program level.

A complete copy of the coding guide for this study can be obtained from the authors.

Coding and Reliability

Coding was performed by nine undergraduate students (four males and five females) at the University of California, Santa Barbara. Coders received extensive training and coding practice before beginning work on the project. Individual coders were randomly assigned to review and code programs.

Reliability was assessed at two distinct levels: (a) agreement on unitizing decisions (identifying sexual content within scenes); and (b) agreement on the context measures. This process mirrors the approach used for the National Television Violence Study (Wilson et al., 1997), which employed comparable units of analysis.

Two separate reliability tests were conducted throughout the coding process without the knowledge of the coders. For unitizing decisions, the CIAM (Close Interval Around the Mode) was calculated. The coders demonstrated agreement between 83% and 100%. For identifying types of talk about sex and sexual behavior, the agreement ranged from 83% to 100%. Agreement on interaction level measures was 100% and agreement on scene level measures ranged from 94% to 100%. Agreement on program level variables ranged from 76% (consequences of sexual behavior by character) to 100% (overall risk and responsibility theme).

RESULTS

Prevalence of Sexual Messages

How often do the programs most popular with adolescents portray sexual talk and behavior? The data indicate sexual content was frequent in these shows. At the program level, 37 of the 45 programs (82% of the sample) contained some talk about sex or sexual behavior (see Table 3.2). Both genres of programming represented in the sample were similar in their likelihood of including sexual content; 82% of sitcoms contained some talk about sex or sexual behavior as did 83% of dramas.

Talk about sex was observed in 67% of the programs analyzed, as compared to 62% for sexual behavior. Almost half (47%) of all programs included both talk and behavior; 20% contained only talk about sex, and 16% contained only sexual behaviors.

Within the 37 programs containing sexual messages, portrayals featuring talk about sex or sexual behavior were numerous, averaging 4.5 scenes per program, or 7.0 scenes per hour with sexual content. However, it is worth

TABLE 3.2
Prevalence of Sexual Messages

	Any Sexual Content	
Of programs with	Percentage of programs with any sexual content	82%
any talk about	Average number of scenes per program containing sex	4.5
sex or sexual	Average number of interactions per program containing sex	7.1
behavior	Average number of scenes per hour containing sex	7.0
	Average number of interactions per hour containing sex	11.1
	No. of programs	37
	No. of hours	23.5
	No. of scenes	165
	No. of interactions	261
	Talk About Sex	
Of programs with	Percentage of programs with any talk about sex	67%
any talk about	Average number of scenes per program	2.7
sex	Average number of interactions per program	3.2
	Average number of scenes per hour	4.2
	Average number of interactions per hour	5.0
	No. of programs	30
	No. of hours	19
	No. of scenes	80
	No. of interactions	95
	Sexual Behavior	
Of programs with	Percentage of programs with any sexual behavior	62%
any sexual	Average number of scenes per program	3.5
behavior	Average number of interactions per program	5.9
	Average number of scenes per hour	5.3
	Average number of interactions per hour	9.0
	No. of programs	28
	No. of hours	18.5
	No. of scenes	99
	No. of interactions	166

Note. Any given scene might contain talk about sex as well as sexual behavior. Due to the occurrence of such overlap within scenes, the data for talk about sex cannot be summed with the data for sexual behavior to yield the numbers for any sexual content overall.

noting that 20% of the shows with sex contained only a single scene of sexually related material.

Within scenes, sexual interactions were also frequent. Shows with sexual material averaged 7.1 sexual interactions per program, or 11.1 interactions per hour.

An adolescent watching these programs would encounter more sexual behavior than talk about sex. From both a per hour and per program perspective, there were nearly twice as many interactions involving sexual be-

havior as talk about sex. Sexual behavior accounted for 64% of all interactions coded, with only 36% comprised of talk interactions. This difference
was statistically significant ($X^2 = 19.8$, $df = 1$, $p < .001$). Shows containing sexual behavior averaged 5.9 behavior interactions per program; those with talk
about sex averaged 3.2 talk interactions. Per hour, there was an average of 9
sexual behavior interactions, compared to 5 interactions involving talk.

Type and Context of Sexual Portrayals

Although the frequency with which sexual messages are found on these
shows is an important consideration, it is the nature of the sexual content
presented that is most critical in understanding its implications for audience effects. Thus, we next turn to the question: What types of talk about
sex and/or sexual behaviors are portrayed and in what context?

Talk About Sex. Most of the sexual conversations identified in this sample centered on people's past, present, or future interests in sexual activity.
Comments about one's own current or future sexual activity and comments
about others' sexual interests accounted for 62% of all talk about sex (see
Table 3.3). These categories can encompass everything from commenting

TABLE 3.3
Types of Sexual Portrayals

Type of Talk About Sex	No.	Average per Hour	% of All Talk About Sex
Comments about one's own current or future sexual activity	31	1.1	32.6%
Comments about others' sexual activity	28	1.0	29.5%
Comments about own past sexual activity	19	0.7	20.0%
Comments about own lack of sexual activity	6	0.2	6.3%
Seeking of advice about sexual activity	6	0.2	6.3%
Talk toward sex	5	0.2	5.3%
Total	95	3.3	100%

Type of Sexual Behaviors	No.	Average per Hour	% of All Sexual Behaviors
Romantic touching	69	2.4	41.5%
Kissing	61	2.1	36.7%
Embracing	21	0.7	12.6%
Flirtatious behavior	6	0.2	3.6%
Intercourse implied	5	0.2	3.0%
Petting/fondling	3	.1	1.8%
Intercourse depicted	1	.04	0.6%
Total	166	5.8	100%

on people's sexual preferences to discussions about future or desired sexual activity, as the following examples demonstrate:

> Marion, a young professional football player, is cooking a romantic dinner for his new girlfriend, Alex. He tells his roommate, Jackie, "Alex and I are having a special evening here tonight." Jackie responds by asking, "Does she know she's going to be dessert?" Marion reacts defensively to the comment. "It's not like that. I've never met anyone like Alex. I'm taking it slow. I'm also taking five cold showers a day!" (*In the House*, NBC)

> Al comes home drunk one night to find his wife, Peggy, visiting with two of their neighbors. After seeing Al, Peggy and the guests discuss the merits of drinking to excess, with Peggy finally explaining the main reason she likes to encourage it. "The only time Al will touch me is when he's had 8 to 10 beers." Al and Peggy then begin to fondle one another, causing her to exclaim, "He's an animal." (*Married with Children*, Fox)

In contrast, seeking advice about sex was very infrequent (6% of interactions) as was talk toward sex (5%).

Sexual Behaviors. Most of the sexual behaviors portrayed were relatively modest in nature, involving romantic touching or kissing (see Table 3.4), as the following examples demonstrate:

> Curtis and Laura, a teenage couple, have just returned from ice-skating. Laura offers to make some hot chocolate to warm them up, but Curtis has other ideas. "I got [sic] a better way to warm up," he says. He then cradles his hand behind Laura's neck, pulls her close, and begins to kiss her passionately. After kissing for a moment, Laura pulls away for fear that her grandmother will come home and catch them. "Won't we hear her when she's coming?" Curtis asks. Laura replies, "Baby, once I start on your lips, I'm not stopping!" (*Family Matters*, ABC)

> Clark Kent and Lois Lane are sharing a romantic candlelit dinner at Clark's home. The two are discussing their upcoming wedding and the conversation turns to how much they really love one another. They both become very emotional as Clark says, "I love you, Lois." Lois, with tears in her eyes, reaches up, softly caresses the side of Clark's face, and replies, "I love you, Clark. You're the man I never thought I'd meet." She then leans over and begins to kiss him deeply, when they are interrupted by a knock at the door. (*Lois and Clark*, ABC)

Intimate behaviors such as petting and intercourse (either depicted or implied) accounted for only 5% of all behaviors observed.

The relationship between participants in behavioral interactions was also assessed. Most sexual behavior (79%) occurred between participants who were not married to one another. At the same time, most of these cases involved participants who, although not married, had an established

TABLE 3.4
Sexual Responsibility Themes

	Scene Level			
	Talk About Sex		Sexual Behavior	
Theme Emphasized	No.	% of All Scenes With Talk About Sex	No.	% of All Scenes With Sexual Behavior
Sexual patience	7	8.8%	1	1.0%
Sexual precaution	2	2.5%	0	0.0%
Depiction of risks	2	2.5%	2	2.0%
Scenes without the above themes	69	86.3%	96	97%
Total	80	100%	99	100%

Program Level		
Theme Emphasized	No.	% of Programs With Sexual Content
Sexual patience	1	2.7%
Sexual precaution	2	5.4%
Depiction of risks	1	2.7%
Programs without the above themes	33	89.2%
Total	37	100%

sexual or romantic relationship (71% of behaviors). Only 26% of interactions involving sexual behaviors took place between characters with no established sexual or romantic relationship.

Infidelity was an infrequent occurrence. In most of the behavior interactions (74%), none of the characters had an established sexual or romantic relationship with someone else. Only a small percentage of sexual behavior interactions (10%) involved characters who did have an established sexual or romantic relationship with someone other than their immediate partner, while in 16% of the cases it could not be determined if any of the characters had a relationship with another person.

Sexual behaviors were rarely explicit, with 86% of the scenes containing sexual behavior including no explicitness at all. Provocative or suggestive dress or appearance occurred in 7% of scenes containing sexual behavior, characters disrobed in 4% of scenes, and discreet nudity occurred in only 3% of scenes. The sample contained no examples of full nudity.

Intercourse. Out of 45 programs, just 3 (7%) contained an instance of intercourse either depicted or strongly implied. Intercourse implied was observed in five scenes, and intercourse depicted was found in only one.

Intercourse Implied: A scene opens with two people in bed kissing and whispering to one another as they engage in sexual foreplay. Suddenly the woman, Susan, sits straight up and says, "No, I'm sorry." She explains to her boyfriend, Brandon, that she is distracted by the romantic problems of two mutual friends. Susan and Brandon talk about her concerns and she decides that a double date with their friends might help the other couple find romance again. Brandon is skeptical and asks,"And hanging out with us is going to do that?" Susan climbs on top of Brandon and begins kissing him passionately before replying: "Honey, it better!" The two then retreat back under the covers and resume their foreplay more aggressively as the scene ends. (*Beverly Hills, 90210*, Fox)

Intercourse Depicted: Monica is alone watching a videotape that her parents made of her prom night. As the home movie concludes, Monica is shocked to find that the footage of her prom night is followed by a video her parents made of themselves having sex. Her parents are shown rolling around under the bed sheets and can be heard moaning each other's names. Monica stares in horror, then quickly reaches to turn the videotape off. (*Friends*, NBC)

All the examples of intercourse involved couples with established sexual or romantic relationships, and in half of the cases the participants were married to one another. Only two of the scenes with intercourse contained any explicitness, both employing discreet nudity.

Characters Involved in Talk About Sex or Sexual Behavior. The characters involved with sexual messages on these programs were split evenly by gender, with 105 being male and 104 being female. Most of the characters were White (75%), 21% were Black, and the remainder were other minorities (2%) or coded as "can't tell." Most interactions (53%) took place between young adults (apparent age 18 to 35), followed by adults aged 36 to 59 (31%), adolescents aged 13 to 17 (11%), elder adults aged 60 and above (3%), and children under the age of 13 (1%). Most characters (68%) were unmarried and 20% were married.

Consequences

What positive and/or negative consequences, if any, do the characters involved in sexual behaviors experience? All characters involved in sexual behavior ($N = 119$) were assessed to determine whether they had experienced any clear positive or negative consequences as a result of their sexual involvement.

Here the most important finding was that the majority of characters (75%) did not experience any clear consequences at all associated with their sexual behavior. Of the minority of characters who experienced any consequences, such outcomes tended to be positive (75%). For example, on

Friends (NBC), Rachel experienced a positive consequence from a sexual behavior when a kiss she shared with Ross allowed them to reestablish their romantic relationship. On the other hand, only 25% of consequences were negative. For example, on *New York Undercover* (Fox), a young police-woman experienced guilt and remorse after deceitfully sharing a kiss with a suspected killer in order to get close to him and try to obtain information about the murder.

Sexual Risk and Responsibility

How often are messages about the risks and responsibilities of sexual be-havior portrayed? This topic was assessed first by examining each scene with any sexual content for an emphasis on sexual patience, sexual precau-tion, or the depiction of risks related to unplanned sexual behavior. We re-port the findings separately for scenes that contained talk about sex only, and scenes that presented overt sexual behaviors. Of the 80 scenes contain-ing only talk about sex, just 11 of them (14%) contained an emphasis on sex-ual risk or responsibility concerns (see Table 3.4). The most prominent theme, sexual patience, accounted for nearly two thirds of all the cases ob-served.

More importantly, there were even fewer scenes containing a risk or re-sponsibility theme when sexual behavior was portrayed, as compared to scenes involving talk interactions only. Only 3 out of 99 scenes (3%) involv-ing sexual behavior contained some theme related to sexual responsibility. The following example illustrates the theme of sexual patience:

> Derek and Ashley, two high school students, have been dating and are think-ing about having sex for the first time. The two have driven to a secluded spot overlooking the city. Derek wants to have sex, but Ashley is hesitant because Derek will soon be leaving to attend college in another town. Sensing her hesi-tation, Derek asks, "Would you rather not do this?" Ashley replies, "I just never thought my first time would be with someone who was leaving me." Derek assures her they will still be seeing each other after he leaves, so Ashley says, "Then we really don't have to rush." Derek agrees and the couple decide not to have sex. Ashley apologizes for not wanting to have sex and Derek reassures her by saying, "Baby, you don't have to apologize to me." (*Fresh Prince of Bel Aire*, NBC).

Interestingly, none of the six scenes in the study presenting sexual inter-course (either depicted or implied) involved a risk or responsibility theme.

Finally, sexual risk or responsibility themes were also uncommon at the overall program level as well. Of the 37 programs in the sample containing talk about sex or sexual behavior, only 4 of these episodes (11%) contained a program level theme related to sexual risk and responsibility. The following example of a program level theme focuses on the risks of unplanned sexual activity:

> Susan, a college student, decided to have an abortion a year earlier. After her sister died in an accident, she got drunk to drown her sorrow and had unprotected sex with Jonathan, her boyfriend at the time, leading to the unplanned pregnancy. Jonathan disagreed with the abortion decision and they broke up as a result. Susan has now written an article for the college newspaper about her experience, but disguised the fact it is about herself. When the article wins an award, she is forced to reveal the secret to her current boyfriend, Brandon. He is supportive, but Susan remains upset and worried about what Brandon thinks of her. It is apparent throughout the episode that her decision still takes a heavy toll emotionally. (*Beverly Hills, 90210*, Fox)

None of the three programs presenting portrayals of intercourse in their stories included a program level risk or responsibility theme.

Summary of Results

Both talk about sex and sexual behaviors were common in this sample of shows favored by adolescents, with 82% of all programs coded containing some sexual content. Sexual behavior was more frequent than talk about sex and tended to occur between participants who were not married to one another. However, most of the sexual behaviors occurred between partners who, although not married, had an established relationship. When sexual behavior was portrayed, the characters involved rarely experienced any clearly positive or negative consequences as a result, though when any consequences were presented, they were overwhelmingly positive.

Intercourse was depicted or strongly implied in 7% of the programs examined, suggesting that most adolescents are likely to encounter such portrayals on occasion. However, explicitness (such as nudity) was infrequent. Finally, depictions or discussions of sexual risks or responsibilities rarely accompanied portrayals of sexual subject matter.

DISCUSSION

The purpose of this study was to provide a greater understanding of adolescents' exposure to sex in the media by documenting the sexual messages contained in the television shows they watch most frequently.

Our data indicate that the programs most popular with teenagers contain a substantial amount of sexual content. Indeed, it would be virtually impossible to watch these programs without encountering some sexually related material. With that stated, the findings for these shows are rather consistent with other studies that have examined a broader range of programming and found sexual talk and behavior to be shown quite frequently.

Similar to the findings reported by Ward (1995), who also examined the programs most popular with teens, we observed that discussions about a variety of sexual topics were common. Characters in our sample of programs discussed everything from when to have sex for the first time to ways of keeping romance alive in sexual relationships. The most common form of talk involved comments that conveyed people's interest in having sex. From a socialization perspective, such talk certainly contributes information about sexual norms and values to the audience, whether it is accompanied by more overt portrayals of sexual behavior.

Sexual behavior was also an important feature of these shows, with nearly two out of three programs containing some sexually related actions. Again consistent with other studies, we found that most of the sexual behaviors portrayed were fairly innocuous, such as kissing, embracing, and touching (Franzblau, Sprafkin, & Rubinstein, 1977; Kunkel et al., 1996). Although these actions pose less of a concern from a health risk standpoint than consummated intercourse, television's consistent depiction of these behaviors may serve as a sort of "script" for young people who are just learning about themselves and others as sexual beings, and may encourage adolescents to place an emphasis on such actions in their own lives.

Sexual intercourse occurred in 1 of every 15 shows in our sample, although rarely with any explicitness. Given that these programs are among the most popular with teens, this finding makes clear that teenagers are regularly encountering television stories involving intercourse. Yet the context surrounding these instances of intercourse diverges somewhat from the pattern observed in most other studies. When intercourse occurred in our sample of programs, the participants were just as likely to be married as unmarried, and all participants had established sexual or romantic relationships with one another. In contrast, previous studies examining more broad-based samples of programming have reported that intercourse on television typically occurs between unmarried partners (Greenberg & Busselle, 1994; Greenberg & D'Alessio, 1985; Kunkel et al., 1996).

From a public health perspective, the pattern of portrayals we have identified raises much less concern than the pattern of depictions of sexual intercourse found elsewhere on television. Whether or not our finding represents a shift in television programming overall or is unique to the shows most popular with adolescents remains to be clarified by future research. And of course the pattern we have observed must be viewed with some caution, as it is based on such a modest number of cases ($N = 6$ scenes of intercourse encountered in a sample of 45 programs).

Despite this relatively positive note, it is still possible that the pattern of portrayals of intercourse we have observed may help to reduce the barriers to sexual intercourse, particularly among those adolescents who find themselves in committed relationships. Research has shown that most intercourse between teenagers tends to occur in monogamous, but not necessarily enduring, relationships (Ehrhardt & Wasserheit, 1992). Here then is the critical link to arguably the greatest concern raised by our findings.

Although teenagers may tend to pursue intercourse most often when they are in a committed relationship, teens also tend to move from one relationship to another more quickly than do adults (Feiring, 1996). This shifting base of partners multiplies the risk of teens contracting sexually transmitted diseases, even within the confines of committed relationships. And although our sample of programs reflected a generally prosocial stance by consistently portraying intercourse within the context of a committed relationship, none of the scenes featuring intercourse included any emphasis on sexual risks or responsibilities (e.g., protecting oneself from unwanted pregnancy or sexually transmitted diseases), nor were such topics addressed in any of these programs as a whole.

In fact, sexual risk and responsibility themes were infrequent throughout the sample. At the scene level, themes related to risks and responsibilities were associated with just 14% of all instances of talk about sex and only 3% of all portrayals of sexually related behavior. At the overall program level, only about one of every nine programs including sexual material (11%) placed strong emphasis on risk and responsibility concerns such as sexual patience or the need for precautions.

In other words, adolescents may be learning a potentially dangerous sexual script from their favorite television shows. These shows may suggest it is normative to have sex if you are in a committed relationship, but more importantly, that people in relationships rarely take any steps to protect themselves against such possible harms as sexually transmitted disease.

Although our findings are generally consistent with previous studies that have reported scarce treatment of sexual risk and responsibility topics (Greenberg & Busselle, 1994; Kunkel et al., 1996; Lowry & Shidler, 1993; Sapolsky & Tabarlet, 1991), our data provide the hint of some increased sensitivity to these issues by television producers. In a composite week's sample of more than 1,000 programs gathered only a year after the data set reported here, Kunkel et al. (1999) found that only 1% of all programs with sexual content placed strong emphasis on risk and responsibility issues. From this perspective, the 11% figure obtained in the teen program sample suggests the prospect that producers may be more receptive to these themes in programs known to be popular with teenagers.

Also of concern was the finding that characters involved in sexual behaviors rarely experienced any negative consequences as a result of their actions. Portrayals of characters engaging in intimate sexual behaviors with little or no regard for preventing disease transmission or unwanted pregnancy is likely to reduce the salience of these considerations for adolescent viewers.

CONCLUSION

Television is but one of many socializing influences in the life of adolescents. Yet for adolescents who are just learning about themselves and others as sexual beings, television may serve as a unique window into this often private realm of "adult" behavior.

That window provides plenty of opportunity to observe messages about sex and sexuality, as sexual content is clearly an important part of television's agenda. In 82% of the programs coded, someone talks about sex and/ or engages in some form of sexual behavior. This focus on sexuality is certainly not lost on adolescent viewers, who may in fact be attracted to these programs precisely because of their frequent treatment of sexual topics.

The nature of the sexual portrayals in these shows certainly is not alarming. Most sexual behavior on television is relatively modest in nature. Sexual intercourse occurs, though not frequently and almost never with any explicitness. And portrayals of intercourse generally involve those in committed relationships. Nonetheless, one aspect of television's treatment of sexual content remains particularly troubling.

In an era of AIDS and widespread sexually transmitted diseases, the real world of sexual activity today necessarily entails serious, potentially life-threatening risks. Those risks are important considerations, and precautions such as the use of condoms can greatly reduce the degree of risk for sexually active teenagers or adults. Yet in the world of television, these risks are generally ignored and rarely portrayed as a factor in sexual decision making. Worse still, the characters who ignore these sexual risks almost never suffer any negative consequences from their actions. Given that television places such strong emphasis on sexual content in its story lines, it remains a disappointment that most programs continue to ignore the importance of sexual risk and responsibility concerns.

REFERENCES

Bandura, A. (1994). Social cognitive theory of mass communication. In J. Bryant & D. Zillman (Eds.), *Media effects: Advances in theory and research* (pp. 61–90). Hillsdale, NJ: Lawrence Erlbaum Associates.
Brown, J. D., Childers, K. W., & Waszak, C. S. (1990). Televison and adolescent sexuality. *Journal of Health Care, 11*, 62–70.

Brown, J. D., & Newcomer, S. F. (1991). Television viewing and adolescents' sexual behavior. *Journal of Homosexuality, 21*(1/2), 77–91.

Brown, J. D., & Steele, J. R. (1995). *Sex and the mass media.* Menlo Park, CA: Henry J. Kaiser Family Foundation.

Bryant, J., & Rockwell, S. C. (1994). Effects of massive exposure to sexually oriented prime-time television programming on adolescents' moral judgment. In D. Zillmann, J. Bryant, & A. C. Huston (Eds.), *Media, children and the family: Social scientific, psychodynamic, and clinical perspectives* (pp. 183–195). Hillsdale, NJ: Lawrence Erlbaum Associates.

Buerkel-Rothfuss, N. L., & Strouse, J. S. (1993). Media exposure and perceptions of sexual behaviors: The cultivation hypothesis moves to the bedroom. In B. S. Greenberg, J. D. Brown, & N. L. Buerkel-Rothfuss (Eds.), *Media, sex and the adolescent* (pp. 225–247). Creskill, NJ: Hampton.

Courtright, J. A., & Baran, S. J. (1980). The acquisition of sexual information by young people. *Journalism Quarterly, 57*(1), 107–114.

Ehrhardt, A. A., & Wasserheit, J. N. (1992). Age, gender, and sexual risk behaviors for sexually transmitted diseases in the United States. In J. N. Wasserheit, S. O. Aral, & K. K. Holmes (Eds.), *Research issues in human behavior and sexually transmitted diseases in the AIDS era* (pp. 97–121). Washington DC: American Society for Microbiology.

Farhi, P. (1998, October 21). On TV, a prime time for teens. *The Washington Post,* pp. A1, A9.

Feiring, C. (1996). Concepts of romance in 15-year-old adolescents. *Journal of Research on Adolescence, 6,* 181–200.

Franzblau, S., Sprafkin, J. N., & Rubinstein, A. (1977). Sex on TV: A content analysis. *Journal of Communication, 27*(2), 164–170.

Gerbner, G., Gross, L., Morgan, M., & Signorielli, N. (1994). Growing up with television: The cultivation perspective. In J. Bryant & D. Zillmann (Eds.), *Media effects: Advances in theory and research* (pp. 17–41). Hillsdale, NJ: Lawrence Erlbaum Associates.

Greenberg, B. S., & Busselle, R. W. (1994). *Soap operas and sexual activity.* Menlo Park, CA: Henry J. Kaiser Family Foundation.

Greenberg, B. S., & D'Alessio, D. (1985). Quantity and quality of sex in the soaps. *Journal of Broadcasting and Electronic Media, 29,* 309–321.

Greenberg, B. S., Stanley, C., Siemicki, M., Heeter, C., Soderman, A., & Linsangan, R. (1993). Sex content on soaps and the prime-time television series most viewed by adolescents. In B. S. Greenberg, J. D. Brown, & N. L. Buerkel-Rothfuss (Eds.), *Media, sex and the adolescent* (pp. 29–44). Creskill, NJ: Hampton.

Huston, A. C., Donnerstein, E., Fairchild, H., Feshbach, N. C., Katz, P. A., Murray, J. P., Rubinstein, E. A., Wilcox, B. L., & Zuckerman, D. (1992). *Big world, small screen.* Lincoln: University of Nebraska Press.

Hyde, J. S., & DeLamater, J. (1997). *Understanding human sexuality* (6th ed.). New York: McGraw-Hill.

Kunkel, D., Cope, K. M., & Colvin, C. (1996). *Sexual messages in "family hour" TV: Content and context.* Menlo Park, CA: Henry J. Kaiser Family Foundation.

Kunkel, D., Cope, K. M., Farinola, W. M., Biely, E., Rollin, E., & Donnerstein, E. (1999). *Sex on TV: A biennial report to the Kaiser Family Foundation.* Menlo Park, CA: Henry J. Kaiser Family Foundation.

Lowry, D. T., & Shidler, J. A. (1993). Prime time TV portrayals of sex, "safe sex" and AIDS: A longitudinal analysis. *Journalism Quarterly, 70,* 628–637.

Nielsen Media Research. (1998). *1998 report on television.* New York: Author.

Peterson, J. L., Moore, K. A., & Furstenberg, F. F. (1991). Television viewing and early initiation of sexual intercourse: Is there a link? *Journal of Homosexuality, 21*(1/2), 93–118.

Sapolsky, B. S., & Tabarlet, J. O. (1991). Sex in prime time television: 1979 versus 1989. *Journal of Broadcasting and Electronic Media, 35,* 505–516.

Ward, L. M. (1995). Talking about sex: Common themes about sexuality in the prime-time television programs children and adolescents view most. *Journal of Youth and Adolescence, 24*(5), 595–615.

Wilson, B., Kunkel, D., Linz, D., Potter, J., Donnerstein, E., Smith, S., Blumenthal, E., & Gray, R. (1997). Violence in television programming overall: University of California, Santa Barbara study. In *National Television Violence Study: Scientific papers* (pp. 3–268). Thousand Oaks, CA: Sage.

4

Daytime Talk Shows:
Up Close and In Your Face

Bradley S. Greenberg
Sandi W. Smith
Michigan State University

The daytime talk show has been a staple on television for more than more than two decades, but its modest beginnings (with Merv Griffin and Phil Donahue) were overshadowed in the 1990s. It has produced one of the wealthiest women, if not the wealthiest, in the nation in Oprah Winfrey. It has produced one of the most controversial television personalities, if not the most controversial, in Jerry Springer. It has competed successfully with daytime soap operas, causing at least two of them to be canceled. Its shift from mild topics and celebrity interviews to extrasensational and increasingly bizarre topics and noncelebrity guests led to the demise of the shows of both of the original hosts, Merv Griffin and Phil Donahue. A score of would-be hosts and hostesses have begun talk shows and failed. Annually, the talk show settles in with about 20 options for viewers, and a dozen tend to survive. The daytime talk show has become an increasingly soft and convenient target for critics who condemn its topics, its guests, and its ambush tactics. Yet, there is little research available to tell us much about it—much less research than for any other genre of television. What is its content? Who are its guests? Who is in the audience? What are its effects? The standard set of questions remains largely without answers.

Are the talk shows also a convenient venue for adolescents to find out about sex? Why not? They are convenient for anyone with some time available in the mid to late afternoon, or to anyone who wishes to program a VCR. Therefore, teenagers and preteens are likely to sample from among the talk show offerings and then to watch heavily what they find most curious, or to follow the advice of their friends. Would they be interested in the sexual topics? Of course they would. In this context, this chapter has been written—with many more questions than answers.

THE ANALYSIS OF DAYTIME
TELEVISION TALK SHOWS

In the summer of 1995, the Henry J. Kaiser Family Foundation requested that the authors do an analysis of daytime television talk shows that paralleled an analysis of soap operas done for the foundation a year earlier. The results of the latter were presented at the first national Soap Summit in Los Angeles and the foundation wished to build on that success by hosting the first national Talk Show summit in New York. We first determined that no prior quantitative content analysis of television daytime talk shows existed, despite the seemingly large number of daytime talk shows available—more than 20 of them. In addition, the growing controversy over the content and demeanor of some of these shows marked a significant need for empirical research. In response, we examined the top 11 shows, whose daily audiences (in December 1994) ranged from 8.9 million households for Oprah (top rated), to 1.9 million for Rolonda Watts (since canceled). At that time, Jerry Springer (number 9) hosted only 2.5 million households daily (Greenberg, Sherry, Busselle, Rampoldi-Hnilo, & Smith, 1997), despite the fact that he already was the center point in the talk show controversy over topics discussed and problematic guests.

As we drafted this chapter in the summer of 1999, the television roster listed 14 daytime talk shows, and an even larger number of talk show variants: five courtroom talk shows, four early morning talk shows, six late night talk shows, one Friday night only talk show (Chris Rock) and one Saturday night only talk show (Howard Stern). Springer's special brand of violence and sex moved him to the lead spot, with 7.2 million households (in August 1998), followed in order by Oprah (6 million), Jenny Jones (4.4 million), Sally Jesse Raphael (4.1 million), Ricki Lake (3.4 million), and Montel Williams (3.9 million)—all shows included in the 1995 study. In the interim, more than a dozen other daytime talk shows started up and failed. The only successful newcomer in the four-year interim was Rosie O'Donnell, with 4 million households daily, but she hosted celebrities rather than problem-oriented guests. And for the fall of 1999, nine new talk shows were on the advance listing, including such hosts as Joan Lunden, Martin Short, Queen Latifah, and Richard Simmons. Thus the talk show genre and its variants held an even stronger position in the television schedule than a half decade earlier.

As interesting as the continuing and increasing popularity of these shows is the continuing and escalating public criticism of them. Many continue to be characterized as pandering to our worst inclinations. Publicly, the criticisms about the violence and the subject matter on Springer led to hearings in the U.S. Congress and the Chicago City Council. These criticisms have then been confounded with the growing need to attempt to understand and explain the seeming outbreak of violent incidents in Littleton, Colorado, in Atlanta, Georgia, and in Fort Worth, Texas, among others. In this context, a Michigan jury made a multimillion dollar award in the spring of 1999 to the family of a guest on the Jenny Jones show; the guest had been slain by a second guest several days after the former declared his homosexual attraction to the latter.

The audience figures mentioned previously reflect household figures, with no breakdown to identify the specific extent of teenage viewing. Talk shows have constituted the only successful challenge to soap operas for afternoon viewers, and a substantial segment of the talk show audience consists of teenagers. In fact, from informal discussions with scores of teenagers, we were hard pressed to find a teenager who was unfamiliar with Springer or Oprah or Jenny or Montel. In one recent study, Davis and Mares (1998) found that 12% of their teenage sample watched talk shows every day and 34% watched sometimes. During the summer, viewing jumped by half, as 68% said they viewed talk shows sometimes or every day in that season. This translates into several million teenage viewers on a daily basis. We believe that large numbers of preteens often become part of the afternoon talk show audience as well.

Despite the growth of entries in this genre, the audience upsurge, and the media-reported criticisms, there has been no increase in research directly focused on the content, the audience, the guests, the advertisers, the hosts, or the production components of this genre of television. There remains almost as little research reported as there was in 1995. In this chapter we summarize what research there is, but the bottom line is the absence of a body of behavioral, quantitative research findings.

Content Studies

As of 1999, three main content analyses have been conducted on television talk shows, all derived from the 1995 talk show analyses initiated by the Kaiser grant and conducted by our research teams at Michigan State University.[1] The first analysis, based on 120 hour-long videotapes, focused on categorization of topics, relationships, physical reactions, verbal reactions, and demographics related to television talk shows (Greenberg et al., 1997). The second content analysis, based on 80 written transcripts, examined the sources, types, and frequencies of personal disclosures on television talk shows (Smith, AhYun, Orrego, Johnson, Mitchell, & Greenberg, in press); the nature of expert advice on television talk shows (Greenberg, Smith, AhYun, Busselle, Rampoldi-Hnilo, Mitchell, & Sherry, 1995); and responses to disclosures about oneself and others in terms of privacy and loss of face (Greenberg et al., 1995; Orrego, Smith, Mitchell, Johnson, AhYun, & Greenberg, 2000). The third study, based on 955 talk show titles from *USA Today* and *TV Guide*, analyzed the ways in which talk show titles reflect the valence of close relationships and types of individual attributes (Smith, Mitchell, AhYun, Johnson, Orrego, & Greenberg, 1999). The main findings of each of these studies are reviewed in the text following.

The time period of the shows analyzed in all of these studies ranged from January 1, 1995, to August 25, 1995. The shows selected were among the 11 most highly rated talk shows, based on Nielsen audience ratings ending December 21, 1994. Listed in order of their ratings, they were: Oprah Winfrey (8.9), Ricki Lake (5.3), Jenny Jones (4.3), Sally Jesse Raphael (4.2), Maury Povich (4.0), Montel Williams (3.8), Phil Donahue (3.6), Geraldo Rivera (3.2), Jerry Springer (2.5), Gordon Elliott (2.4), and Rolonda Watts (1.0).[2]

---

[1]This research was supported by a grant from the Henry J. Kaiser Family Foundation, for which the two authors were the coprincipal investigators.

[2]In Nielsen ratings, 980,000 households constitute one rating point.

Videotape Analysis. The first content analysis, based on 110 hour-long videotapes, focused on talk show guests, the topics they discussed, and their interactions with others on the shows. In addition, when possible, the theme or title of each show was recast as a proposition that reflected contemporary community standards, for example, "Prostitution is not a good thing to do," or "Husbands should not beat their wives" (Greenberg et al., 1997). Ten shows from each of the 11 top-rated hosts were selected by systematic probability sampling and were videotaped between July 18 and August 25, 1995, for our subsequent systematic content analysis. Ten episodes of a 12th show, Christina (in Spanish), also were taped, but are not included in these results.

Family relations were discussed most frequently across all these talk shows. Major parent–child discussions—a principal focus of the interview—were found on one half the shows; marital discussions were major topics on one third of the shows. The next most frequently discussed issue was general sexual activity, found on one third of the shows. In addition, 1 in 5 shows focused on sexual infidelity, and 1 in 10 focused on sexual orientation. Shows featuring one or more of these three sexual themes were found most often on Geraldo, Jenny, Rolonda, and Springer and least often on Oprah and Donahue.

The relationships between individuals in a group, as identified from their own perspective, included 26% parent–child combinations, 12% married couples, 11% lovers, 9% former lovers, 16% nonromantic friends, 14% acquaintances, and 13% siblings. Thus, 51% were family relationships, and 33% of the guests in the sample had been or were presently in a romantic relationship.

The distribution of physical reactions found 19% of the guests in an embrace, which included hugging, kissing, and/or holding hands; 11% laughing; 10% yelling or shouting to be heard; 5% crying due to sadness; 2% crying for joy; and 1% hitting someone. Hugging occurred more among married pairs and lovers, laughing among married couples, and crying among children and their parents.

The distribution of verbal reactions among guests included 15% affectionate statements; 14% denial; 10% rejection; 7% surprise, shame, or embarrassment; 6% anger; 2% fear; and 2% apology. In 50% of the relational pairs, no feelings toward the other were expressed; in the remainder, 29% expressed positive feelings; 17% negative feelings; and 4% mixed feelings.

Of the 1,041 guests in the sample, females outnumbered males 2:1. Guests were relatively young: 16% were under 20; 46% were in their 20s; 25% were in their 30s; 9% were in their 40s; and 4% were 50 or older. Seventy-five percent of the guests were White, 18% were Black, and 5% were Hispanic. Black guests were more likely to be young and male than were the other guests, and women were consistently younger than men and less likely to be African American. Guests under 20 were predominantly female and White.

The overall theme in two thirds of the shows analyzed could be cast as propositions that reflected contemporary community standards. One half of these dealt with sexual propriety; the remainder was divided about equally among personal safety, marital relations, family relations, and self-presentation. Audience responses to questions and statements related to these propositions were analyzed. Over 80% of the responses to statements made by guests and individual audience members were supportive, and more than 60% of the responses to the hosts were supportive of general community norms.

Transcript Analysis. Three different areas were content analyzed from 10 transcripts obtained from each of 8 talk shows aired between June 27 and July 21, 1995. In all, 80 transcripts were obtained from independent transcription services for the following hosts: Oprah Winfrey, Jenny Jones, Sally Jesse Raphael, Maury Povich, Phil Donahue, Geraldo Rivera, Jerry Springer, and Rolonda Watts. The sources, types, and frequencies of personal disclosures on talk television (Smith, AhYun, et al., in press), the nature of expert advice on television talk shows (Greenberg et al., 1995), and responses to self- and other disclosures in terms of privacy and loss of face (Orrego et al., in press) were the focus of our transcript-based analyses.

Talk show critics have argued that the primary function of guests on these shows is to reveal traumatic or unusual information about themselves in order to draw an audience, and that these self-disclosures come at a rapid pace (Heaton & Wilson, 1995). These claims can be turned into three testable questions: (a) Do disclosures usually originate with the featured guests to whom they refer? (b) What is the content of these disclosures? and (c) What is the average rate of these disclosures? The unit of analysis here was the televised disclosure: "a televised outpouring of personal information usually revealed only to one's close friends, family, rabbi, minister, or therapist" (Priest, 1995).

The first question, "Who are the primary sources of the televised disclosures on these talk shows?", is important because a large percentage of self disclosures would indicate that the featured guests controlled the disclosures of personal information about themselves and the frequency with which this information was revealed. High percentages of disclosures by hosts or those in personal relationships with the featured guests would indicate that the featured guests had little or no control over the disclosures, thus they could be "ambushed" with public airing of private information. We coded the source of all of the televised disclosures in the 80 transcripts and found that self-disclosures accounted for less than half of the televised disclosures, at 42%. Disclosures about guests by hosts accounted for 28% of the televised disclosures. Disclosures about guests by those in personal relationships with them, such as family members, friends, or romantic partners, accounted for 30% of the total televised disclosures. These results indicate that guests controlled televised disclosures about themselves less than half of the time and had little or no control over the personal information that was revealed about them in 58% of the cases in this sample. In one example of what could be termed an "ambush disclosure," a young woman revealed that her sister, who also was on the show, had begun having sexual intercourse at age 8.

The second and third questions concerned the content and rate of televised disclosures on an average show in our sample. Six categories of televised disclosures were found:

1. *Sexual activity* was comprised of disclosures about general sexual activity, pregnancy, sexual infidelity, general sexual issues, safe sex, sexual advances, rape, abortion, and sexually transmitted diseases. An example of a sexual activity self-disclosure occurred when a young woman who claimed that her sister began having sexual intercourse at age 8 disclosed that she herself was 11 when she began having sex.

2. *Sexual orientation* was comprised of disclosures about being gay, transsexual, transvestite, lesbian, or bisexual. An example of a sexual orientation disclosure is that a young woman said that it had been kept secret that her father was gay, and that he killed her mother when his sexual orientation was made public.

3. *Abuse* disclosures included general, physical, sexual and verbal abuse, and exploitation. An example of an abuse disclosure occurred when a mother claimed that her daughter's boyfriend hit her with a baseball bat when she was 3 months pregnant.

4. *Embarrassing situation* disclosures are those about relational secrets, negative feelings for one's partner, concealed relationships, past hidden experiences, and positive feelings for someone other than one's relational partner. An example of an embarrassing situation disclosure occurred when a man and woman who had conceived a child while he was married to another woman revealed it to their daughter, whom he had never met.

5. *Criminal activity* disclosures occurred with revelations that guests had engaged in unlawful activity. This ranged from writing bad checks to theft, rape, child abuse, and murder. For example, one woman claimed that her ex-husband hired a hit man to murder her.

6. *Personal attribute* disclosures were about mental and physical health, addiction, personality traits, and race. One example of this was a whole show devoted to "Housewives Hooked on Heroin," in which five women talked about being addicted to heroin.

Some disclosures could be coded as an instance of more than one category: For example, a disclosure about rape was coded as an instance of sexual activity, abuse, and criminal activity. A person who watched a typical talk show from our sample would witness 4 sexual activity, 1 sexual orientation, 3 abuse, 2 embarrassing situation, 2 criminal activity, and 4 personal attribute disclosures, for a total of 16 televised disclosures in a 1-hour span.

In addition to a concern with televised disclosures, critics of talk shows have also claimed that experts on these shows receive little airtime to offer solutions to the problems posed on the shows. In order to investigate this claim, the percentage of speaking turns was analyzed. A speaking turn occurs each time a particular person initiates talk and ends when another person begins talking. There were a total of 38,400 speaking turns across the 80 transcripts.

Experts, defined as people who claimed special training related to the main issue of the show, received only 3% of, or an average of 13, speaking turns per show. Speaking turns for experts were highest on Oprah, with 10%; Jerry Springer and Jenny Jones had no experts on the shows in our sample. Guests received 53% of the speaking turns, or an average of 252 per show. Guest turns were highest on Sally Jesse Raphael, Jerry Springer, and Geraldo Rivera, with about 60% each, and lowest on Oprah, with 40%.

Hosts received 39% of the speaking turns, or an average of 189 per show. Host turns were highest on Oprah and Phil Donahue, with about 42%, and lowest on Sally, with 32%. The audience received 5% of the speaking turns overall, or an average of 26 turns per show. Audience turns were highest on Rolonda Watts, with 14%, and lowest on Jerry Springer, with 3%. Based on the results from our sample, we can say that critics of talk shows are correct when they claim that experts are given little opportunity to solve the problems that are posed on talk shows.

Orrego et al. (2000) reviewed and extended the findings of Greenberg et al. (1995) in terms of the two types of responses that immediately followed disclosures. They found that the responses to self-disclosures by hosts most often were requests for more information, but that the responses to self-disclosures by those close to the self-discloser were most often negative in nature. These negative reactions served to create relational distance between the parties. In contrast, the responses to other disclosures were most often requests for more information, perhaps due to the surprise element of ambush disclosures. The immediate response to an ambush is to ask for more information, whereas the responses signaling loss of face, breach of privacy, and betrayal are likely to come later in the sequence.

Title Analysis

Because critics often claim that talk shows focus on negative relationships, a sample of television talk show titles for the 11 shows listed previously was drawn from *TV Guide* and *USA Today* from January 1, 1995, to June 30, 1995

(Smith et al., 1999). Of the 955 titles, 294 (30%) referred to family relationships and 254 (27%) referred to personal relationships. Sixty percent of the family relationships titles were negative (e.g., "Feuding Families"); 51% of the personal relationship titles were negative (e.g., "Betrayal by Friends"). In addition, personal attributes such as personality traits were coded from the titles. A large percentage of these (74%) were negative as well (e.g., "Liars and Cheaters").

To confirm that content reflects the categories of the titles, a secondary analysis of the disclosure data was performed. Fifty-four percent of the shows in the transcript sample could be coded as instances of family or personal relationship shows, with family relationship shows having a mean of 2.5 sexual activity disclosures per hour; personal relationship shows, alternately, had a significantly higher mean of 6.3 sexual activity disclosures per hour.

THE SURVEY AND EXPERIMENTAL RESEARCH

The content analyses conducted and summarized previously can now be supplemented by our reporting of a meager listing of quantitative survey and experimental studies, which total only five as of the fall of 1999. We do this here because the results of content analyses should serve primarily as a harbinger of subsequent studies of the effects of that content. That appears to have been the basis for some of the studies to be reported. However, we omit the substantial literature on talk shows provided by qualitative analysts (cf. Abt & Seesholtz, 1994; Gamson, 1998; Nelson & Robinson, 1994).

Cress and Rapert (1996) surveyed a primary group of more than 100 teenagers in introductory communication courses. More women (63%) than men (37%) participated in the study. The questionnaire contained an adaptation of Rubin's (1983) questions about television viewing motives; demographic measures (gender, age, employment); and questions regarding respondents' frequency of talk show viewing, including their videotaping of talk shows. Results showed that respondents' three strongest motives for viewing talk shows were to be entertained, to pass time, and to relax. The females reported viewing 3.2 hours of talk shows per week and the males reported an average of 2 hours. Males and females did not differ in their reported viewing motives.

Frisby and Weigold (1994) asked respondents to view one episode of Oprah, Donahue, or Geraldo during a week in the fall of 1993. Before viewing, respondents completed a self-esteem scale and were given a booklet in which they were to record their thoughts while viewing the talk show, and to indicate any feelings they were experiencing on an accompanying set of scales (e.g., positive–negative, calm–excited, curious–bored). They also were asked to rate the host's attractiveness, to compare themselves with the guests (e.g., happier–sadder, better–worse), and to answer items about their talk show viewing habits and motives.

Participants were 182 respondents, 89 of whom were regular viewers of the show they had chosen to watch. The major results included:

1. Motives for watching were not predictive of either emotional valence (positive or negative feelings) or emotional intensity (excited or bored feelings).
2. Regular viewers experienced significantly more positive feelings while viewing, and more positive, happy, and "cool" thoughts than did nonviewers, but did not differ from nonviewers on the number of negative feelings.
3. Positive feelings experienced were positively related to the previewing level of self-esteem; downward comparison (favorable evaluation of oneself in comparison to guests on the show) was positively correlated with postviewing self-esteem. Neither measure of self-esteem was related to the number of talk shows viewed, but both were positively correlated with perceptions of host attractiveness.
4. The number of negative feelings was inversely related to the number of shows the respondents viewed and to the perceived attractiveness of the host. In other words, the more the respondents viewed talk shows, the less negative they felt about the shows' content and hosts.

Frisby (1999) assessed self-esteem (a 10-item scale) and measured life satisfaction (a 40-item scale) in an experiment she conducted with 232 college undergraduates who were talk show viewers. Subjects of high or low self-esteem were assigned to watch a 6-minute excerpt that showed a guest solving an interpersonal problem (upward social comparison), or an excerpt where a guest failed to solve a similar problem (downward social comparison). Frisby expected those with low self-esteem to gain more on the life satisfaction measure in the downward social comparison, and those with high self-esteem to gain more from the upward social comparison treatment. The results indicated that watching both upward and downward social comparison treatments increased the life satisfaction measure for both the low- and high-self-esteem subjects, but that the high-self-esteem viewers got an even bigger boost from viewing the downward social comparison treatment.

Davis and Mares (1998) examined the effects of talk show viewing on adolescents. Their sample consisted of 282 students in grades 9 to 12; 58% were female and 76% were White. Their instrument asked the teenagers about the following:

1. Their estimates of the percentage of people who engage in activities commonly discussed on talk shows, such as teen pregnancy, adultery, and premarital sex.
2. Social judgments about typical talk show problems (agreement with statements such as "It's hard to keep close relationships going").
3. Desensitization (students read vignettes in which one person was harmed by another, through substance abuse or sexual relations, and indicated how wrong they thought the perpetrators' actions were and how much they thought the victim had suffered).
4. Issue complexity (students rated the seriousness and complexity of two topics often discussed on talk shows—drug abuse and pregnancy—and two topics seldom discussed—homelessness and AIDS). Their predictor variable measures included: talk show viewing, perceived realism of talk shows, and overall television viewing.

Twelve percent of the sample watched talk shows every day, 34% watched sometimes, 29% rarely, and 25% never watched. During the summer, 68% of the sample viewed talk shows sometimes or every day. Females were more likely to watch sometimes or every day than were males (54% vs. 34%).

The study tested several specific hypotheses, with these results:

1. Talk show viewing was significantly related to estimates of behaviors discussed on talk shows for teen-related topics, but not for nonteen topics. The teenagers overestimated the frequency that these topics occur and heavy viewers made even higher estimates for the teen-related issues. Heavy viewers also were less likely to agree that "People are pretty decent to each other" and "You can rely on people to be there when you need them."

2. Talk show viewing was not negatively related to beliefs about the complexity and severity of the issues of drug abuse and pregnancy, common topics on talk shows. However, talk show viewing was positively related to ratings of the seriousness of the problem of teen pregnancy, a finding that was counter to the predicted outcome.

3. Heavy viewers did not rate situations where one person harms another as less morally wrong.

4. The expectation that the effects of talk show viewing on social reality beliefs would depend on the teenagers' perceptions of the realism of these shows had little support.

In a recent experiment, Greenberg, Mastro, and Woods (1999) exposed teenage college students to alternatively constructed versions of Jerry Springer episodes in order to assess viewer acceptance or rejection of verbal and physical aggression. Participants were randomly assigned to high, moderate, or no-exposure aggression conditions. Based on social learning theory, it was hypothesized that subjects in the high aggression condition would report the highest acceptance of verbal and physical aggression, followed by the moderate group, and then the control group. The treatments yielded no differences in verbal aggression. However, exposure to high levels of physical aggression in the constructed examples diminished the acceptability of physically aggressive behavior. On three separate measures of physical aggression, the lowest aggression response came from those exposed to the high aggression episode of the Jerry Springer show. This result was the opposite of the predicted outcome. Further analyses indicated that the female subjects, the more devoted viewers of talk shows, provided these significant results, with no meaningful differences among the males. The authors speculated that the source of this aberrant result might be that the talk show "models" were not attractive and were not rewarded for their often obnoxious behavior, thereby muting the predicted effects from the social learning perspective.

In this same study, participants provided information about their viewing of daytime talk shows, together with their estimates of the frequency of problems in different interpersonal relationships and their estimates of the occurrence of a set of unusual behaviors, for example, collecting dozens of pets, excessive sexual activity. Hypotheses positively linking viewing with these real-world estimates were supported.

STRATEGIC RESEARCH ISSUES

The concluding section of this chapter offers a strategy for research designed to enhance the meager information now available on the audiences, uses, and outcomes of daytime television talk shows. When a substantive area of mass media has been so completely neglected by academic social scientists and so heavily embraced as a focus for severe condemnation by politicians of typically opposing ideologies, it is reasonable for social scientists to shift a portion of their attention to this genre. Perhaps there is a bit of snobbery in the content choices of the academy: to belittle daytime content—soaps and talk shows—in comparison with the more glamorous areas of prime-time entertainment and/or news.

Content issues remain. One quantitative examination of talk shows is on the record. No trend studies exist, whereas both Oprah and Springer announced that their shows were shifting from what they were (and then Springer reneged). Regardless, to plot trends in specific talk shows (e.g., the most popular ones), it is more reliable to analyze 40 to 50 episodes for each host in order to be able to make comparisons between shows as well as among them. Then, within those episodes, one may examine the guests, the hosts, the audiences, the topics, the interactions, the titles, the interruptions, the commercials. If the interest is in teenagers, then the data set needs to be large enough to focus on teenage guests, as well as topics of particular interest to teenagers.

Viewing data are mandatory. From a broad, preferably national sample of teenagers, what daytime talk shows do they watch and prefer? How do those findings merge with their overall diet of television, and how do they blend with teenagers' broader media diet, inclusive of teen magazines, preferences for music, Internet options, and so on. No genre of television content exists in a social vacuum; it is likely that one must concurrently determine the alternative media and nonmedia sources that provide complementary entertainment or information or gratification options.

The research summary identifies gratifications sought from talk shows as falling within the gratifications found in other television content (Cress & Rapert, 1996). That study suffers from not offering the respondents an opportunity to identify gratifications that may come primarily, if not exclusively, from this genre of content. Viewers of talk shows may watch in part for the voyeurism opportunity it provides, what may be labeled a "peeping Tom motive," although a less sexist label would acknowledge the predominantly female audience. Second, the literature speculates that a key motive for viewing this content is that of "social comparisons." Given the unattractive nature of the guests and their problems, viewers may react with a comparative response that says their own problems aren't nearly as bad as the ones they're hearing about and watching. At any rate, finding motives for teenage viewing of daytime talk shows demands that additional thought be given to the development and identification of specific gratifications. Or do these shows, indeed, primarily provide momentary entertainment for teenagers who are otherwise quite savvy and unperturbed by the strange people and strange behaviors found on many of these shows?

Perceptions of content provide another research realm. Assessments of the realism of the problems, the credibility of the guests, the honesty of the confrontations, the role of the host—all these provide fodder for subsequent studies. Importantly, most research models would posit that these perceptions mediate or intervene in the viewers' acceptance of what they see and hear on such shows.

Then, if we move to what might be considered some critical effects of talk shows on teenage viewers, we can begin with an interest in the extent to which these shows introduce teenage viewers to issues and situations not before confronted by them. Their understanding of such issues, if talk shows are the original source of information, may be a key element in identifying specific important effects of this genre. It becomes a question of what they think they know about certain social issues with which they have not had direct experience, and that have been mediated for them primarily in such shows. One can then move from the origination of information to examine the transfer of that information to real-life estimates or likelihoods of occurrence, à la the cultivation perspective. Perhaps second-order effects should be given a more central role: If teenagers consistently see parent–child or spousal conflicts (common topics on talk shows), does this generalize to a worldview regarding the nature and extent of interpersonal problems in general? Are they less likely to see marriage as a lasting phenomenon?

Sexual information is the focus on over one third of shows (Greenberg et al., 1977). Sexual relationships, sexual fidelity, and sexual orientation are frequent topics on these shows. Guests are not shy, perhaps they are even eager, to talk about intimate sexual issues. Important questions about teenage viewers and this sexual information remain. Do frequent viewers make higher estimates of the occurrence of both normal and bizarre sexual activity? Is this likely to impact on their own sex lives or sex life expectations? How should sexuality education in the schools cope with this "sex information" readily available in after-school television time?

Not all teenagers, of course, are alike. Discernible differences in response to the talk shows and their content should be evident in different subgroups of teenagers. Specifying the origin of those differences provides another research venue. The socially alienated versus socially integrated teenager, the shy versus outgoing teenager, the more and less worldly teenager—all provide opportunities for theory development and research questions. Some further distinctions among adolescents may be paths to understanding different responses to the same talk shows. For example, there is an "overrepresentation" of minority and female and younger guests on these shows (Greenberg et al., 1997). Does this suggest to young viewers that they are a greater source or cause of the problems discussed? Does it bias majority group perceptions of the minorities portrayed, as the latter are more steeped in those types of unusual dilemmas? Does it alter young females' images of romance and other interpersonal relationships?

So little has been studied about talk shows in general, let alone their relevance to teenagers in particular, that the available research landscape has limitless boundaries.

REFERENCES

Abt, V., & Seesholtz, M. (1994). The shameless world of Phil, Sally, and Oprah: Television talk shows and the deconstructing of society. *Journal of Popular Culture, 28*, 171–191.

Cress, S. L., & Rapert, K. D. (1996, November). *Talk show viewing motives: Does gender make a difference?* Paper presented at the annual meeting of the Speech Communication Association, San Diego, CA.

Davis, S., & Mares, M. L. (1998). Effects of talk show viewing on adolescents. *Journal of Communication, 48,* 69–86.

Frisby, C. M. (1999). *When bad things happen to bad people: Will social comparison theory explain effects of viewing TV talk shows.* Paper presented at the convention of the Association for Education in Journalism and Mass Communication, New Orleans, LA.

Frisby, C. M., & Weigold, M. F. (1994). *Gratifications of talk: Esteem and affect related consequences of viewing television talk shows.* Paper presented at the annual meeting of the Association for Education in Journalism and Mass Communication, Atlanta, GA.

Gamson, J. (1998). *Freaks talk back: Tabloid talk shows and sexual nonconformity.* Chicago: The University of Chicago Press.

Greenberg, B. S., Mastro, D., & Woods, M. (1999). *Aggression responses to verbal and physical violence on the Jerry Springer show.* Paper presented at the annual meeting of the International Communication Association, San Francisco.

Greenberg, B. S., Rampoldi-Hnilo, L., Sherry, J. L., & Smith, S. W. (1997). Television talk shows: Making intimacies public. *SIECUS Report, 25,* 8.

Greenberg, B. S., Sherry, J. L., Busselle, R., Rampoldi-Hnilo, L., & Smith, S. W. (1997). Daytime television talk shows: Guests, content and interactions. *Journal of Broadcasting and Electronic Media, 41,* 412–426.

Greenberg, B. S., Smith, S. W., AhYun, J., Busselle, R., Rampoldi-Hnilo, L., Mitchell, M., & Sherry, J. L. (1995). *The content of television talk shows: Topics, guests, and interactions.* Report prepared for the Henry J. Kaiser Family Foundation, Menlo Park, CA.

Heaton, J. A., & Wilson, N. L. (1995). *Tuning in trouble: Talk TV's destructive impact on mental health.* San Francisco: Jossey-Bass.

Nelson, E. D., & Robinson, B. W. (1994). "Reality talk" or "telling tales"? The social construction of sexual and gender deviance on a television talk show. *Journal of Contemporary Ethnography, 23,* 51–78.

Orrego, V. O., Smith, S. W., Mitchell, M. M., Johnson, J. A., AhYun, J., & Greenberg, B. S. (2000). Disclosure and privacy issues on television talk shows. In S. Petronio (Ed.), *Balancing disclosure, privacy, and secrecy.* Hillsdale, NJ: Lawrence Erlbaum Associates; 249–259.

Priest, P. (1995). *Public intimacies: Talk show participants and tell-all TV.* Cresskill, NJ: Hampton Press.

Rubin, A. M. (1983). Television uses and gratifications: The interactions of viewing patterns and motivations. *Journal of Broadcasting, 27,* 37–51.

Smith, S. W., AhYun, J., Orrego, V. O., Johnson, A. J., Mitchell, M. M., & Greenberg, B. S. (in press). The sources, types, and frequencies of personal disclosures on talk television. In L. Klein (Ed.), *Talking up a storm: The social impact of daytime talk programs.* Westport, CT: Greenwood.

Smith, S. W., Mitchell, M. M., AhYun, J., Johnson, A. J., Orrego, V. O., & Greenberg, B. S. (1999). The nature of close relationships as presented in television talk show titles. *Communication Studies, 50,* 175–187.

5

Would That Really Happen? Adolescents' Perceptions of Sexual Relationships According to Prime-Time Television

L. Monique Ward
Benjamin Gorvine
Adena Cytron
University of Michigan

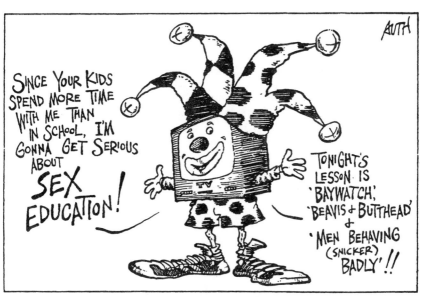

AUTH © The Philadelphia Inquirer. Reprinted with permission of
UNIVERSAL PRESS SYNDICATE. All rights reserved.

"I thought you wanted me to. I mean, the way you looked at me . . ."
—Molly to David after kissing him (*Roseanne*)

"She didn't tell you because women aren't as smart as they think they are.
They don't realize how little we actually know."
—Father offering advice to his son, Brad, about why
his date is upset with him (*Home Improvement*)

It is widely believed that television has become an important source of information for today's youth about sexuality, dating, and sexual relationships (Brown & Steele, 1995; Huston, Wartella, & Donnerstein, 1998; Strasburger, 1995). From daytime soap operas to prime-time situation comedies, television presents viewers with countless verbal and visual examples of how dating, intimacy, sex, and romantic relationships are handled. Studies report that an average of 10 instances of sexual behavior appear per hour on soap operas (Greenberg & Busselle, 1996; Heintz-Knowles, 1996), and that 29% of the interactions on prime-time programs popular among youth contain verbal references to sexual issues (Ward, 1995). In a comprehensive analysis of 942 programs aired on 10 networks during one week, Kunkel et al. (1999) reported that 54% of all programs and 65% of prime-time network programs included some talk about sexuality.

However, whereas the prevalence of sexual content on today's programming is well documented, less is known about how younger viewers perceive this material. Among parents and politicians, concern is often expressed that today's sexual portrayals are "too much" for younger viewers—too frequent, too explicit, and too unrealistic. Indeed, because much of popular programming was created with adult viewers in mind, the sexual situations typically depicted are complex, sophisticated, and innuendo laden, leaving them open to multiple, and sometimes incorrect, interpretations. Moreover, content analyses report that the sexual messages conveyed are frequently misleading—overglamorizing sex and underemphasizing its risks and consequences (see Huston et al., 1998, for review). Depictions of courtship and sexual relationships are often limited and stereotypical, with sex-driven males competing with each other for females, who are viewed as sexual objects or prizes (Ward, 1995).

Yet is this what adolescents see? Do American youths view these portrayals as realistic and these messages as acceptable? In the popular mind, adolescents and college students are perceived as worldly, cynical, and not likely to be fooled by "the man behind the curtain." Indeed, if you were to ask an 18-year-old what he or she thought about TV's portrayals, you might get a disdainful look followed by, "Nobody really believes that stuff." Yet given adolescents' limited experience with dating and sexual relationships, coupled with their hunger for knowledge in this area, it is important to understand what they see when they view these complex yet often misleading portrayals of sexuality. This is the central issue of this chapter.

GOALS OF THE STUDY

In examining this issue, we addressed three main goals or questions. The first goal was to examine adolescents' general perceptions of TV's sexual content. How do young viewers interpret TV's sexual situations? In accordance with the active audience approach to media effects (e.g., Dorr, 1986; Levy & Windahl, 1985), our assumption was that viewers would not necessarily see TV's sexual situations in the same way, but instead would offer diverse interpretations based on their preexisting beliefs, biases, experiences, and intended uses. Evidence indicates that viewers do indeed offer diverse readings of TV's sexual/romantic content (e.g., Brown & Schulze, 1990; Kalof, 1993; Livingstone, 1990), with even the most straightforward scenes drawing multiple interpretations. Therefore, in response to the question, "What is the main message of this scene?" we would expect substantial variation in students' perceptions of select sexual content. This does not mean that the number of interpretations possible is unlimited; instead, the options will be constrained by both the homogeneity of the content typically available (Signorielli, 1986), and the common cultural values shared by viewers and the programs' creators (Biocca, 1988; Dorr, 1986).

In addition to surveying viewers' general interpretations of TV's sexual situations, we were also interested in assessing their evaluations of particular content, namely their judgments of the realism of the portrayals, their personal connections with the main characters, and their level of approval of the characters' actions. These dimensions were selected because each is believed to mediate the potential impact of media content. Theories such as Bandura's Cognitive Social Learning Theory (1986; 1994) and Greenberg's "drench" hypothesis (1988) each highlight the importance of a scene's realism and relevance in determining the strength of its impact. The expectation is that portrayals perceived as fake, inappropriate, or irrelevant will be dismissed and will be less likely to shape viewers' attitudes or behaviors. Findings typically support this premise (e.g., Basil, 1996; Perse, 1986; Potter, 1986), indicating, for example, stronger effects on behaviors and attitudes of television content rated higher in actual or perceived realism (e.g., Huesmann, 1986; Rubin, Perse, & Taylor, 1988). Our intent, therefore, was to assess viewers' evaluations of specific sexual portrayals and situations, focusing on those judgments believed to mediate their eventual impact.

Our second goal was to identify some of the dominant personal and experiential factors that shape viewers' perceptions. In other words, what factors determine whether people see the same sexual content differently? Although previous work addressing this question typically has focused on contributions of gender, race, or age (e.g., Brown & Schulze, 1990; Kalof, 1993), we believed that a complex assortment of variables would contribute to the diversity present in young viewers' perceptions of sexual content.

According to the Adolescents' Media Practice Model developed by Steele and Brown (1995), adolescents' selections, interpretations, and uses of the media are heavily influenced by basic sociocultural factors such as gender and race; by their developing identities; and by a multitude of conditions in their lives, labeled "lived experience," which encompasses neighborhood influences, family life, friendships, peer culture, and religious backgrounds and beliefs. The notion is that adolescents carry their particular life histories with them, and that their perceptions of media content are filtered through these experiences. Working from this model, our goal was to identify some of the central variables that affect viewers' perceptions of sexual content. Assessing all possible contributors would be an overwhelming task for one study; our choice, therefore, was to focus on the contributions of a few central domains.

Our third goal was to assess the consistency with which these factors exert their influence. In other words, do factors shaping viewers' perceptions do so for all content in all circumstances? An unstated assumption in much of the previous work has been that a factor (e.g., age) found to predict viewers' perceptions of one or two clips would do so in all cases. Yet might people bring different "baggage" to different types of content, perhaps with their gender or race being relevant for some content but not for other content? Are there certain constants that transcend clip-specific content? This chapter attempts to answer these questions, examining whether there are, in fact, global predictors of interpretations (i.e., personal attributes that predict viewer interpretations across different types of television clips), or whether predictors are situation- or content-specific.

Perhaps the most challenging task for this type of project was constructing a list of factors, suggested by either existing evidence or theoretical arguments, that might shape viewers' interpretations and evaluations of television's sexual content. Because only a few studies have examined factors predicting perceptions of sexual content (e.g., Brown & Schulze, 1990; Greenberg, Linsangan, & Soderman, 1993; Walsh-Childers, 1990), we expanded our search to include factors reported to affect perceptions of nonsexual content as well (e.g., Surlin & Tate, 1976). Our review of the research in these areas led us to focus on three sources of potential variance: demographics, television viewing behaviors, and existing sexual attitudes and experiences.

The first group of factors emerging is demographics. Research examining the forces shaping viewers' perceptions of TV content have frequently focused on this domain, with gender, age, ethnicity, socioeconomic status (SES), and culture emerging as strong contributors. One of the most dominant forces in this domain has been gender, with men and women frequently offering different interpretations and evaluations of and connections with both sexual and nonsexual content (e.g., Basil, 1996; Greenberg et al., 1993; Kalof, 1993; Livingstone, 1990). For example, women have been found to perceive female characters as less stereotypically feminine than men do (Reep & Dambrot, 1990). Comprehension and perceptions of TV content also have been found to vary developmentally (e.g., Greenberg et al., 1993; Granello, 1997; Silverman-Watkins & Sprafkin, 1983; Walsh-Childers, 1990), especially among children and adolescents. Finally, substantial variation has been reported in viewers' perceptions based on SES (e.g., Press, 1989; Sprafkin, Silverman, & Rubinstein, 1980), ethnicity (e.g., Brown & Schulze, 1990; Brigham & Giesbrecht, 1976; Cooks & Orbe, 1993), and cultural background (e.g., Katz & Liebes, 1985; Katz, Liebes, & Iwao, 1991; Surlin & Tate, 1976). Thus, we expected that multiple aspects of viewers' demographic backgrounds would shape how they perceived sexual content on television.

A second domain of factors frequently reported to affect viewers' perceptions is their typical viewing behaviors or approach to TV. Within this domain, a prominent agent has been amount of viewing. According to cultivation theory (Gerbner & Gross, 1976; Gerbner, Gross, Morgan, & Signorielli, 1994), television's consistent images and portrayals construct a specific portrait of reality. As viewers watch more and more TV, they gradually come to cultivate or adopt attitudes and expectations about the world that coincide with this portrait. Thus, based on this premise and on findings from cultivation studies, we anticipated that students' regular viewing amounts would predict their evaluations of individual content. In particular, we anticipated that frequent TV viewers would attribute more reality to the portrayals (e.g., Elliott & Slater, 1980; Potter, 1988), and would be more inclined to accept stereotypical portrayals and situations (e.g., Reep & Dambrot, 1990; Slater & Elliott, 1982).

Given the richness of our experiences with television, we suspected that components of viewing behavior other than amount would also affect how TV content was perceived. For example, Basil (1996) revealed that it was viewers' emotional reliance on TV, not their viewing amounts, that predicted the strength of their identification with a popular celebrity spokesperson. Therefore, we believed that viewers' general level of connection with TV and its portrayals would also shape how they perceived and evaluated its sexual content. In assessing the global construct of connection or involvement, we chose to focus on two dimensions in particular: level of active viewing and viewing motivations. The notion of the active viewer is a staple of constructivist perspectives of media use. The active viewer is seen as one who is selective, attentive, involved, and apt to apply the messages received (e.g., Levy & Windahl, 1984). Being active in these ways is believed to enhance media effects, with some empirical support for this premise (e.g., Rubin & Perse, 1987). Similarly, although viewers choose to watch TV for various reasons, those who intend to use TV content to learn about the world are believed to experience enhanced media effects (e.g., Van Evra, 1998). Thus we expected that viewers' perceptions of TV content would vary based on their viewing amounts and general viewing involvement, with both heavier and more involved viewers offering greater acceptance of the portrayals and messages presented.

A third domain of factors reported to shape viewers' perceptions of television content are their existing attitudes and related experiences. The assumption is that if viewers come to the viewing situation with a certain belief or expectation, they are more inclined to interpret TV content in a way that supports this existing belief. Although few studies have examined the impact of selective perception in regard to sexual content, existing findings indicate that viewers' attitudes about sex do matter (Sprafkin et al., 1980; Walsh-Childers, 1990). For example, interviews with adolescent girls about their media use and perceptions of its sexual content indicated striking differences in how sexual content was perceived, depending on the girls' level of physical, personal, and sexual development (Brown, White, & Nikopoulou, 1993). Some girls were uninterested in and disgusted by sexual content, some were intrigued and solicitous, and others were oppositional. Moreover, it appeared that the girls with more actual sexual experience were more critical of media portrayals of sexuality. Additional support for the impact of preexisting attitudes on viewers' perceptions was found in research on perceptions of racist portrayals (e.g., Brigham & Giesbrecht, 1976; Vidmar & Rokeach, 1974; Wilhoit & de Bock, 1976); in this research, participants offered differing impressions of a program (*All in the Family*) and its characters based on the level of their preexisting racial attitudes. Therefore, based on findings examining both sexual and nonsexual content, we predicted that viewers' existing sexual attitudes and experiences would likely affect their perceptions of sexual content presented on television. Thus overall, we expected that young viewers' interpretations and evaluations of TV's sexual content would be influenced by who they are (demographically), how they typically use TV, and their preexisting attitudes about gender and sexuality.

In summary, this chapter examines how adolescents perceive sexual/romantic content in prime-time TV programs, and attempts to determine which factors (i.e., demographics, attitudes, media behaviors) best predict these perceptions. Our plan was to present a selection of clips representative of TV's sexual content, obtain students' interpretations and evaluations of those clips, and examine which of several dimensions of their daily lives and experiences most affect these perceptions. Driving our efforts were the following research questions:

1. What are viewers' interpretations of the central themes and messages depicted in a selection of TV clips addressing various themes about sexual relationships? Is there much variance in these impressions or do a majority of the people tend to see the scenes in the same way? In their evaluations, to

what extent do participants perceive the content as realistic, appropriate, and relevant to their own lives?

2. To what extent are viewers' perceptions of sexual content influenced by demographics, media viewing behaviors, and sexual attitudes and experiences?

In keeping with previous research, we expected that gender would emerge as an important determinant of viewers' perceptions. Students' preexisting sexual attitudes and experiences were also expected to play a strong role, such that those already endorsing more casual or recreational notions about sexuality would be more accepting of the content presented. Finally, we expected that viewers' perceptions of TV content would vary based on their viewing amounts and general viewing involvement—with more frequent and more involved viewers being more accepting of the portrayals and messages presented.

3. How do these perceptions vary across different clips? Are predictors global or specfic to the clip content?

Based on findings reported by Greenberg et al. (1993) and Sprafkin et al. (1980), we expected that perceptions would be more content specific than universal.

METHOD

Participants

Participants were 314 university undergraduates (55% female) from the University of Michigan (N = 158) and the University of California, Los Angeles (N = 156), who agreed to participate to fulfill a course requirement. Although the students ranged in age from 18 to 24 (Mean = 19.36), 97% were between the ages of 18 and 20. Based on students' responses to an open-ended survey question about their racial/ethnic background/identity, the following ethnic group breakdown was compiled: 54% White/Euro-American; 26% Asian American/Pacific Islander/Middle Eastern; 12% Latino(a); 8% Black/African American. Approximately 95% of the participants had spent their formative years (ages 5 to 15) in the United States.

A variable representing socioeconomic status (SES) was constructed for each participant, based on information about his or her mother's education (Mean = 15.3 years), father's education (Mean = 16.2 years), and each parent's occupation. Occupations first were rated for prestige, using the 1989 Socioeconomic Index of Occupations (Nakao & Treas, 1992). A z-score was then calculated for each of the parental education and occupational prestige variables. Finally, these four z-scores were summed to create a z-score representing the relative SES of each participant. With this information, the following five demographic variables were used in this study: age, sex, ethnicity, SES, and school (UCLA or UMICH).

Stimuli

Serving as stimuli were four clips selected from the Ward (1995) analysis of TV's sexual content. They included excerpts from *Roseanne, Martin, Home Improvement*, and *Family Matters*, which were among the 12 shows teens watched most during the 1992–1993 broadcast season, and were still airing in syndication during the course of this study. Each clip was approximately 3 minutes in length. A range of material was selected in order to reflect different ethnic groups (two with Black casts and two with White casts), different stages of relationships (newly dating to married), and different ages of key characters (preteen to middle age). In addition, we selected clips that featured typical yet relatively complex situations that could yield a range of interpretations. Pilot testing of several clips indicated that the four particular segments selected met these needs appropriately.

In the clip from *Roseanne*, teenage neighbor Molly visits the Connor household looking for a homework assignment from classmate Darlene. Darlene is not home. Instead, her boyfriend, David, is baby-sitting her younger brother, D. J., who soon exits. Molly decides to wait for Darlene's return. She eyes David's comic book drawings on the table and compliments the female bodies depicted. David assures her that her body is fine, too. Molly leans over and kisses David. David pulls away in shock because Molly is aware that he has a girlfriend. Molly asserts that she had sensed that David wanted her to kiss him, and that he deserves better than his current girlfriend, Darlene. David defends his relationship. The parents enter, ending the conversation.

In the clip from *Martin*, single male Martin discusses a sexual dilemma with his two closest friends, also single males. He tells his friends that he loves Gina, his current girlfriend, but is attracted to a new coworker, with whom he wants to sleep. Martin believes that his coworker is interested in him as well. He asks his friends for advice. His friends offer conflicting advice. One friend tells him that it is his duty as a man to fool around with his coworker (i.e., "conquer that territory"). The other friend belittles this advice and warns Martin not to jeopardize his relationship. He believes Martin needs to reject his coworker's advances. Martin's girlfriend arrives and the conversation ends.

In the clip from *Home Improvement*, preteen Brad sits outside dejectedly, dressed in his Halloween costume. Brad is upset about a dispute he just had with Jennifer, a girl he likes. His dad comes out to give him advice. He tells Brad to talk to Jennifer and try to see her side. Dad reminds Brad that "women are always right," and that all will be resolved and forgiven if Brad says "I understand." Brad confronts Jennifer about their disagreement. He tries his father's advice, but the approach does not work. Jennifer explains that she was mad at Brad for not picking her to be on his kickball team. Brad explains that he wanted to win the game and picked the girl who was good. They discuss the issue and apologize to each other.

In the clip from *Family Matters*, wife and mother Harriet is just completing her first at-home piano lesson. She is laughing with the handsome male piano teacher, who is preparing to exit. Her husband, Carl, is not amused. He hurries the piano teacher out of the house and slams the door in his face. Harriet questions Carl's behavior. Carl explains that he thought the piano teacher was "groping, pawing, and touching" her and was trying to make a move on her. Harriet accuses Carl of being too jealous. Carl explains his reasons and insecurities. Harriet reassures Carl of her love for him and they hug.

Measures

Perceptions of Television Clips. Participants were asked to rate the situation presented in each clip for its realism, likelihood to happen in their own lives, appropriateness of the male and female characters' behavior (only two scenes had prominent female characters), and for their level of identification with the main character (all main characters were male for consistency). Perceptions were rated on a scale of 1 to 4, with a score of 1 reflecting less of each construct. Participants also were asked three open-ended questions about each clip: "Please describe what just occurred in this scene"; "Why do you think the main character, ——, acted that way or did what he did?"; "What do you think the writers of this scene are trying to say about how males and females interact or view each other?" These open-ended questions were coded later, using a group of 16 categories developed for this study.

Developing the Coding System. Several steps were taken to develop an effective system for coding the open-ended responses. Preliminary coding categories were first established based on reviews of random portions of the data. These categories were then tested and refined over several rounds of coding until inter-rater reliability consistently averaged .8 or above. During each round, three coders worked independently to code the responses of a small subset of the data (i.e., data from approximately 15 to 20 participants), checked reliability, and discussed discrepancies. Resulting from this process were the 16 categories listed in Table 5.1. This list was finally tested using 20% of the data, revised slightly, and a final reliability check was run on the same 20% plus an additional 10% of the data. Inter-rater reliability was .83.

With the coding system firmly established, each rater coded two thirds of the data, thereby ensuring that all responses were coded by two people.

TABLE 5.1
Categories Used for Coding Open-Ended Responses

Coding Category	Examples
1. Importance of communication and of reading verbal and nonverbal communication and behavior	• "They need to talk to understand each other" • "That girl got the wrong impression"
2. Maintaining a relationship is hard but valuable. Relationship challenges like jealousy, being torn and tempted by another person. Importance of love, trust, respect, commitment, and other positive "shoulds" to a relationship	• "Sometimes you have to get the other person's perspective" • "Insecurity often gets in the way of relationships and can lead to jealousy"
3. Men are jealous, insecure, and easily threatened	• "Men will become jealous or protective of women they love if they feel threatened or insecure" • "That males get jealous very easily"
4. Issues of sex drive, sexual urges, and the power of physical attraction	• "Martin acted the way he did because it's exciting to have someone express their interest in him when he feels the same way" • "He was acting on hormones"
5. Men and women play games, compete, manipulate each other, and have power struggles	• "That Martin has his game on and all the honeys are tryin' to hook up" • "That sex relationships are a game or more like a battle between women and men"
6. Men and women are different: "Men are this, women are that." Nonsexual generalities and stereotypes	• "That women get mad easily about things men usually don't know are affecting them. Also men are more clueless as to how to evaluate and conclude matters/problems." • "Males are into trying to get away with things while females are so honest"
7. Relational and emotional nature of men	• "This clip presents males as somewhat blind to emotions and feelings of women, not purposely, but because they interact differently" • "Men have trouble seeing the good things they have when other options come along"
8. Relational and emotional nature of women	• "The writers are saying women get the wrong impression(s) from actions that really have nothing to do with them" • "Females will do anything to get what they want"
9. Stereotypical expectations of male sexuality—prominence of male sex drive	• "That males never stop looking" • "The writers are showing how a man may take an innocent relationship and turn it into something bad or lustful"

(Continued)

104

TABLE 5.1
(Continued)

Coding Category	Examples
10. Men are faithful; can be loyal to one person; can control their sex drive	• "Not all men will jump at the chance to be with women other than their girl-friends"
	• "That it is OK for males to say no when they have opportunity to have sex"
11. Stereotypical expectations of female sexuality—female as temptress/seducer	• "Aggressive sexual advances are not limited to males"
	• "The writers were showing that women also make sexual advances toward men"
12. Women are faithful; can be loyal to one person; can control their sex drive	• "She will be true"
	• "Unusual for girl to make the first move"
13. Receiving advice from someone because he/she does not know what to do	• "He takes opinions from his father because he doesn't know what to do"
14. Age issues: Youth, inexperience, nature of teen relationships or teens in them	• "He was young and naive"
	• "He was young and inexperienced"
15. Bad behavior or bad choices (e.g., being insensitive, lacking values)	• " 'Brad' was only thinking of himself—not wanting to care how the other person may feel"
	• "He said he wanted to win. This may be true, but he was insensitive to what his girlfriend was feeling"
16. Scared might get caught	• "David was scared they might get caught and he really liked Darlene"
	• "He might have been feeling guilty for having checked Molly out and probably thinking about what his girlfriend would do or say if she found out"
Response was left blank; response was not codable.	• "I don't know"
	• "No answer"

For each participant, raters coded a perceived "main message" of each scene, and a perceived motive of the main character's actions. Efforts were made to assign one code for each open-ended response; however, if a dominant code was not distinguishable, multiple codes could be assigned to more accurately reflect the complexity of the answer. Approximately 16% of the 1,760 responses coded were given more than one code. After all responses had been independently coded, raters compared their codes. Differences were discussed, and if agreement could not be reached, the third rater determined which code would be used. Inter-rater reliability averaged .87. This procedure was repeated two weeks later, with each rater recoding data from 20 subjects. The resulting mean test-retest reliability was .93.

General Television Viewing Behaviors. Five variables assessed participants' typical viewing behaviors (Ward & Rivadeneyra, 1999). To measure
viewing amount, a list was provided of all network comedies and dramas
that had aired regularly (at least four times) on one of the six major networks (ABC, CBS, NBC, Fox, UPN, and WB) during the previous school term.
Using a 5-point scale, participants indicated how often they had viewed
each of the more than 150 programs listed during an average month during
the previous school term. The prime-time and weekend daytime syndicated
programs were rated using five frequency markers ranging from *every week*
to *never/not this season*. Soap operas and weekday syndicated programs
(that aired five times a week) were rated using five frequency markers ranging from *once a day/almost every day* to *never/not this season*. The key variables of interest resulting for each participant were the Monthly Hours of
Prime Time Viewing, the Monthly Hours of Soap Opera Viewing, and the Total Monthly Viewing Hours (of comedies and dramas).

The next measure examined the degree to which viewers watch TV to
learn about the world. Here, participants rated each of 11 possible motivations for watching television comedies and dramas that had been extracted
from previous research (see Ward & Rivadeneyra, 1999 for more details).
To rate each motivation, participants used a 6-point scale that ranged from
1 (*strongly disagree*) to 6 (*strongly agree*). Examples of motivations included
"because they help me to learn about myself and others" and "to help me
understand the world." Ratings of agreement with the 11 motivations were
summed to produce one Learning Motive Score for each participant.

To assess level of active viewing, participants rated the extent to which
each of 34 statements in the Active Viewing Measure (Ward & Rivadeneyra,
1999) reflected their own viewing style. Eight items reflected selectivity
(e.g., "I often plan my day around the TV shows I like to watch"), 17 reflected
involvement during exposure (e.g., "I often try to guess what will happen
next or how an episode will end"), and 9 reflected postexposure use (e.g., "I
frequently talk to others about what I have recently seen on TV shows").
Agreement with each statement was rated using a 6-pt scale that ranged from
not at all like me to *very much like me*. Through factor and reliability analyses,
the Active Viewing Measure was reduced to 27 items (alpha = .91; see Ward
and Rivadeneyra [1999], for more about these measures).

In summary, the following five variables assessing participants' general
TV viewing were included in this study: Monthly Hours of Prime Time
Viewing, Monthly Hours of Soap Opera Viewing, Total Monthly Viewing
Hours, Level of Active Viewing, and Learning Motive.

Sexual Attitudes and Experiences. A set of four outcome measures was
used to capture viewers' attitudes about both gender roles and sexuality, as
well as their actual experiences with sexual relationships. Participants' attitudes about dating, sexual roles, and sexual relationships were examined

using the Attitudes Toward Dating and Relationships measure (Ward & Riva-deneyra, 1999) that assessed recreational, traditional, and relational orientations to sexuality. A *recreational orientation* to sexuality was represented by 18 statements that portrayed dating and sexual relations as a game or competition. Here, the sexual double standard prevailed, and males and females were viewed as being on opposing teams ("battle of the sexes"), taking different roles, and using sex as the object of exchange. A *procreational* or *traditional orientation* to sexuality was represented by eight statements that centered sexuality around religious dictates and traditional courtship norms. Here, sex was seen to belong in marital relationships only. Finally, a *relational orientation* to sexuality was represented by seven statements that viewed sex as part of a loving relationship based on friendship, mutuality, trust, responsibility, and open communication. Participants rated their level of agreement with each of the 33 statements using a 6-point scale that ranged from 1 (*strongly disagree*) to 6 (*strongly agree*). Reliability analyses conducted on the sample of 314 undergraduates in this study indicated acceptable levels of reliability for the traditional and recreational subscales (with alphas of .84 and .75, respectively). However, appropriate levels of reliability were not reached for the relational subscale, which was dropped.

Gender role attitudes were measured by the Attitudes Toward Women Scale for Adolescents (Galambos, Peterson, Richards, & Gitelson, 1985). This 12-item measure assesses attitudes about the roles and appropriate behaviors of girls in relation to boys. Participants rated their level of agreement with each statement using a 4-point scale that ranged from 1 (*strongly disagree*) to 4 (*strongly agree*). Sample statements include "Swearing is worse for a girl than a boy," and "Boys are better leaders than girls." Scores were summed across the items to yield a total score ranging from 12 to 48, with higher scores reflecting more traditional gender attitudes.

The final sexual background measure assessed participants' own levels of sexual experience. As part of an exploratory effort to include a behavioral component, participants at the UMICH site were asked: "How would you describe your current level of experience with dating and sexual relationships?" Responses were made on a 0 to 10 scale that ranged from *just starting out* (0 or 1) and *some dating* (2 or 3) to *have had several sexual relationships* (6 to 10).

The four sexual background measures (more fully described in Ward and Rivadeneyra, 1999) included Endorsement of Traditional Gender Role Attitudes, Endorsement of Recreational Attitudes Toward Sex, Endorsement of Traditional Dating Norms, and Own Level of Sexual Experience.

Procedure

Students viewed the TV clips in small groups of two to nine, depending on their schedules and availability. On arrival at the experimental session, participants were introduced to the experimenter and the study. They were told that it was a study about students' perceptions of how dating and relationships are portrayed on television. After the experiment was introduced and consent was granted, each participant received a packet of surveys to complete containing all of the television viewing and sexual attitude measures for the study. Participants watched the four clips either before or after completing the questionnaires. The clips were presented one at a time, with ample opportunity given between each clip for participants to evaluate it. For each clip, participants described the scene's main message, indicated whether they had seen that scene or episode before, and rated the content along the following four dimensions: realism, likelihood to happen in own life, identification with the main character, and approval of the characters' behaviors. When all measures and evaluations were completed, participants returned their packets, were thanked for their participation, and received a written debriefing sheet providing more information about the study (UMICH sample only).

Several steps were taken during the execution of this study to reduce potential bias through randomization. First, two viewing conditions were established in which the placement of clip evaluation varied. In one condition ($N = 163$; 52% of sample), participants watched and responded to the clips first, and then completed the questionnaires assessing their sexual attitudes and media habits. In the second condition ($N = 151$), the order was reversed. Second, the ordering of the individual media questionnaires and the sexual attitude questionnaires was randomized across the entire sample. Finally, the clips were presented in one of four orders, and these orderings were equally represented across the two viewing conditions.

RESULTS

Our first goal was twofold: (a) to examine students' interpretations of the major themes and messages of specific clips featuring sexual content, and (b) to assess their evaluations of this content along four specific dimensions (e.g., realism).

Open-Ended Questions

Our analysis of students' responses to the open-ended questions revealed that viewers saw a variety of different messages within the same clip. Three or four themes generally emerged as the most dominant messages of each scene, accounting for 73% to 88% of the responses given. Some clips appeared to be more complex than others. Table 5.2 summarizes the most popular interpretations of the main message of each clip.

TABLE 5.2
Viewers' Interpretations of the Main Message of Each Clip:
Top Responses to Open-Ended Questions

Program	Message	Total %	Male %	Female %
Family Matters	Relationship challenges	41.9	**46.4**	**35.8**
	Men are jealous	30.6	**26.3**	**36.4**
	Male–female communication issues	15.0	14.8	15.2
Home Improvement	Male–female communication issues	46.2	39.3	43.8
	Men and women are different	36.2	37.4	34.6
	Game playing	10.4	**13.6**	**6.2**
	Relationship challenges	6.9	7.0	6.2
Martin	Prominence of male sex drive	48.7	47.3	50.6
	Relationship challenges	15.0	14.9	15.2
	Power of male–female physical attraction	9.7	8.6	11.4
	Male–female communication issues	6.6	**9.0**	**3.2**
Roseanne	Male–female communication issues	25.5	26.4	24.2
	Woman as sexual aggressor	23.0	23.6	22.2
	Men are loyal and faithful	14.9	16.2	15.7
	Relationship challenges	13.6	12.0	13.1

Note. X^2 for bolded male–female percentages differ significantly at the $p < .05$ level.

In the clip from *Family Matters*, a seemingly straightforward clip in which a jealous husband shares his insecurities with his wife, viewers saw more than jealousy as the central theme. In fact, only 30.6% of the responses asserted that the message was that men, in particular, are jealous. As one viewer put it, "Men get jealous because they view their significant other as someone special—beautiful and intelligent for example—that other men would want to have." A larger portion of interpretations (41.9%) focused on the general challenges of a relationship and the difficulties and value in maintaining one: "No matter how secure you feel in a marriage, couples need to support and continually express their love for each other." An additional 15% of the responses asserted that the clip was about the difficulties and challenges of male–female communication: "They [males and females] need to talk to understand each other."

In *Home Improvement*, where a preadolescent male discusses with his father his difficulty understanding the behavior of girls, viewers also offered a range of interpretations. The most popular response (46.2%) was that the clip demonstrated the difficulties and challenges of male–female communication. As one viewer expressed it: "Men and women often interpret how the other acts incorrectly." Close behind (36.2%) was the view that the clip highlighted the differing natures of men and women: "Women care about relationships. Men care about sports." A minority of responses suggested that the clip was about the game playing or competitive aspect of dating (10.4%): "Males and females are kind of childish. It's a game that they play."

In the clip from *Martin*, in which the main character contemplates cheating on his girlfriend, the most popular interpretation offered was the prominence of the male sex drive (48.7%). One viewer summarized this viewpoint quite succinctly: "Men will have sex with anyone who offers whether [or not] he is in a relationship right now." Responses offered less frequently included the notion that relationships are challenging (15.0%; "Relationships are hard to keep monogamous") and that sexual attraction between males and females is powerful (9.7%; "They [men and women] look at each other as sex objects").

The final clip, from the program *Roseanne*, yielded the most complex array of interpretations. In this clip, a teenage male rejects the advances of a female out of commitment to his current girlfriend. A quarter of the responses (25.5%) noted the difficulties and nuances of male–female communication: "Mixed signals between men and women can lead to uncomfortable situations." Close behind (23.0%) was the interpretation that females could be just as sexually aggressive as males: "The stereotypical gender roles (men coming on to women) are sometimes reversed." Two less common interpretations were that men could be loyal and faithful (14.7%; "Not all guys think girls are sex objects"), and that relationships are fraught with challenges (13.6%; "If you care for someone else, you resist temptations").

As gender of the viewer was expected to exert a strong influence in several areas, we examined its influence on both the number and type of interpretations offered. Data reported in Table 5.2 indicate a sizable contribution of gender, with males and females differing in four specific instances in the frequency with which they expressed a particular interpretation. The number of interpretations offered also differed by gender: Summing across the four clips, males provided a larger total number of interpretations than did women ($t = 4.46$, $p < .001$; $Ms = 5.00$ and 4.39, respectively).

Evaluations of TV Sexual Content

Ratings were obtained representing participants' evaluations of each situation's realism, likelihood to happen in their own life, approval of the main characters' behavior, and identification with the main character. Ratings were based on 4-point scales, with higher scores reflecting more of each construct. Means are reported in Table 5.3, as are the percentage of people scoring a 3 or 4 for that construct.

In general, the sexual situations depicted were seen to be quite realistic, with 85% to 95% of participants rating them as *realistic* or *very realistic*. The clip from *Roseanne,* in which a teen male rejects the sexual advances of an attractive female, was seen as significantly less realistic than the other clips. Still, 85% of the sample rated this situation as *realistic* or *very realistic*.

TABLE 5.3
Viewers' Perceptions of the Four Clips

Program	Perceived Realism		Likely to Happen in Own Life		Approve of Man's Behavior		Approve of Women's Behavior		Identify With Main Character	
	Mean	% Realistic	Mean	% Likely	Mean	% Approve	Mean	% Approve	Mean	% Identify
Roseanne	2.94_a	84.7	2.35_b	40.4	3.56_a	98.1	1.63	4.0	2.98_a	79.5
Martin	3.29_b	94.7	2.50_b	51.0	2.34_d	40.8			2.81_b	69.5
Family Matters	3.18_b	90.0	2.67_a	58.3	2.56_c	51.3			2.99_a	78.7
Home Improvement	3.20_b	92.1	2.66_a	56.3	2.84_b	72.0	2.69	67.5	2.84_b	73.5

Note. Within each construct, mean ratings with different subscripts differ significantly at the $p < .05$ level.

Although the scenes were judged to be quite realistic, the participants were less apt to perceive the situations as likely to happen in their own lives. As expected, this perception varied somewhat based on the content of the individual clip. Actions depicted in the *Roseanne* clip were seen as least likely to happen, whereas the issues of jealousy and miscommunication depicted in *Family Matters* and *Home Improvement* were seen as most likely. Approximately half of the sample, 58.3% and 56.3%, respectively, could see the situations portrayed in these shows happening to them.

The one judgment that varied most across the clips was approval of the male characters' behavior. Participants saw David in the *Roseanne* clip as "doing the right thing" and he received a 98% approval rating. Participants were more ambivalent about the behavior of the other characters, whose approval ratings ranged from 41% to 72%. For the female characters, Molly's hitting on David in *Roseanne* was approved by only 4% of the sample; by contrast, 67.5% approved of Jennifer's behavior with Brad in the clip from *Home Improvement*. Results therefore indicate that approval varied widely based on the specific behavior of individual characters; it was not guaranteed.

The final variable examined viewers' level of identification with the main character. Once again, these ratings were quite high, ranging from 70% to 80%. Viewers identified least with lecherous Martin and with confused Brad in *Home Improvement*, and most with loyal David in *Roseanne* and jealous and insecure Carl in *Family Matters*.

Thus, despite differences in the ages, ethnic backgrounds, relationships, and behaviors of the characters involved, the four clips were perceived quite similarly. All four were seen as realistic, and participants readily identified with the main characters. At the same time, most participants placed some distance between the portrayals and their own lives, perceiving the situations as somewhat unlikely to happen to them. Yet viewers' approval ratings suggest that they did see the characters in totality, flaws and all, and perceived some actions as more appropriate than others.

Predicting Viewer Perceptions

Our second goal was to examine the demographic, attitudinal, and media factors predicting viewers' general perceptions of the sexual situations depicted. We first ran a series of correlational analyses to determine which of the 16 variables surveyed correlated most consistently and significantly with participants' perceptions of the four clips. Included in these analyses were the following variables: 7 Demographic Variables (Age, Gender, Asian, Black, Latino, SES, School); 6 Viewing Behaviors (Prime-time Hours, Soap Opera Hours, Total Hours, Active Viewing, Viewing to Learn, and Seen That Clip Before); and 3 Attitudinal Variables (Endorsement of Traditional Gender Role Attitudes, Endorsement of Recreational Attitudes About Sex, and Endorsement of Traditional Dating Norms). Zero-order correlations were run between each of these factors and the 18 variables representing participants' perceptions of the clips (i.e., perceived realism, identification) listed in Table 5.2. Variables correlating significantly (at the $p < .075$ level) with more than one third of the perception variables (7/18 or greater) were selected as factors to be included in regression analyses. The following variables reached this predetermined cutoff level: Gender (10/18 significant correlations), Total Viewing Hours (8/18), Viewing to Learn (8/18), Endorse Recreational Sex (8/18), and Endorse Traditional Dating Norms (7/18). Although Seen That Clip Before correlated with only two perception variables, it was included as an experimental control in appropriate regression equations. Standardized regression coefficients can be found in Tables 5.4 and 5.5.

Perceptions of Realism. The first series of regression analyses examined how well these five factors predicted viewers' perceptions of the realism of the sexual situations depicted in each clip. Each of the four regression equations (one for each clip) was statistically significant, and the predictors contributed from 2.5% to 5.2% of the variance. Emerging as the biggest predictor was Viewing to Learn. The more participants watched TV to learn about the world, the more realistic they perceived its content to be. Other factors contributed as well. Females generally perceived the clips as more realistic than males did. In addition, offering stronger endorsement of a recreational orientation toward sex contributed to seeing the behavior of Martin, a lusty male, as more realistic, and the behavior of David in *Roseanne*, a male in control of his sexual urges, as less realistic. Similarly, giving stronger endorsement of traditional dating norms was associated with viewing the sexual situation in *Roseanne* as less realistic.

Likelihood to Happen. The second series of analyses explored factors predicting viewers' perceptions of each situation's likelihood to happen in their own lives. Again, each of the four regression equations was statistically or notably significant $(p < .10)$, with the predictors accounting for 1.5% to 13.8% of the variance. Although Viewing to Learn dropped out as a predictor, Total Viewing Hours emerged as a robust predictor for all four clips. Here, those who frequently watch TV comedies and dramas were more likely to perceive the events presented as likely to happen in their own lives. At the same time, however, those endorsing traditional dating norms saw the sexually-charged situations of *Martin* and *Roseanne* as less likely to happen in their own lives. Being female and endorsing recreational notions about sex made minor contributions as well.

TABLE 5.4

Predictors of Viewers' General Perceptions of Clip Content (Standardized Regression Coefficients)

	Perceived Realism				Likely to Happen				Identification			
	FM	HI	MT	RS	FM	HI	MT	RS	FM⁺	HI	MT	RS⁺⁺
Sex (F)	.122⁺	.124⁺	.118⁺		.153*	.140*	.103⁺	-.192**	.163*			
Total Viewing Hours	.164**							.278***			.110⁺	
Viewing to Learn			.148*	.165**								
Recreational Sex			.142*	-.133*			.166**				.245***	
Traditional Dating Norms				-.159**			-.165***	-.233***			-.140*	
R²	.055	.042	.068	.064	.044	.032	.094	.153	.038	.009	.113	.044
Adj. R²	.038	.025	.052	.047	.027	.015	.078	.138	.018	-.008	.097	.024
F	3.34	2.53	4.22	3.93	2.65	1.90	5.94	10.38	1.91	.52	7.28	2.20
Signif. F	.005	.028	.005	.028	.022	.09	.022	.09	.08	.75	.08	.75

Note. FM = *Family Matters*; HI = *Home Improvement*; MT = *Martin*; RS = *Roseanne*.

⁺$p < .075$; *$p < .05$; **$p < .01$; ***$p < .001$.

⁺⁺Includes as a covariate whether clip has been previously seen; for *Roseanne*, the standardized regression coefficient for the covariate is $-.158$ ($p < .01$).

114

TABLE 5.5
Predictors of Viewers' Approval of the Behavior of Male and
Female Characters (Standardized Regression Coefficients)

	Approve of Male's Behavior				Approve of Female's Behavior	
	FM	HI	MT	RS	HI	RS
Sex (F)	.126*		−.155*	.138*		−.323***
Total Viewing Hours						
Viewing to Learn				−.133*	.140*	
Recreational Sex	.132*	.146*	.197**			
Traditional Dating Norms			−.108+			−.152**
R^2	.022	.022	.102	.059	.031	.151
Adj. R^2	.005	.005	.086	.043	.015	.136
F	1.31	1.34	6.50	3.66	1.88	10.23
Signif. F	.25	.24	.25	.24	.09	.09

Note. FM = Family Matters; HI = Home Improvement; MT = Martin; RS = Roseanne.
+p < .075; *p < .05; **p < .01; ***p < .001.
++Includes as a covariate whether clip has previously been seen.

Identification With the Main Character. A third series of analyses examined factors predicting viewers' identification with the main characters of the clips. Here, results were much more equivocal, with none of the variables serving as reliable predictors across clips. In fact, none of the variables predicted viewer identification for either the *Roseanne* or *Home Improvement* clip. The only factor that predicted identification for the *Family Matters* clip was Gender, with females indicating stronger identification than males with the main character, Carl. For *Martin*, several factors emerged as significant predictors. Most notably, stronger endorsement of Recreational Attitudes About Sex was associated with a higher level of identification, while stronger endorsement of Traditional Dating Norms was associated with a lower level of identification. Overall, it appears as if the set of factors determining viewers' identification with individual characters was not well captured by the variables tested here.

Approval of Character Behavior. A final series of regression analyses addressed factors influencing viewers' approval of the behavior of the men and women in the clips. For approval of the man's behavior, Gender, not surprisingly, was an important predictor. Women were more likely than men to approve of the man's behavior in the *Family Matters* and *Roseanne* clips, and less likely to approve of Martin's contemplating cheating. Endorsing a Recreational Orientation Toward Sex was an important factor as well, predicting higher levels of approval of the male characters in the *Family*

Matters, *Home Improvement*, and *Martin* clips. For approval of the woman's behavior (only relevant for the clips from *Home Improvement* and *Roseanne*), predictors differed depending on the clip. For *Home Improvement*, the only significant predictor was Viewing to Learn, with participants who watched TV to learn about the world more likely to approve of the female's behavior. For the clip from *Roseanne*, being female and endorsing Traditional Dating Norms were each associated with less approval of Molly's hitting on David.

    Role of Sexual Experience as a Predictor. For half of the sample, information was also available about viewers' general level of experience with dating and sexual relationships. To explore whether sexual experience was a predictor of their evaluations, we first calculated a median split of the sexual experience score. Sexual experience had been rated from 0 to 10, with scores of 0 to 3 indicating minimal experience, scores of 4 to 5 indicating one sexual relationship, and scores of 6 to 10 indicating having had several sexual relationships. The median fell at 4.6, dividing the sample into one group that had moderate to high levels of sexual experience (HIGH), and a second group that had moderate to low levels (LOW). A series of one-way ANOVAs was then run to determine if these groups differed in their evaluations (e.g., perceived realism) of the four clips. Whereas there were no differences between the LOW and HIGH groups in their perceptions of the *Family Matters* or *Home Improvement* clips, several differences emerged concerning perceptions of both the *Martin* and *Roseanne* clips. Viewers in the HIGH sexual experience group perceived the events portrayed in *Martin* as more likely to happen in their lives than did viewers in the LOW group ($F = 9.33$, $p < .01$; Ms = 2.47 and 2.05, respectively). Viewers in the HIGH group also identified with the main character in *Martin* more than viewers in the LOW group ($F = 14.48$, $p < .001$; Ms = 2.90 and 2.42, respectively). Similar results were found for the *Roseanne* clip: Viewers in the HIGH sexual experience group thought that the events portrayed were more likely to happen in their own life than did viewers in the LOW group ($F = 8.48$, $p < .01$; Ms = 2.36 and 2.03, respectively). Viewers in the HIGH sexual experience group also identified marginally more with the main character than did viewers in the LOW group ($F = 3.43$, $p < .07$; Ms = 3.00 and 2.80, respectively). Unfortunately, because the sample size for each of these groups was quite small, it was not possible to explore further whether gender interacted with sexual experience.

Are Predictors Global or Specific to the Clip Content or Evaluation in Question?

Our final goal was to assess the consistency with which the central predictor variables exerted their influence. Sixteen factors were initially selected for examination, but only five correlated consistently enough with the perception variables to be included in the regression analyses. Of these five, the most influential factor across the board was the viewer's gender, which emerged as a significant predictor (at the $p < .075$ level) in 50% of the regression equations. Gender consistently predicted both perceived realism and the level of approval given for the male character's behavior. The second most global predictor was Attitudes About Recreational Sex, which emerged as a significant predictor ($p < .05$) for 7 of the 18 regression equations. Its most consistent contribution was to viewers' judgments about the male character. Overall, however, most predictors were not global, but were specific to the scene or evaluation in question. Some predictors worked strongly and consistently for one question or evaluation, but not for others. For example, Total Viewing Hours was a robust predictor of perceived relevance (i.e., likelihood to happen in own life), but was not a predictor for the other perception questions. These patterns highlight the complexity of viewers' reactions to complex stimuli.

DISCUSSION

This study examined undergraduates' perceptions of a sample of romantic and sexual content drawn from prime-time television. Our first goal was to document students' general impressions of this content, as assessed both through open-ended questions about each scene's main message and through ratings of particular features. In accordance with constructivist perspectives, we expected that interpretations by student viewers would be quite variable, perhaps due to their less experience with sexual relationships, their youthful values and perspectives, or the general complexity of the content itself. This expectation was met, with substantial variability emerging in viewers' interpretations of the scenes presented. No one interpretation of a scene accounted for more than 50% of the responses; instead, for each clip, two or three interpretations typically shared the floor. The gender of the viewer played a prominent role, with men offering both significantly more and frequently different interpretations of the scenes than women. We speculate that because the clips focused on male characters, male viewers were able to see greater complexity in the behaviors than were female viewers, able, perhaps, to offer more rationales and justifications. Moreover, male participants often interpreted the actions in a way that painted men in a better light, for example, interpreting the actions in *Family Matters* as relationship challenges rather than as male insecurity and jealousy. Overall, these findings illustrate the utility of conducting descriptive analyses of viewers' interpretations. Because both content analyses and effects studies typically assume a uniform interpretation of TV content, it is informative to be reminded of the variability offered by actual viewers. Content analyses do have a role and place, but researchers need to acknowledge that their perceptions of specific sexual content may differ from those of other viewers.

As a further analysis of viewers' perceptions, we examined students' ratings of various features of the content (e.g., realism). Two of the more surprising outcomes were the high degree of realism viewers attributed to the situations, and their strong identification with the main characters. It is possible that unusually realistic clips were selected as stimuli (although this was not our intent), or that asking viewers to rate concrete vignettes elicited higher realism and identification scores than might have been obtained if standard questionnaires had been employed. Yet whatever the source, portrayals and situations perceived to be so realistic and with which viewers can strongly identify carry a high level of potential influence—as noted earlier. Of particular concern is the power of these portrayals to shape viewers' attitudes about their own sexual experiences, as well as their expectations about sexual relationships in the real world. For example, research indicates that adolescents who identified closely with TV personalities and believed their TV role models to be more sexually skilled than they were also reported being less satisfied with their status as virgins or with their own intercourse experiences (Baran, 1976a, 1976b; Courtright & Baran, 1980). Similarly, female undergraduates who identified strongly with TV's portrayals of sexuality also held higher expectations of the level of sexual activity of their peers (Ward & Rivadeneyra, 1999).

These findings suggest an interesting circle of relationships. It is likely that viewers with recreational or casual attitudes about sexual relationships will identify more strongly with many of TV's sexual portrayals, which in turn validate and strengthen their beliefs about sex. It is also likely that among younger viewers with less well-formed attitudes, those who build stronger personal connections to TV characters and who see these portrayals as realistic may be especially open to accepting the accompanying messages. Thus, data reported here validate concerns that TV's portrayals of sexuality hold the potential to shape viewers' sexual attitudes and assumptions. To determine if they actually do, longitudinal and experimental research is needed in which students' attitudes are examined both before and after exposure to specific types of sexual content.

Despite the high level of perceived realism, it would be inaccurate to conclude that undergraduate viewers are gullible and indiscriminate. Instead, our data indicate that respondents did not blindly approve of all behavior, nor did they necessarily see each situation as likely to happen in their own lives. Indeed, weaker identification was reported with the men whose behavior was most negative. In addition, even when viewers identified with a particular character (e.g., Martin), they did not necessarily approve of his behavior in a particular situation. It appears, then, that although participants saw these clips as realistic, they did place some distance between these images and their own lives, perhaps seeing them as realistic for and likely to happen to other people, but not to themselves (i.e., the "third-person effect"). It would be informative to explore further the nuances of perceived realism. How do viewers define realism in television's portrayals of sexuality (i.e., realistic for whom)? What standards are used in deciding what is realistic? What exactly do viewers see as realistic about these portrayals: Is it the dialogue, the situations, or the characters' responses? Future research must also consider that simply viewing or even enjoying a program does not constitute acceptance of its sexual messages.

The second and third goals of this study were to explore the range of factors that shape and differentiate viewers' perceptions of TV's sexual content. As noted earlier, contributions from the central predictors varied based on the particular evaluation in question. A strong predictor of the perceived realism of the situations was Viewing to Learn, with viewers who use TV to learn about the world perceiving greater levels of realism. It makes sense that if viewers come to TV to learn, then on some level they must assume that TV is realistic enough to learn from. In terms of perceived relevance, the chief influence was Total Viewing Hours. Being a frequent TV viewer was related to perceiving the sexual situation depicted in each of the four scenes as more likely to happen in one's own life. Existing attitudes about sexuality were also important, with those endorsing more traditional dating norms perceiving the situations in *Martin* and *Roseanne* as less personally relevant. Finally, both gender and existing sexual attitudes were solid predictors of viewers' approval of the characters' behaviors. Women appeared to be more approving than men of behaviors that were "relationship-maintaining" (i.e., jealous husband protecting wife in *Family Matters*, man rejecting woman's advances in *Roseanne*) and less approving of relationship threats (i.e., Martin's contemplating cheating, Molly's making advances in *Roseanne*). At the same time, endorsing more recreational attitudes about sexuality was associated with greater approval of the male character's behavior for three of the four clips. Together, these findings validate the existence of selective perception and the strong role of gender and sexual attitudes in it. Whereas the content-specific nature of the outcomes makes it difficult to generalize these findings across all content, the solid contributions made by gender and sexual attitudes, as expected, indicate that some personal attributes affect perceptions more regularly.

Concerning participants' identification with the main character, the interesting outcome was the lack of results. We had suspected that gender, race, and viewing amounts would figure prominently, such that males and more frequent viewers would identify more strongly with the main characters, and that Blacks would identify more strongly than Whites with the Black characters. None of these expectations was met. However, because participants did identify strongly with these portrayals, we must question what factors affected these connections, if not the ones examined here. Perhaps we should look toward more idiosyncratic aspects of the viewers' personalities, such as jealous tendencies or confidence with the opposite sex. It is also possible that the programs and characters selected for study were so popular that everyone identified with them, thereby reducing the variance available for analyses. In the future, using programs that are less popular, or selecting more controversial characters, might more strongly highlight the personal or attitudinal factors that determine who identifies with whom.

Two additional factors that played a smaller role than anticipated were viewing amounts and level of sexual experience. Of the three viewing amounts variables created, Total Viewing Hours predicted Perceived Relevance only, and neither of the other two amounts variables was even robust enough to be included in the regression analyses. This meager showing validates the need to look beyond viewing amounts as the only avenue of media influence. Participants' level of sexual experience played only a moderate role, as well. Results indicated that for the clips with more explicit sexual content (i.e., scenes from *Roseanne* and *Martin*), participants with more sexual experience identified more strongly with the characters and felt that such situations were more likely to happen in their own lives. It is probable that these viewers could relate to this content more easily because they had been in sexual relationships. However, these findings run counter to those reported by Brown et al. (1993), in which adolescent girls with more sexual experience appeared to be more critical of media portrayals. Further research is needed to help determine how and under what circumstances a viewer's level of sexual experience mediates her perceptions of fictional sexual content.

Our efforts to examine adolescents' perceptions of TV's sexual content lead us to several interesting conclusions. First, it appears that perceptions of sexual content vary widely from person to person, highlighting the role of selective perception. It may be difficult to state with certainty that there is a dominant "read" of any particular scene, for, in fact, multiple interpretations are typically offered. Findings also confirmed that a number of variables contribute to this variance in viewers' perceptions. Although some predictors worked across several scenes and perception constructs, it is still necessary to include multiple factors in order to truly understand viewers' impressions. At the same time, there was consistency in several areas. Although students did not take home the same messages, they did see the scenes selected as realistic and could easily identify with the main characters. Similarly, both gender and existing sexual attitudes were consistent influences on their perceptions, regardless of the specific content or judgment. It is likely that such high levels of identification and perceived realism enhance the power of the media to shape students' sexual attitudes and assumptions. Further research with both younger and older populations is needed to fully explore these implications. Overall, our pattern of results confirms that media portrayals are complex, and so are the viewers watching them.

REFERENCES

Bandura, A. (1986). *Social foundations of thought and action: A social-cognitive theory*. Englewood Cliffs, NJ: Prentice-Hall.

Bandura, A. (1994). Social cognitive theory of mass communication. In J. Bryant & D. Zillman (Eds.), *Media effects: Advances in theory and research* (pp. 61–90). Hillsdale, NJ: Lawrence Erlbaum Associates.

Baran, S. J. (1976a). How TV and film portrayals affect sexual satisfaction in college students. *Journalism Quarterly, 53*, 468–473.

Baran, S. J. (1976b). Sex on TV and adolescent self-image. *Journal of Broadcasting, 20*, 61–68.

Basil, M. D. (1996). Identification as a mediator of celebrity effects. *Journal of Broadcasting and Electronic Media, 40*, 478–495.

Biocca, F. (1988). Opposing conceptions of the audience: The active and passive hemispheres of mass communication theory. In J. A. Anderson (Ed.), *Communication Yearbook 11*. Beverly Hills, CA: Sage.

Brigham, J., & Giesbrecht, L. (1976). "All in the Family": Racial attitudes. *Journal of Communication, 26*, 69–74.

Brown, J. D., & Schulze, L. (1990). The effects of race, gender, and fandom on audience interpretations of Madonna's music videos. *Journal of Communication, 40*, 88–102.

Brown, J. D., & Steele, J. R. (1995). *Sex and the mass media*. Menlo Park, CA: Henry J. Kaiser Family Foundation.

Brown, J. D., White, A. B., & Nikopoulou, L. (1993). Disinterest, intrigue, resistance: Early adolescent girls' use of sexual media content. In B. S. Greenberg, J. D. Brown, & N. L. Buerkel-Rothfuss (Eds.), *Media, sex, and the adolescent* (pp. 177–195). Cresskill, NJ: Hampton Press.

Cooks, L. M., & Orbe, M. P. (1993). Beyond the satire: Selective exposure and selective perception in "In Living Color." *The Howard Journal of Communication, 4*, 217–233.

Courtright, J. A., & Baran, S. J. (1980). The acquisition of sexual information by young people. *Journalism Quarterly, 1*, 107–114.

Dorr, A. (1986). *Television and children: A special medium for a special audience*. Beverly Hills, CA: Sage.

Elliott, W. R., & Slater, D. (1980). Exposure, experience, and perceived reality for adolescents. *Journalism Quarterly, 57*, 409–414.

Galambos, N. L., Peterson, A. C., Richards, M., & Gitelson, I. B. (1985). The attitudes toward women scale for adolescents (AWSA): A study of reliability and validity. *Sex Roles, 13*, 343–354.

Gerbner, G., & Gross, L. (1976). Living with television: The violence profile. *Journal of Communication, 26*, 173–199.

Gerbner, G., Gross, L., Morgan, M., & Signorielli, N. (1994). Growing up with television: The cultivation perspective. In J. Bryant & D. Zillman (Eds.), *Media effects: Advances in theory and research*. (pp. 17–41). Hillsdale, NJ: Lawrence Erlbaum Associates.

Granello, D. H. (1997). Using *Beverly Hills, 90210* to explore developmental issues in female adolescents. *Youth & Society, 29*, 24–53.

Greenberg, B. S. (1988). Some uncommon television images and the drench hypothesis. In S. Oskamp (Ed.), *Television as a social issue* (pp. 88–102). Newbury Park, CA: Sage.

Greenberg, B. S., & Busselle, R. W. (1996). Soap operas and sexual activity: A decade later. *Journal of Communication, 46,* 153–160.

Greenberg, B. S., Linsangan, R., & Soderman, A. (1993). Adolescents' reactions to television sex. In B. S. Greenberg, J. D. Brown, & N. L. Buerkel-Rothfuss (Eds.), *Media, sex, and the adolescent* (pp. 196–224). Cresskill, NJ: Hampton Press.

Heintz-Knowles, K. E. (1996). *Sexual activity on daytime soap operas: A content analysis of five weeks of television programming.* Menlo Park, CA: Kaiser Family Foundation.

Huesmann, L. R. (1986). Psychological processes promoting the relation between exposure to media violence and aggressive behavior by the viewer. *Journal of Social Issues, 42,* 125–139.

Huston, A. C., Wartella, E., & Donnerstein, E. (1998). *Measuring the effects of sexual content in the media.* Menlo Park, CA: Kaiser Family Foundation.

Kalof, L. (1993). Dilemmas of femininity: Gender and the social construction of sexual imagery. *The Sociological Quarterly, 34,* 639–651.

Katz, E., & Liebes, T. (1985). Mutual aid in the decoding of Dallas: Preliminary notes from a cross-cultural study. In P. Drummond & R. Paterson (Eds.), *Television in transition* (pp. 187–198). London: British Film Institute.

Katz, E., Liebes, T., & Iwao, S. (1991). Neither here nor there: Why *Dallas* failed in Japan. *Communication, 12,* 99–110.

Kunkel, D., Cope, K. M., Maynard Farinola, W. J., Biely, E., Rollin, E., & Donnerstein, E. (1999). *Sex on TV: Content and context.* Menlo Park, CA: Kaiser Family Foundation.

Levy, M., & Windahl, S. (1984). Audience activity and gratifications: A conceptual clarification and exploration. *Communication Research, 11,* 51–78.

Levy, M., & Windahl, S. (1985). The concept of audience activity. In K. E. Rosengren, P. Palmgreen, and L. Wenner (Eds.), *Media gratification research: Current perspectives.* Beverly Hills, CA: Sage.

Livingstone, S. M. (1990). Interpreting a television narrative: How different viewers see a story. *Journal of Communication, 40,* 72–85.

Nakao, K., & Treas, J. (1992). *The 1989 Socioeconomic Index of Occupations: Construction from the 1989 Occupational Prestige Scores* (General Social Survey Methodological Rep. No. 74). Chicago: University of Chicago, National Opinion Research Center.

Perse, E. M. (1986). Soap opera viewing patterns of college students and cultivation. *Journal of Broadcasting and Electronic Media, 30,* 175–193.

Potter, W. J. (1986). Perceived reality and the cultivation hypothesis. *Journal of Broadcasting and Electronic Media, 30,* 159–174.

Potter, W. J. (1988). Perceived reality in television effects research. *Journal of Broadcasting and Electronic Media, 32,* 23–41.

Press, A. (1989). Class and gender in the hegemonic process: Class differences in women's perceptions of television realism and identification with television characters. *Media, Culture, and Society, 11,* 229–251.

Reep, D. C., & Dambrot, F. H. (1990). Effects of frequent television viewing on stereotypes: "Drip, drip" or "drench"? *Journalism Quarterly, 66,* 542–550, 556.

Rubin, A. M., & Perse, E. M. (1987). Audience activity and television news gratifications. *Communication, 14,* 58–84.

Rubin, A. M., Perse, E. M., & Taylor, D. S. (1988). A methodological examination of cultivation. *Communication Research, 15,* 107–134.

Signorielli, N. (1986). Selective television viewing: A limited possibility. *Journal of Communication, 36,* 64–76.

Silverman-Watkins, L. T., & Sprafkin, J. N. (1983). Adolescents' comprehension of televised sexual innuendoes. *Journal of Applied Developmental Psychology, 4,* 359–369.

Slater, D., & Elliott, W. R. (1982). Television's influence on social reality. *Quarterly Journal of Speech, 68*, 69–79.

Sprafkin, J. N., Silverman, L. T., & Rubinstein, E. A. (1980). Reactions to sex on television: An exploratory study. *Public Opinion Quarterly, 44*, 303–315.

Steele, J. R., & Brown, J. D. (1995). Adolescent room culture: Studying media in the context of everyday life. *Journal of Youth and Adolescence, 24*, 551–576.

Strasburger, V. (1995). *Adolescents and the media: Medical and psychological impact.* Thousand Oaks, CA: Sage.

Surlin, S. H., & Tate, E. D. (1976). "All in the Family": Is Archie funny? *Journal of Communication, 26*, 61–68.

Van Evra, J. (1998). *Television and child development.* Mahwah, NJ: Lawrence Erlbaum Associates.

Vidmar, N., & Rokeach, M. (1974). Archie Bunker's bigotry: A study in selective perception and exposure. *Journal of Communication, 24*, 36–47.

Walsh-Childers, K. B. (1990). *Adolescents' sexual schemas and interpretations of male–female relationships in a soap opera.* Unpublished doctoral dissertation, University of North Carolina, Chapel Hill.

Ward, L. M. (1995). Talking about sex: Common themes about sexuality in the prime-time television programs children and adolescents view most. *Journal of Youth and Adolescence, 24*, 595–615.

Ward, L. M., & Rivadeneyra, R. (1999). Contributions of entertainment television to adolescents' sexual attitudes and expectations: The role of viewing amount versus viewer involvement. *Journal of Sex Research, 36*, 237–249.

Wilhoit, G. C., & de Bock, H. (1976). "All in the Family" in Holland. *Journal of Communication, 26*, 75–84.

6

Media's Impact on Adolescents' Body Dissatisfaction

Linda J. Hofschire
Bradley S. Greenberg
Michigan State University

Reprinted with permission from FOR BETTER OR FOR WORSE © UFS

The mass media present a narrowly defined body type ideal (e.g., Brumberg, 1997; Fouts & Burggraf, 1999). For females, this ideal is slender and toned; for males, it is slim and muscular. Although the current emphases the media place on weight control and muscle development help to promote a more health-conscious society, negative impacts, such as body dissatisfaction, preoccupation with attaining a certain body type ideal, and eating disorders, have emerged as well. In the United States, people are becoming increasingly dissatisfied with their bodies: A 1993 national survey of women between the ages of 18 and 70 showed that nearly 50% negatively evaluated their appearance and reported concern about being or becoming overweight (Cash & Henry, 1995). In a similar study conducted in 1985 (Cash, Winstead, & Janda, 1986), just 30% reported such concerns.

Adolescents are particularly at risk for experiencing body dissatisfaction and engaging in eating disordered behaviors because the onset of puberty leads to increased concerns about the physical changes of their bodies (Brooks-Gunn & Reiter, 1990; Lauber, 1982). Further, this period is also marked by increased interest in the opposite sex (Brooks-Gunn & Reiter, 1990), and many teens strive to have the "right body" so that they will be found desirable and attractive. To the extent that the media define this right body that the opposite sex seeks, teens are faced with largely unattainable ideals. On television, popular actresses such as Jennifer Aniston (Rachel on *Friends*), Tori Spelling (Donna on *Beverly Hills, 90210*), and Jennifer Love Hewitt (Sarah on *Party of Five*) attract men with the seemingly impossible combination of a large bust and a waiflike body. And actors such as Scott Wolf (Bailey on *Party of Five*) and James Van Der Beek (Dawson on *Dawson's Creek*) regularly reveal their muscular physiques in the presence of women.

Adolescents' body dissatisfaction is a widespread problem in our society. In a survey of more than 3,000 high school students (Felts, Tavasso, Chenier, & Dunn, 1992), 25% thought they were too fat and 68% were trying to lose weight. The pressure to improve one's figure is evident. A study (Newman, 1991) of more than 2,000 high school students showed that 66% were doing something to change their weight. Brumberg (1997) reported an even more disturbing statistic: "By age thirteen, 53% of American girls are unhappy with their bodies; by age seventeen, 78% are dissatisfied" (p. xxiv).

When considering the prevalence of this dissatisfaction, certain questions must be raised. Why are people increasingly unhappy with the shape of their bodies? What sources convince them they need to alter their figures? Researchers theorize that sociocultural factors are largely responsible for these high levels of body dissatisfaction and the increasing number of eating disorders reported, particularly among women (Fallon, 1990; Heinberg & Thompson, 1992; Rodin, Silberstein, & Striegel-Moore, 1985). Current societal standards of attractiveness overly emphasize the desirability of a thin, muscular figure (Tiggemann & Pickering, 1996). Because the media are among the most prominent conveyors of these sociocultural ideals, it is important to determine whether they play a causal role (Silverstein, Perdue, Peterson, & Kelly, 1986).

Adolescents consume large quantities of media that emphasize these standards of attractiveness—for example, television, movies, and magazines—and it is possible that they apply these standards to their own bodies. Existing research about body dissatisfaction has focused largely on adult women. The purpose of this chapter is to expand on previous findings by investigating the relationship between the media and adolescents' dissatisfaction with their bodies. Further, adolescents are influenced by a range of sources other than the media. Therefore, two primary predictors of body dissatisfaction that have been identified in prior research—interpersonal sources (e.g., Heinberg & Thompson, 1992) and body type characteristics (e.g., Mortenson, Hoerr, & Garner, 1993)—are also examined.

LITERATURE REVIEW

Prior research has focused on the body type ideals prevalent in popular media (i.e., magazines and television) as well as the impact of these ideals on audiences.

Media Images

Analyses focusing specifically on teen magazines indicate that readers of such magazines are bombarded with messages emphasizing the importance of appearance. Evans, Rutberg, Sather, and Turner's analysis (1991) of *Sassy, Seventeen*, and *Young Miss* (now *Young and Modern*, or *YM*) found that advertisements for appearance-related products predominated (21% were for beauty care products, 11% were fashion-related, and 4% were related to health and hygiene). Further, the most prevalent theme among the feature articles—interpersonal relations—focused primarily on dating issues. Based on these findings, the authors concluded that these magazines "reinforc[e] an underlying value that the road to happiness is attracting males for successful heterosexual life by way of physical beautification" (p. 110).

Such themes also carry over to the nonadvertising content of these magazines. In an analysis of *Seventeen* magazine content from three time periods (1961, 1972, and 1985), Pierce (1990) found that articles about appearance were dominant in each decade (48% in 1961, 52% in 1972, and 46% in 1985).

One concern brought to the forefront by these studies is that the combination of body image content and "attracting the opposite sex" articles reinforces the notion that achieving a certain body type ideal is central to making oneself desirable. For example, in Duffy and Gotcher's (1996) rhetorical analysis of *YM*, they argued that the magazine creates a world where

> young women must attempt to discern the minds and desires of young men in order to attract them. It is a place where they must costume and beautify themselves to achieve an almost impossible physical beauty ideal. And, it is a place where sexuality is both a means and an objective, where the pursuit of males is almost the sole focus of life. (p. 43)

Some studies have investigated the discrepancies between adult men's and women's magazines, many of which are read by older teens. Nemeroff, Stein, Diehl, and Smilack (1994) compared women's and men's magazines across a 12-year time span (1980 to 1991). Although weight loss, beauty, fitness, and health-related content was found significantly more often in women's magazines, there was an increase in weight loss content in the men's magazines across the time period studied.

Another comparison study (Silverstein et al., 1986) found that popular women's magazines contained over 200% more ads for diet foods than men's magazines. This difference was also found when comparing the amount of ads for nonfood figure-enhancing products in the two sets of magazines.

Petrie et al. (1996) studied the men's magazines *Esquire* and *GQ* from 1960 to 1992, and found that although the number of messages concerning physical fitness and health have increased, messages regarding weight and attractiveness have decreased since the late 1970s. However, no significant change in male models' body sizes was found in these two magazines.

These analyses, particularly of women's magazines, indicate that magazines provide both images of the ideal body type as well as various means to achieve this ideal (e.g., dieting regimens, figure-enhancing products). Therefore, it is possible that such magazines make issues such as dieting and improving one's figure salient for females.

Media Effects

Research investigating the relationship between magazine readership and body dissatisfaction indicates that the media may play an influential role. For example, Newman and Dodd (1995) found a negative correlation for both male and female undergraduates between self-esteem and reading sports magazines and television and movie guides.

Other researchers have measured participants' body dissatisfaction after exposure to images of the thin body type ideal. Waller, Hamilton, and Shaw (1992) found that eating disordered women overestimated their body dimensions significantly more than did normal women (i.e., women who did not display eating disordered symptomatology) after viewing fashion magazine pictures of female models. In general, those women with more abnormal eating attitudes showed a greater tendency to respond negatively to the fashion images.

In a study of female undergraduates, Stice and Shaw (1994) found that exposure to magazine pictures of ultrathin models produced more depression, stress, guilt, shame, insecurity, and body dissatisfaction than exposure to pictures of average-weight models or pictures containing no models.

Very little research exists analyzing body types portrayed on television. A recent analysis (Fouts & Burggraf, 1999) found that the main female characters in 28 popular situation comedies tended to be below average weight and received significantly more positive reinforcement from male characters about their body shape and weight than did female characters above average weight.

Studies examining the effects of television have consistently shown a positive correlation between television viewing and body dissatisfaction. For example, Myers and Biocca (1992) found that watching just one half hour of body-image-oriented television programming (i.e., programming focused on the display of thin female bodies) significantly increased women's dissatisfaction with their figures.

In a survey of male and female undergraduates, Harrison and Cantor (1997) found that media use (i.e., television and magazine consumption), particularly magazine readership, predicted disordered-eating symptomatology, drive for thinness, and body dissatisfaction in women. For men, media use was associated positively with endorsement of personal thinness and dieting, and favorable attitudes toward thinness and dieting for women.

Another study (McMullen, 1984) also identified television's effects among both men and women. In a survey of undergraduates, McMullen found that regular viewing of popular television programming (defined as the top 20 shows in the Nielsen ratings) was positively correlated with depression after viewing physically attractive television characters.

Heinberg and Thompson (1992) examined more closely this impact of media characters on people's evaluations of their bodies. They found that women who rated celebrities as strong influences on their appearance were significantly more dissatisfied with their bodies and exhibited more eating-disordered behaviors.

Similarly, among college undergraduates, Harrison (1997) found that attraction to thin media celebrities (measured by how much the respondents liked, felt similar to, and wanted to be like each celebrity) was positively related to respondents' dissatisfaction with their bodies and desire to become thinner.

The few studies that exist involving adolescent respondents report similar findings. For example, Tiggemann and Pickering (1996) found that among a sample of adolescent females, body dissatisfaction was positively correlated with the amount of time they spent watching soaps and movies on television, and negatively correlated with their sports viewing.

The research on media effects reveals several factors that influence body dissatisfaction. Exposure to both magazines and television, as well as identification with media characters, have been demonstrated to negatively impact people's evaluations of their bodies.

Related Factors

In addition to the media, interpersonal and biological factors that have a significant impact on body dissatisfaction have been identified. In a survey measuring the importance of different entities on personal appearance, Heinberg and Thompson (1992) found that (a) friends were rated most influential; (b) classmates, other students at school, and celebrities came next; and (c) families and the general public were ranked least important. Researchers have focused on the influence of two of these groups: friends and family.

One study (Crandall, 1988) examined the influence of social groups on binge eating in two college sororities. In both sororities, Crandall found that the more a woman binged, the more popular she was among her sorority sisters. Peer pressure among the sorority members was so high that by the end of the academic year, a sorority member's binge eating could be predicted by the binge eating level of her friends.

The influence of family on eating-disordered behavior has also been examined. Through interviews with mother and daughter pairs, Pike and Rodin (1991) found that mothers of daughters with eating disorders were more likely than other mothers to have engaged in eating-disordered behaviors themselves. Moreover, these mothers thought their daughters should lose more weight than other mothers thought.

Body type, or body composition, has also been identified as a predictor of body dissatisfaction. This variable can be measured in numerous ways; one of the most common is the Body Mass Index (BMI). BMI is considered the most valid and reliable of weight indices, because it is highly correlated with independent measures of body fat (Keys, Findanza, Karvonen, Kimura, & Taylor, 1972). It is calculated by dividing weight (in kilograms) by height (meters squared). Generally, normal weight ranges fall between indices of 19 and 24; a score of 25 or more is considered overweight. A number of studies indicate that BMI is positively correlated with body dissatisfaction, that is, the higher the respondent's BMI, the higher her reported body dissatisfaction (e.g., Dionne et al., 1995; Mortenson et al., 1993).

Research using male participants indicates that men are similarly affected by their body composition. Weight and percentage of body fat have been positively correlated with body dissatisfaction among male bodybuilders (Blouin & Goldfield, 1995) as well as normal populations (e.g., Huddy, Nieman, & Johnson, 1993). Because both interpersonal and biological factors have been demonstrated to significantly impact body dissatisfaction, they are used as control variables in the present study.

THEORY AND HYPOTHESES

The principles of social cognitive theory ground this study. Bandura (1977) theorized that we "acquire attitudes, emotional responses, and new styles of conduct through filmed and televised [models]" (p. 39). If these models are reinforced, it is likely that we will mimic them. In the context of this study, adolescents may compare themselves to media figures who are rewarded for their appearance. If they feel they do not resemble these models, they may be dissatisfied and attempt to become more like them.

Traditional learning theorists proposed that we acquire attitudes and behaviors through direct experience; that is, we respond to our environments and then "experience the effects" (Tan, 1985, p. 243). If we are rewarded for these responses, we are likely to repeat them. Bandura expanded on this theory by suggesting that we can learn from observing others (models) as well as through direct experience (Tan, 1985). Thus, social cognitive theory is relevant to the study of media effects because the media offer an easily accessible source of attractive models (DeFleur & Ball-Rokeach, 1989).

Harrison and Cantor (1997) used social cognitive theory to explain their findings because modeling "provides a theoretical means by which [people] may acquire a body ideal, the motivation to engage in extreme dieting behavior, and the instructions on how to do so from the media" (p. 44). They highlighted two components of the social learning model that are relevant to this chapter—prevalence and incentives—to provide an explanation of how dieting behaviors and the stereotypical body type ideal may be socially learned from the mass media.

Prevalence is a relevant component because television and magazines heavily emphasize diet imagery and advertising, as well as slender characters. Because images of thinness and dieting dominate popular media, modeling of diet behaviors is a logical outcome of exposure (Harrison & Cantor, 1997). Incentives also are highlighted because numerous television characters are rewarded for their slim, muscular appearances (e.g., they receive attention from the opposite sex, they are popular, they appear happy and satisfied). Thus, observers may feel that they, too, will be rewarded by others and become personally satisfied by achieving the stereotypical body type ideal.

Based on social cognitive theory, it was predicted that (a) television viewing, (b) magazine readership, and (c) identification with female models and television stars for female respondents, and with male athletes and television stars for male respondents, are positively correlated with body dissatisfaction, belief in the stereotypical body type ideal, and attempts to improve one's figure through dieting and exercise behaviors.

METHODS

In December 1996, a preliminary questionnaire was completed by 10th- and 11th-grade students ($N = 71$) from a Michigan high school. The students were asked open-ended questions in order to: (a) identify the sources (both media and nonmedia) that influenced them about their bodies (i.e., that make them feel good or bad about the way their bodies look); (b) determine the range of media they use; (c) assess their level of satisfaction with their bodies; and (d) learn the language they use when discussing these issues.

A survey instrument was created based on the students' responses to this preliminary questionnaire. It was pretested with 9th- and 10th-grade students ($N = 83$) from a Michigan high school and then administered to 382 students in the 9th and 10th grades from five Midwestern high schools during spring 1997. The mean age of the students was 15; 90% were White, and 46% were female.

Variables and Indices

The survey instrument measured the following variables:

Antecedent variables:
  Demographics (age, gender, ethnicity)

Independent variables:
  Media exposure (to television and magazines)
  Desire to look like media celebrities
  Interpersonal sources' influence on body dissatisfaction
  Body type (respondents' height and weight)

Dependent variables:
  General body dissatisfaction
  Specific body dissatisfaction
  Desire to be thinner
  Belief in the stereotypical body type ideal
  Diet and exercise behaviors

Independent Variables

Television Exposure. Television exposure was assessed in three ways. First, to measure sheer exposure, respondents were asked to estimate the amount of television they viewed on an average school day. This question was divided into three time periods: in the morning before school, in the afternoon before dinner, and after dinner. Response categories ranged from 0 to 4 or more hours per time period. Respondents also were asked how many hours of television they watched on a typical Saturday and Sunday, with response categories ranging from 0 to 9 or more hours per day. Second, to investigate the types of programming that were popular, respondents were asked approximately how many hours per week they watched the following types of television genre: sports, soap operas, and music videos. Response categories ranged from 0 to 11 or more hours per week. Third, the respondents were asked whether they watched 17 shows that aired in prime time or on Saturday morning on six major broadcast networks (ABC, CBS, FOX, NBC, UPN, and WB). These shows, referred to as "body image shows," were selected because they often portrayed the stereotypical ideal body type (i.e., slender women and muscular, toned men), and, based on pretest results, were popular with this age-group (see Table 6.1). Fourteen of these shows aired weekly; thus, responses were measured on a 5-point scale (never = 1, less than once a month = 2, about once a month = 3, once every 2 to 3 weeks = 4, almost every week = 5). The remaining three shows could be seen daily. Frequency of viewing was measured on a 5-point scale with the following response categories: never (1), about once a month (2), once every 2 to 3 weeks (3), once a week (4), and several times a week (5).

Magazine Exposure. Respondents were asked how often they read a group of magazines selected from the top 200 paid-circulation magazines for the first half of 1996 (Kelly, 1996). Magazines were chosen from this list based on the following criteria: (a) portrayal of the stereotypical body type ideal; (b) emphasis on figure-enhancing products; and (c) presence of diet-

TABLE 6.1
Body Image Shows

Weekly Shows	Daily Shows
Beverly Hills, 90210	Baywatch
Boy Meets World	California Dreams
Clueless	Saved by the Bell
ER	
Friends	
Hang Time	
Lois & Clark	
Melrose Place	
Moesha	
NYPD Blue	
Party of Five	
Relativity	
Suddenly Susan	

TABLE 6.2
Magazines

Sports Magazines	Teen Magazines	Women's Magazines
Inside Sports	Sassy	Allure
Runner's World	Seventeen	Cosmopolitan
Ski	Teen	Elle
Sport	YM	Glamour
Sports Illustrated		Mademoiselle
Tennis		Marie Claire
The Sporting News		Vogue

or exercise-related content (see Table 6.2). Female respondents were asked how frequently they read 11 monthly fashion magazines (4 were teen magazines and 7 were women's). Frequency of reading was measured on the 5-point scale used for weekly TV shows, with response categories ranging from never (1) to almost every week (5). Using the same response categories, male respondents were asked how frequently they read seven sports magazines (male fashion magazines were not included because more than 90% of the pretest respondents did not read them). Although the magazines chosen for this survey were monthly magazines, this scale was used because respondents may either read a magazine more than once or may read it across a period of several sittings.

Desire to Look Like Media Celebrities. In the preliminary questionnaire and the pretest, respondents were asked to list celebrities they desired to look like. From their responses, a list of celebrities who have the stereotypical ideal body type was developed. Female respondents were shown a list of six television actresses and six female fashion models. Desire to look like these women was measured on a 4-item, 5-point summated scale (strongly disagree = 1 to strongly agree = 5). The scale for desire to look like media celebrities (models, alpha = .75, television stars, alpha = .86, and the combined scale—both models and television stars—alpha = .87) included these items:

I wish I looked like these women.

I admire women like these.

I think that these women are attractive.

I would like to have the body that these women have.

Male respondents were shown a list of six television actors and six male athletes. Desire to look like these men was measured on a 5-point summated scale (strongly disagree = 1 to strongly agree = 5). The scale for desire to look like television stars (alpha = .77) included these items:

I wish I looked like these men.

I admire men like these.

I would like to have the body that these men have.

An additional item, "I think these men are handsome," was dropped from the television stars scale because the pretest results demonstrated that it lowered the scale's reliability. It was included in the athletes scale (alpha = .78) because it did not affect the scale's reliability in the pretest results. The alpha value for the combined scale (both television stars and athletes) was .83.

Interpersonal Sources. The influence of interpersonal sources, such as family, peers, and friends, on body dissatisfaction was also measured. To assess the importance to respondents of other people's opinions about their appearance, respondents were asked to rate on a 4-point scale the importance of various people's opinions. Response categories ranged from not applicable (0) to very important (4). Included were mother, father, friends, classmates, brother(s), and sister(s). Working with the same list of people, respondents then were asked whether the opinions these people expressed about the respondent's appearance were positive (1), neutral (0), negative (−1), or not applicable (0).

Body Type. Respondents' self-reported height (in feet/inches) and weight (in pounds) were converted by the author into a BMI, using the following calculation:

$$\frac{kilograms}{meters^2}$$

Dependent Variables

Three scales were used to measure respondents' body dissatisfaction:

General Body Dissatisfaction. These measures were adapted from Huddy et al.'s (1993) body-image questionnaire. The original study's alpha was .72. General body dissatisfaction was measured on a 5-point summated scale (strongly agree = 1 to strongly disagree = 5). The general body dissatisfaction scale (alpha = .90 for the entire sample and for female respondents only; alpha = .88 for male respondents only) included these items:

I am satisfied with the shape of my body.

I'm satisfied with my weight.

When I look into a full-length mirror, I'm satisfied with what I see.

I'm confident that when other people look at me, they are favorably impressed.

Specific Body Dissatisfaction. Adapted from the body dissatisfaction subscale of Garner, Olmstead, and Polivy's (1983) Eating Disorder Inventory, these items asked respondents whether they believed that their specific body parts were too small (1), just right (0), or too large (1). These items were coded so that responses of "too small" and "too large" were considered dissatisfaction, whereas a response of "just right" was considered satisfaction. The original study's alpha was .90. In the specific body dissatisfaction scale (for females, alpha = .70, and for males, alpha = .78), respondents were asked about their arms, thighs, stomach, waist, butt, and hips, as well as their bust (for females) and their chest (for males).

Desire to Be Thinner. These measures also were adapted from Huddy et al.'s (1993) body-image questionnaire. The original study's alpha was .72. The desire to be thinner scale (alpha = .92 for the entire sample; .91 for the female respondents, and .89 for the male respondents) was assessed with the following items, using a 5-point summated scale (strongly disagree = 1 to strongly agree = 5):

I'm too heavy.

I wish I could gain some weight. (reversed in scoring)

I would be happier with my body if I could get rid of some of my body fat.

I wish I could lose some weight.

I diet because I wish to have a thinner body.

I wish I were thinner.

The three measures of body dissatisfaction—general body dissatisfaction, specific body dissatisfaction, and desire to be thinner—were significantly correlated with each other, ranging from .50 to .58 ($p < .001$). Consequently, they were converted into z scores and collapsed into one overall measure of body dissatisfaction.

Belief in the Stereotypical Body Type Ideal. Respondents were shown the ideal body subscale (Cogan, Bhalla, Sefa-Dedeh, & Rothblum, 1996) for both male and female figures (see Fig. 6.1).[1] From the 12 figures, they were asked to identify the one ideal figure, as well as all figures they believed

---

[1]Although this scale contains a wide range of body sizes, it is limited by the fact that it does not portray one female shape that is commonly found (and emphasized as attractive) in popular media: the large bust/waiflike body.

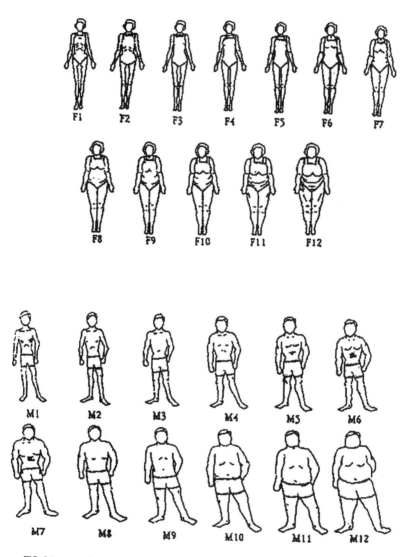

FIG. 6.1. Ideal body subscale (Cogan, Bhalla, Sefa-Deheh, & Rothblum, 1996).

were too small and too large. Female respondents were also asked what they thought was the ideal clothing size for women their age (response categories ranged from 1/2 to 11/12), as well as the ideal measurements for women their age for bust (less than 30 to more than 40 inches), waist (less than 19 to more than 28 inches), and hip (less than 26 to more than 36 inches). Each of these items was reverse scored, so that the higher the score, the smaller the dimension desired.

Because the bust, hip, and waist measures were significantly correlated with each other, ranging from .23 to .56 ($p < .01$), they were converted to z scores and collapsed into a single measure of the stereotypical ideal body.

Diet and Exercise Behaviors. Respondents were asked how often they did the following: lift weights, play sports, skip meals, diet in order to control their weight, and engage in cardiovascular activities like running, swimming, aerobics, or biking. These items were measured on a 6-point scale that included: never (1), less than once a month (2), once every month (3), once every two weeks (4), once a week (5), and several times a week (6). For the entire sample, the alpha for the diet scale was .48 (females = .50, males = .28) and the alpha for the exercise scale was .65 (females = .68, males = .63).

RESULTS

The means for the entire sample, female respondents only, and male respondents only, as well as *t*-test results for the comparisons between the male and female respondents' means are in Tables 6.3 and 6.4. In Table 6.3, where gender comparisons are possible, the boys watched more television overall and sports shows in particular, and fewer soap operas and body image shows. The two groups did not differ in terms of their viewership of music videos. In Table 6.4, the girls were more dissatisfied with their bodies in general, wanted to be thinner, and favored more dieting and less exercise than the boys did.

Tests of Hypotheses

The results of the hypotheses tests are reported by the entire sample (where possible), girls only, and boys only, in order to provide more depth to the analyses, and are listed in Table 6.5. Major findings are summarized in the text following.

Television Findings. The first set of hypotheses predicted that the amount of television viewing (both overall and of specific genres) would be positively correlated with body dissatisfaction and related variables (i.e.,

TABLE 6.3
Means and *t*-Test Values for the Independent Variables—Entire Sample
(N = 382), Females Only (N = 179), and Males Only (N = 203)[2]

Independent Variables	Means			t-Value
	Entire Sample	Females	Males	
Television:				
Total weekly TV hours	23.78	21.12	26.12	3.72**
Soaps	0.59	1.03	0.19	−5.92**
Sports	2.93	1.73	3.99	7.34**
Music videos	2.72	2.61	2.82	0.63
Body image shows	31.50	33.85	29.43	−4.47**
Magazines:				
Teen magazines	N/A	9.99	N/A	N/A
Women's magazines	N/A	9.08	N/A	N/A
All magazines	N/A	19.08	N/A	N/A
Sports magazines	N/A	N/A	9.13	N/A
Media character identification:				
TV star identification	N/A	14.26	8.52	N/A
Models/athletes identification	N/A	13.67	12.26	N/A
Combined identification (TV				
star and models/athletes)	N/A	27.92	20.78	N/A
Body type characteristics:				
BMI	21.40	20.57	22.09	4.48**
Interpersonal sources:				
Mother	0.45	0.34	0.54	1.82
Father	0.39	0.43	0.36	−0.59
Sister	0.17	0.26	0.08	−1.53
Brother	0.06	0.01	0.11	0.84v
Friends	0.40	0.51	0.31	−2.43*
Classmates	0.10	0.10	0.10	0.08

Note. [2]Standard deviation and range data are available from the authors. N/A = Not applicable. *p < .05, **p < .01

belief in the stereotypical body type ideai, and attempts to improve one's figure through dieting and exercise behaviors). For the entire sample, viewing the body image shows (r = .15, p < .01) and soaps (r = .12, p < .05) was positively correlated with body dissatisfaction. The relationship between viewing sports and dissatisfaction also was significant, but in the direction opposite to what had been predicted (r = −.17, p < .01). The overall measure of television viewing was not significantly related to body dissatisfaction. For girls only, this relationship was significant for music videos (r = .16, p < .05). No significant relationships were found among the boys.

Magazine Findings. The second set of hypotheses predicted that magazine readership would be positively correlated with body dissatisfaction and related variables. For girls, reading teen magazines (r = .23), women's

TABLE 6.4

Means and *t*-Test Values for the Dependent Variables—Entire Sample
(N = 382), Females Only (N = 179), and Males Only (N = 203)

Dependent Variables	Means			t-Value
	Entire Sample	Females	Males	
General body dissatisfaction	14.40	15.51	13.29	−5.07**
Specific body dissatisfaction	2.41	3.24	1.67	N/A
Desire to be thinner	17.21	20.05	14.72	−8.85**
Combined dissatisfaction measures	0.00	0.57	−0.50	N/A
Dieting	5.49	6.66	4.45	−7.41**
Exercise	13.72	13.16	14.21	2.66**
Ideal body type	N/A	7.25	5.83	N/A
Ideal clothing size	N/A	6.05	N/A	N/A
Ideal measurements	N/A	0.00	N/A	N/A

Note. *p < .05. **p < .01.

TABLE 6.5

Summary of Hypotheses Tests

Hypothesis	Outcome
Hypothesis 1 (Television viewing is positively correlated with body dissatisfaction)	For the entire sample, supported for BIS[3] (r = .15**) and soaps (r = .12*). A significant relationship also was found for sports (r = −.17), but in the opposite direction than had been predicted. For females only, supported for music videos (r = .16*).
Hypothesis 2 (Television viewing is positively correlated with body type, measurements, and clothing size)	For girls only, supported for BIS and the ideal body type (r = .16*), soaps and the ideal clothing size (r = .17**), and the total weekly hours watched (r = .25**) BIS (r = .20**), and soaps (r = .19**) with the ideal measurements. For boys only, supported for music video viewing and the ideal body type (r = .14*).
Hypothesis 3 (Television viewing is positively correlated with diet and exercise)	For the entire sample, supported for the correlation between BIS (r = .13*), music videos (r = .19**), soaps (r = .22**) and diet. A significant relationship also was found for sports (r = −.15**), but in the opposite direction than had been predicted.

(Continued)

TABLE 6.5
(Continued)

Hypothesis	Outcome
	The viewing of soaps (r = −.12*) and sports (r = .31**) was significantly correlated with exercise, although only sports was in the predicted direction. For girls only, watching music videos (r = .31**) and soaps (r = .23**) was significantly correlated with dieting, and viewing sports (r = .15*) was significantly correlated with exercise. For boys only, viewing the BIS (r = .15*) and sports (r = .37**) was significantly correlated with exercise.
Hypothesis 4 (Magazine readership is positively correlated with body dissatisfaction)	Supported for girls only (r = .23** for teen magazines, r = .21** for women's magazines, r = .26** for both sets combined).
Hypothesis 5 (Magazine readership is positively correlated with ideal body type)	Supported for boys only (r = .14*).
Hypothesis 6 (Magazine readership is positively correlated with diet and exercise)	For girls only, magazine readership was significantly (r = .30**). For boys only, magazine readership was significantly correlated with exercise (r = .37**).
Hypothesis 7 (Females' identification with media celebrities is positively correlated with body dissatisfaction)	Supported for models (r = .37**), television stars (r = .36**), and both scales combined (r = .40**).
Hypothesis 8 (Females' identification with media celebrities is positively correlated with ideal body type, measurements, and clothing size)	Supported for models and ideal body type (r = .19*), models and measurements (r = .18*), and television stars (r = .20**), models (r = .20**), and both scales combined (r = .22**), all with ideal clothing size.
Hypothesis 9 (Females' identification with media celebrities is positively correlated with diet and exercise)	Supported for models (r = .17*) and both scales combined (r = .16*) with diet, and models (r = .21**) and both scales combined (r = .19*) with exercise.
Hypothesis 10 (Males' identification with media celebrities is positively correlated with body dissatisfaction)	Supported for athletes (r = .21**), television stars (r = .22**), and both scales combined (r = .24**).
Hypothesis 11 (Males' identification with media celebrities is positively correlated with ideal body type)	Not supported.
Hypothesis 12 (Males' identification with media celebrities is positively correlated with diet and exercise)	Supported for exercise only (r = .16*).

Note. [3]BIS = Body Image Shows. *$p < .05$ **$p < .001$

magazines (r = .21), and both sets of magazines combined (r = .26), (all at $p <$ .01) was positively correlated with body dissatisfaction. This relationship was not significant for boys.

Findings Identification With Media Characters. The third set of hypotheses predicted that respondents' identification with media characters would be positively correlated with body dissatisfaction and related variables. Female respondents' identification with female models (r = .37), female television stars (r = .36), and both scales combined (r = .40), (all at $p <$ .01) were positively correlated with body dissatisfaction. Male respondents' identification with male athletes (r = .21), male television stars (r = .22), and both scales combined (r = .24), (all at $p < .01$) were positively correlated with body dissatisfaction.

Multiple Regression Analyses

Multiple regression analyses were performed to examine the media's impact on adolescents' body dissatisfaction while controlling for other predictor variables (i.e., BMI, interpersonal sources). Only variables that were significantly correlated with each other were entered in the regression equations.

For girls, multiple regression analyses showed identification with media characters (β = .16, $p < .05$); and BMI (β = .29, $p < .01$) significantly predicted body dissatisfaction (R^2 = .13, $p < .01$), (see Table 6.6). BMI complemented identification with media characters: The two variables together predicted body dissatisfaction better than identification with media characters did alone.

For boys, multiple regression analyses showed BMI significantly predicted body dissatisfaction (β = .34, $p < .01$), (R^2 = .13, $p < .01$), (see Table 6.7). The results demonstrate that the BMI variable is neither suppressed nor complemented by adding identification with media characters into the regression equation; the two together predict dissatisfaction no better than the correlation of BMI with dissatisfaction.

Watching videos (β = .19, $p < .05$), BMI (β = .23, $p < .01$) and watching soaps (β = .16, $p < .05$) significantly predicted dieting (R^2 = .20, $p < .01$) among girls, and identification with media characters (β = .16, $p < .05$) significantly predicted exercise (R^2 = .06, $p < .01$). For boys, magazine readership (β = .20, $p < .01$), viewing sports on television (β = .25, $p < .01$), and friends' opinions regarding appearance (β = .15, $p < .01$) significantly predicted exercise (R^2 = .22, $p < .01$). The three variables together predicted frequency of exercise better than any of them did alone. However, in the regression equation, the effects of both magazine readership and sports viewing become smaller compared to their independent correlation coefficient values.

TABLE 6.6
Regression Analyses of Body Dissatisfaction, Ideal Body Type,
and Diet and Exercise Measures—Females Only (N = 179)[4]

Variable	Predictors	Beta	p Value	Outcome
Body dissatisfaction	Magazines	.03	.66	R = .38
	Celebrity ID[5]	.16	.03	R^2 = .13
	Friends	−.12	.09	F = 7.42, p < .01
	BMI	.29	.00	
Diet	Music videos	.19	.02	R = .48
	Soaps	.16	.03	R^2 = .20
	Magazines	.12	.15	F = 6.39, p < .01
	Celebrity ID	.08	.30	
	Mother	−.12	.14	
	Father	−.07	.41	
	BMI	.23	.00	
Exercise	Sports	.12	.11	R = .29
	Magazines	.09	.25	R^2 = .06
	Celebrity ID	.16	.03	F = 3.88, p < .01
	Classmates	.12	.10	
Ideal body type	Total weekly TV hours	−.14	.06	R = .26
	Celebrity ID	−.14	.06	R^2 = .05
	Classmates	−.15	.05	F = 4.29, p < .01
Ideal clothing size	Soaps	−.10	.17	R = .37
	Celebrity ID	−.14	.06	R^2 = .12
	BMI	.26	.00	F = 9.32, p < .01
Ideal body measurements	BIS[6]	−.06	.46	R = .35
	Total weekly TV hours	−.18	.03	R^2 = .10
	Soaps	−.11	.15	F = 4.57, p < .01
	Model ID	−.11	.15	
	Brother	.13	.08	

Note. [4]Only variables that were significantly correlated with each other were entered in the regression equations. [5]ID = Identification. [6]BIS = Body Image Shows.

Classmates' opinions about the respondents' appearance (β = −.15, p < .05) predicted ideal body type (R^2 = .05, p < .05) among girls. In contrast, the variables of magazine readership (β = .15, p < .05), watching music videos (β = −.15, p < .05), and BMI (β = .21, p < .01) predicted ideal body type (R^2 = .08, p < .01) among boys.

Finally, total hours of weekly television viewing (β = −.18, p < .05) predicted the ideal body measurements (R = .35, p < .01), and BMI (β = .26, p < .01) predicted ideal clothing size (R^2 = .12, p < .01) among girls.

DISCUSSION

The purpose of this study was to measure the effect of media exposure on adolescents' body dissatisfaction. In popular television programs and magazines, physical attractiveness tends to be equated with having a slim,

TABLE 6.7
Regression Analyses of Body Dissatisfaction, Ideal Body Type,
and Diet and Exercise Measures—Males Only ($N = 203$)

Variable	Predictors	Beta	p Value	Outcome
Body dissatisfaction	Celebrity ID	.08	.19	$R = .37$
	BMI	.34	.00	$R^2 = .13$
				$F = 15.80, p < .01$
Exercise	BIS	.06	.28	$R = .47$
	Magazines	.20	.00	$R^2 = .22$
	Sports	.25	.00	$F = 9.17, p < .01$
	Celebrity ID	.06	.33	
	Father	.04	.57	
	Friends	.15	.03	
Ideal body type	Music videos	−.15	.03	$R = .30$
	Magazines	.15	.03	$R^2 = .08$
	BMI	.21	.00	$F = 6.55, p < .01$

physically fit figure, and this "ideal" figure is frequently displayed. Thus, it was proposed that more frequent television viewers and magazine readers would be more likely to (a) express dissatisfaction with their bodies, (b) admire body types similar to the ones idealized by the media, and (c) attempt to improve their bodies through diet and exercise. These propositions were grounded in the principles of social cognitive theory, which suggests that people learn behaviors and attitudes by viewing models who are positively reinforced for their actions. A second goal of the study was to analyze media influence on adolescents' evaluations of their bodies when controlling for other significant predictors of body dissatisfaction. The hypotheses based on this theory were for the most part supported: More frequent television viewers and magazine readers expressed greater dissatisfaction with their bodies, idealized body types like those found in popular media, and modeled figure-enhancing behaviors (diet and exercise).

Interpretation of Results

With a mean BMI of 21, the respondents in this study were well within the normal weight range. Garrow and Webster (1985) indicate that normal BMIs range between 19 and 24. Despite this, the girls expressed dissatisfaction with specific areas of their body ($M = 3.24$, possible range = 0–7) as well as a desire to be thinner ($M = 20.05$, possible range = 6–30).

The respondents also spent a significant amount of time watching television—the equivalent of nearly one full day per week ($M = 23.78$ hours). This result, combined with their low to moderate level of magazine reading (for females, $M = 19.08$, possible range = 11–55; for males, $M = 9.13$, possible range = 5–25), demonstrates that they are exposed to a steady diet of media that emphasize slender, fit people.

The results indicate that the types of television shows viewed, and not just the sheer amount, mattered most when predicting body dissatisfaction (Tiggemann & Pickering, 1996). Interestingly, total weekly hours viewing television did not have a significant effect on body dissatisfaction. However, more frequent viewers of body image shows or soaps were more dissatisfied with their bodies, whereas sports viewers expressed less dissatisfaction. Music video viewing also increased girls' body dissatisfaction.

The one area where sheer television exposure formed a significant relationship was in girls' choice of the ideal body type and measurements. The more hours of television girls viewed weekly, the more they preferred thinner bodies and smaller body measurements. Boys, however, were influenced in their choice of the ideal body type by music videos—the more they watched, the thinner the bodies they chose—perhaps because videos do not focus solely on athletic male figures.

Watching certain types of television also influenced respondents' attempts to improve their figures. Viewing body image shows, soaps, and/or music videos increased dieting behaviors, whereas viewing sports decreased them. Not surprisingly, respondents who watched sports exercised more frequently. However, soaps viewers were less likely to exercise.

Magazine readership also led to body dissatisfaction for girls, whereas for boys, frequent magazine readers chose larger body types as ideal. This relationship may be explained by the fact that boys were asked only about sports magazines, which emphasize muscular, athletic figures. Female magazine readers also were more likely to diet, whereas male magazine readers were more likely to exercise. The results for the girls support the findings of magazine content analyses (e.g., Nemeroff et al., 1994; Snow & Harris, 1986), which have consistently found a strong emphasis on dieting.

Desiring to look like media celebrities also had a significant influence on body dissatisfaction. For girls, identification with models led to body dissatisfaction; the idealization of smaller body types, measurements, and clothing sizes; and an increase in diet and exercise behaviors. Identification with television stars also led to body dissatisfaction, idealization of smaller clothing sizes, and more frequent exercising. Boys were less influenced by media celebrities, yet those who identified with them expressed more body dissatisfaction and spent more time exercising.

Because other factors influence teens besides the media, it is important to consider the impact of these factors on body dissatisfaction. The multiple regression analyses enabled us to examine these relationships further. For boys, none of the media variables emerged as significant predictors of body dissatisfaction. Identification with media characters had no effect when controlling for BMI. In contrast, identification with media characters increased girls' body dissatisfaction even when controlling for the effects of BMI and magazine reading. However, BMI emerged as the stronger predictor in the regression equation.

Not surprisingly, boys who read sports magazines and watched sports on television exercised frequently. These predictors, along with friends' opinions about their appearance, were significant in the regression equation. However, only identification with media characters emerged as a significant influence on girls' exercising habits: The greater their desire to look like these characters, the more they exercised. Media variables were significant in boys' and girls' choices of ideal body types. Reading magazines led boys to choose larger body types as ideal, whereas watching music videos caused them to choose smaller bodies as ideal, even when controlling for BMI. When controlling for classmates' opinions, the total hours of television viewed weekly had no effect on girls' choice of ideal body type. However, media influences were significant factors in girls' choice of ideal body measurements and clothing size. Total weekly hours of television viewing led girls to idealize smaller body measurements, even when controlling for the body image shows, soaps, identification with models, and the opinions of classmates.

Clearly, marked gender differences were present in our results. Watching certain types of television, reading magazines, and identifying with slender or "buff" media characters tended to correlate positively with body dissatisfaction, with acceptance of stereotypical body type ideals, and with engagement in diet or exercise behaviors; these relationships were stronger for girls. Those boys who expressed dissatisfaction with their bodies had different concerns and methods for improving themselves. Whereas girls favored thinness and diet as a means for achieving improvement, boys idealized larger, more muscular figures and were more likely to exercise. It is possible that these findings reflect societal standards that socialize girls to believe that their worth is defined by their physical appearance (Brumberg, 1997).

Study Limitations

This study provided an exploratory analysis of the media's relationship with other predictor variables in influencing adolescents' body dissatisfaction. It was limited by several factors that would be useful to consider in subsequent studies.

First, the lack of ethnic diversity among the sample (90% White) prevented racial comparisons. Prior research in this area indicates that African American females have more positive body images (Cash & Henry, 1995) and are less likely to be dissatisfied with their weight (Felts et al., 1992) than are White females.

Second, the media variables were affected by their restriction in range. Respondents were neither frequent magazine readers nor frequent viewers of the body image shows, soaps, and music videos, which may have caused attenuation of the correlation coefficients. Stronger correlations between media exposure and body dissatisfaction might have emerged if these variables had been normally distributed.

Third, this study was limited by its correlational nature. Although it is easy to conclude that heavy media doses and identification with media celebrities lead to body dissatisfaction, the cross-sectional design does not permit us to infer cause and effect relationships. It is possible that people who are already dissatisfied with their bodies seek out certain types of television or magazines to establish an ideal for themselves and to learn how to achieve it. By using either longitudinal or experimental methods, future research could determine causality and maintain better control over the types of media content to which individuals are exposed.

Study Implications

This study established a relationship between media exposure and body dissatisfaction, the idealization of certain body type characteristics, and dieting and exercise. To impress the opposite sex or for other reasons, dissatisfied adolescents may become preoccupied with attaining a body type that is largely unachievable. In extreme cases, they may develop eating disorders. Further research in this subject area may help to better define the relationships between predictor variables and body dissatisfaction. However, given the potentially negative outcomes of body dissatisfaction, it is also important to investigate whether certain factors may counter the harmful effects of exposure to the ideal body stereotypes portrayed in the media. Such analyses may encourage society to take a more active role in helping teens develop positive body images.

Finally, the use of 9th- and 10th-grade students in this study masks the origin of the relationships we have uncovered. Certainly, television is a preeminent pastime for younger teens and preteens; in fact, they spend more time with television than the age-groups used here. In addition, magazines targeting younger readers may also reinforce the gender-normative body ideal evidenced in the media used by our high school students. Subsequent research, then, is obliged to examine even younger segments of society to determine not only how, but when, the mass media make this impression on physical self-images.

REFERENCES

Bandura, A. (1977). *Social learning theory*. Englewood Cliffs, NJ: Prentice-Hall.
Blouin, A. G., & Goldfield, G. S. (1995). Body image and steroid use in male bodybuilders. *The International Journal of Eating Disorders, 18*(2), 159–165.

Brooks-Gunn, J., & Reiter, E. O. (1990). The role of pubertal processes. In S. S. Feldman & G. R. Elliott (Eds.), *At the threshold* (pp. 16–53). Cambridge, MA: Harvard University Press.

Brumberg, J. J. (1997). *The body project: An intimate history of American girls.* New York: Random House.

Cash, T. F., & Henry, P. E. (1995). Women's body images: The results of a national survey in the U.S.A. *Sex Roles, 33*(1–2), 19–28.

Cash, T. F., Winstead, B. W., & Janda, L. H. (1986). The great American shape-up: Body image survey report. *Psychology Today, 20*(4), 30–37.

Cogan, J. C., Bhalla, S. K., Sefa-Dedeh, A., & Rothblum, E. D. (1996). A comparison study of United States and African students on perceptions of obesity and thinness. *Journal of Cross-Cultural Psychology, 27*, 98–113.

Crandall, C. S. (1988). Social contagion of binge eating. *Journal of Personality and Social Psychology, 55*(4), 588–598.

DeFleur, M. L., & Ball-Rokeach, S. J. (1989). *Theories of mass communication.* White Plains, NY: Longman.

Dionne, M., Davis, C., Fox, J., & Gurevich, M. (1995). Feminist ideology as a predictior of body dissatisfaction in women. *Sex Roles, 33*, 277–287.

Duffy, M., & Gotcher, J. M. (1996). Crucial advice on how to get the guy: The rhetorical vision of power and seduction in the teen magazine *YM. Journal of Communication Inquiry, 20*, 32–48.

Evans, E. D., Rutberg, J., Sather, C., & Turner, C. (1991). Content analysis of contemporary teen magazines for adolescent females. *Youth & Society, 23*(1), 99–120.

Fallon, A. (1990). Culture in the mirror: Sociocultural determinants of body image. In T. Cash & T. Pruzusky (Eds.), *Body images: Development deviance and change* (pp. 80–109). New York: Guilford.

Felts, M., Tavasso, D., Chenier, T., & Dunn, P. (1992). Adolescents' perceptions of relative weight and self-reported weight loss activities. *Journal of School Health, 62*(8), 372–376.

Fouts, G., & Burggraf, K. (1999). Television situation comedies: Female body images and verbal reinforcements. *Sex Roles, 40*(5/6), 473–481.

Garner, D. M., Garfinkel, P. E., Schwartz, D., & Thompson, M. (1980). Cultural expectations of thinness in women. *Psychological Reports, 47*, 483–491.

Garner, D. M., Olmstead, M. P., & Polivy, J. (1983). Development and validation of a multidimensional eating disorder inventory for anorexia nervosa and bulimia. *International Journal of Eating Disorders, 2*, 15–34.

Harrison, K. (1997). Does interpersonal attraction to thin media personalities promote eating disorders? *Journal of Broadcasting and Electronic Media, 41*(4), 478–500.

Harrison, K., & Cantor, J. (1997). The relationship between media consumption and eating disorders. *Journal of Communication, 47*(1), 40–67.

Heinberg, L. J., & Thompson, J. K. (1992). Social comparison: Gender, target importance ratings, and relation to body image disturbance. *Journal of Social Behavior and Personality, 7*, 335–344.

Huddy, D. C., Nieman, D. C., & Johnson, R. L. (1993). Relationship between body image and percent body fat among college male varsity athletes and nonathletes. *Perceptual and Motor Skills, 77*, 851–857.

Kelly, K. J. (1996, August 26). Magazines stay on downward course in 1st half. *Advertising Age, 67*(35), 25.

Keys, A., Findanza, F., Karvonen, M. J., Kimura, N., & Taylor, H. L. (1972). Indices of relative weight and obesity. *Journal of Chronic Disease, 25*, 329–343.

Lauber, C. A. (1982). *Perception of body image in adolescents aged 14–16.* Unpublished master's thesis, Michigan State University, East Lansing.

McMullen, J. L. (1984). *The effects of physical stereotypes of males and females in media on body-image and self-esteem.* Unpublished doctoral dissertation, University of Texas, Austin.

Mortenson, G. M., Hoerr, S. L., & Garner, D. M. (1993). Predictors of body satisfaction in college women. *Journal of the American Dietetic Association, 93*(9), 1037–1039.

Myers, P. N., & Biocca, F. A. (1992). The elastic body image: The effect of television advertising and programming on body image distortions in young women. *Journal of Communication, 42*(3), 108–133.

Nemeroff, C. J., Stein, R. I., Diehl, N. S., Smilack, K. M. (1994). From the Cleavers to the Clintons: Role choices and body orientation as reflected in magazine article content. *International Journal of Eating Disorders, 16*(2), 167–176.

Newman, I. M. (1991). *Eating and exercising: Nebraska adolescents' attitudes and behaviors.* (Report No. CG-023-954). Lincoln, NE: Health Education, Inc. (ERIC Document Reproduction Service No. ED 340 997)

Newman, L. B., & Dodd, D. K. (1995). Self-esteem and magazine reading among college students. *Perceptual and Motor Skills, 81,* 161–162.

Petrie, T. A., Austin, L. J., Crowley, B. J., Helmcamp, A., Johnson, C. E., Lester, R., Rogers, R., Turner, J., & Walbrick, K. (1996). Sociocultural expectations of attractiveness for males. *Sex Roles, 35*(9/10), 581–602.

Peirce, K. (1990). A feminist theoretical perspective on the socialization of teenage girls through *Seventeen* magazine. *Sex Roles, 23*(9/10), 491–500.

Pike, K. M., & Rodin, J. (1991). Mothers, daughters, and disordered eating. *Journal of Abnormal Psychology, 100*(2), 198–204.

Rodin, J., Silberstein, L. R., & Striegel-Moore, R. H. (1985). Women and weight: A normative discontent. In T. B. Sonderegger (Ed.), *Nebraska symposium on motivation: Vol 32. Psychology and gender* (pp. 267–307). Lincoln: University of Nebraska Press.

Silverstein, B., Perdue, L., Peterson, B., & Kelly, E. (1986). The role of the mass media in promoting a thin standard of bodily attractiveness for women. *Sex Roles, 14,* 519–532.

Snow, J. T., & Harris, M. B. (1986). An analysis of weight and diet content in five women's interest magazines. *The Journal of Obesity and Weight Regulation, 5*(4), 194–214.

Stice, E., & Shaw, H. F. (1994). Adverse effects of the media portrayed thin-ideal on women and linkages to bulimic symptomatology. *Journal of Social and Clinical Psychology, 13*(3), 288–308.

Tan, A. S. (1985). *Mass communication theories and research.* New York: Macmillan.

Tiggemann, M., & Pickering, A. S. (1996). Role of television in adolescent women's body dissatisfaction and drive for thinness. *International Journal of Eating Disorders, 20*(2), 199–203.

Waller, G., Hamilton, K., & Shaw, J. (1992). Media influences on body size estimation in eating disordered and comparison subjects. *British Review of Bulimia and Anorexia Nervosa, 6*(2), 81–87.

MAGAZINES

7

From "Just the Facts" to "Downright Salacious": Teens' and Women's Magazine Coverage of Sex and Sexual Health

Kim Walsh-Childers
University of Florida

Alyse Gotthoffer
University of Miami

Carolyn Ringer Lepre
California State University–Chico

Magazine cover headlines from 1999:

> *"Guys and Sex: What They Think About Foreplay, Experienced Women, and Lust vs. Love"*
>
> —*Mademoiselle,* July 1999

> *"Orgasm Dos and Don'ts Survey"*
> *"Is Your Sexual Health in Danger? Immediate Steps to Protect Your Female Parts Now"*
>
> —*Glamour,* July 1999

> *"Love Lessons: Why Guys Cheat—Shocking Confessions"*
>
> —*YM,* July 1999

> *"Free Instruction Cards! Sex Tricks He's Never Seen Before: The Outrageous 'Rock' Technique and 21 Other Moves That Will Make His Thighs Go Up in Flames"*
> *"Guy Butt Watch '99: Tons of Taut, Tan, Utterly Fant-ass-tic Naked Star Buns"*
>
> —*Cosmopolitan,* July 1999

> *"How to Cast Your Own Love Spell"*
> *"Should You Tell Him You're Not a Virgin?"*
> *"Quiz: Innocent Crush or Mad Obsession?"*
>
> —*Seventeen,* November 1999

To anyone who ever has given more than a passing glance to the covers of magazines sold at any supermarket checkout counter, there's nothing new in the revelation that articles about sex have become a staple in American women's magazines and even in many of the magazines targeted at teenage girls. Indeed, as the headlines above illustrate, it sometimes seems the women's magazines compete to offer the raciest content. In addition to instruction in how to "make his thighs go up in flames," however, these magazines offer readers a type of sexual health education in the form of information about contraception, pregnancy, sexually transmitted diseases (STDs), and other sex-related health concerns. The question this chapter addresses is this: What is the balance teens' and women's magazines are striking between sex instruction and sexual health education?

Teenage Girls' Sexual Health

Understanding what types of sexual health and other sex-related information magazines may provide to their teenage readers is important for a number of reasons. First, research indicates that teenage girls today face numerous sexual health risks. More than half of all 17-year-old girls have had sex; by age 19, more than three quarters of all girls are sexually active (Alan Guttmacher Institute, 1998). According to the Centers for Disease Control's 1997 Youth Risk Behavior Survey, the prevalence of sexual experience declined 15% between 1991 and 1997 among boys but not among girls (CDC, 1998a). Another cause for concern is the prevalence of multiple sex partners among teenage girls. About 14% of high school girls responding to the Youth Risk Behavior Survey reported having had four or more partners (CDC, 1998a).

Teenage girls' use of contraception at first intercourse increased during the 1980s and early 1990s, so that by 1995, 78% of teenage girls used birth control the first time they had sex. Ninety percent of teenage girls now report using a contraceptive method, but not always consistently or correctly. The result is that almost one million teenage girls—11% of all 15- to 19-year-old girls—become pregnant each year. About 8 of every 10 of those pregnancies are unplanned. Among women who first gave birth in their teens, 28% of them are poor in their 20s and early 30s, compared with only 7% of women who first give birth after adolescence. One third of pregnant teens receive inadequate prenatal care, and as a result, babies born to teens are more likely than those of older mothers to have low birth weight and to have childhood health problems leading to hospitalization (Alan Guttmacher Institute, 1998).

In addition to unplanned pregnancies, sexually active girls are at risk from STDs, including the human immunodeficiency virus (HIV). According to the Alan Guttmacher Institute (1998), up to 15% of sexually active teenage girls in some studies were infected with the human papilloma virus (HPV); many of these cases involved a strain of the virus linked to cervical cancer. Teenage girls have a higher hospitalization rate than older women for acute pelvic inflammatory disease (PID), which can lead to infertility and ectopic pregnancy (Alan Guttmacher Institute, 1998; see also chapter 1 of this book).

Teenage girls also are at risk of contracting HIV and dying of AIDS. According to the Centers for Disease Control, men who have sex with men still account for the majority of HIV infections among 13- to 24-year-olds; however, the results of one CDC study of HIV rates in 25 states with standardized HIV/AIDS reporting procedures showed that 44% of the 13- to 24-year-olds with HIV were young women (CDC, 1998b). Among disadvantaged youth, HIV infection rates from 1990 to 1996 were 50% higher for young women than for young men, and young women are infected at younger ages (CDC, 1998c).

Magazines as Sex Information Sources

Given the sexual health risks teenage girls now face, it is crucial that they have access to sources of accurate information about those risks. Research shows that magazines may be among the most important mass media sources to which teenagers, especially girls, turn for sex information. First, as Table 7.1 shows, magazines targeted to teenage girls reach large percent-

TABLE 7.1
Teenage Girls' Readership of Popular Teens' and Women's Magazines

Magazine	% of Girls 12–15 Who Read Regularly	% of Girls 16–19 Who Read Regularly
Seventeen	85.6	55.8
Teen	53.2	23.0
YM	50.0	48.6
Glamour	20.5	28.5
Vogue	15.1	23.6
Good Housekeeping	13.2	14.0
Cosmopolitan	12.6	31.2
Redbook	9.6	12.8
Mademoiselle	8.5	25.3
McCall's	8.1	10.4
Elle	5.7	13.2
Self	5.45	10.7

Note. 1998 Simmons Teen-Age Research (STARS). Percentages are weighted by population.

ages of them, with nearly 86% of 12- to 15-year-old girls and almost 56% of 16- to 19-year-old girls reading *Seventeen* magazine alone. Among older girls, readership of magazines targeted at young adult women is also common; nearly one third of 16- to 19-year-old girls read *Cosmopolitan* regularly (Simmons Market Research Bureau, 1998).

Although fashion and makeup tips and stories about favorite celebrities may draw teens to these magazines, there also is evidence that they find sexual health information between the makeovers and clothing ads. For instance, a Gallup Organization survey about STDs indicated that 28% of adults and 11% of teens said they first had learned about STDs from books, magazines, or television, making mass media the second most important initial source of STD information, after schools. In addition, one fourth of the teens surveyed and more than two thirds of the adults said books, magazines, and TV are current sources of information about STDs (American Social Health Association, 1995). In a Henry J. Kaiser Family Foundation survey of teenagers, 70% of the girls reported reading magazines such as *Teen*, *YM*, and *Seventeen* regularly, and half of the readers (36% of all the girls in the survey) said these magazines are an important source of information about sex, birth control, and STDs. Nearly 70% of the regular magazine readers—more than one of every five girls—said the information magazines provide often isn't available to them from other sources (Henry J. Kaiser Family Foundation, 1996, 1998). In another survey, more than 60% of high school-age girls said they had learned about pregnancy prevention, birth control, or contraception from magazines (Sutton, Brown, Wilson, & Klein, 1999).

Magazines also have served as important sources of AIDS information for teenagers. A 1985 study revealed that high school students who received AIDS information from magazines knew more about the disease than those who had not (Price, Desmond, & Kukulka, 1985). However, studies of magazines popular with teenagers also have shown that discussion of teens' risk of AIDS and of safe sex behaviors such as condom use are rare (Endres, 1990; Stephenson & Walsh-Childers, 1993), and that articles about AIDS in magazines geared toward children and teenagers do not provide enough information to help prevent the spread of the disease (Wysocki & Harrison, 1991).

If magazines are important sources of sex and sexual health information, particularly for teenage girls, then it is critical that those concerned about adolescent health know what kinds of information these magazines are providing. It is important to note here that the teen-targeted magazines are not the only magazines of concern. One 1994 survey showed that *Cosmopolitan*, *Glamour*, and *Mademoiselle* were among the top 15 magazines read by teenage girls (Simmons Market Research Bureau, 1995); and older teenagers in particular may be far more likely to read these and other magazines targeted to young adult women than they are to read even the most popular teens' magazines: *Teen*, *YM*, and *Seventeen*.

RESEARCH QUESTIONS

The original study from which these results were drawn involved a content analysis of 50 consumer magazines, including teens', women's, men's, African American, and health magazines. For this chapter, however, we focused on a subset of 16 teens' and women's magazines published between 1986 and 1996. We investigated the following questions:

- What was the volume of content devoted to sex? How much of that content focused on sexual health issues, and how did that content change between 1986 and 1996?
- What sex-related topics did the magazines focus on, and how did those focuses change over the decade? How did women's magazines differ from teens' magazines in the topics they focused on?
- Within sex-related items, what specific types of sexual health information were most likely to be included? Did the types of sexual health information included in women's versus teens' magazines differ?
- What was the context in which sexual health information appeared? What non-health sex topics were covered in women's and teens' magazines? Did this change over time?

METHODS

Analyses focused on the editorial content of 16 consumer magazines, including the 4 most popular teens' magazines—*Seventeen, Teen, Sassy,* and *YM*—and 12 of the most popular women's magazines—*Cosmopolitan, Glamour, Mademoiselle, Vogue, Elle, Ladies' Home Journal, Good Housekeeping, McCall's, Woman's Day, Redbook, Self,* and *Ms.* The sample included 6 randomly selected issues of each magazine dated between June 1995 and May 1996 (June, August, and October 1995 and January, April, and May 1996). The 9 years from June 1986 to May 1995 were divided into 3-year blocks (June 1986–May 1989, June 1989–May 1992, and June 1992–May 1995). Then, using a table of random numbers, we randomly selected 10 months/issues of each magazine from each 3-year block, for a total sample of 36 issues of each magazine.[1]

If a magazine was published more frequently than once a month, the issue coded was that published the first full week of the selected month. In some cases, magazines combined issues for 2 months; if both months had been selected for sampling, only the one issue was coded. This strategy was chosen as the best way of fairly representing the amount of reproductive and sexual health information, on average, to which magazine readers would be exposed.

Every effort was made to find copies of every selected issue of every magazine, and the magazines were located in libraries, purchased from the magazine publishing companies or, in a few cases, were coded at the magazines' New York City offices. Some issues originally selected for the sample could not be located through any of these methods. However, there is no reason to believe that anything distinguishes the issues that could not be located from those included in the analysis. The results described here reflect the contents of 470 magazine issues.

Eight coders were trained to analyze the magazines. All items of editorial content were coded if they concerned any issue directly related to sexual activity. For purposes of this study, "sexual health" topics were defined as those focused on pregnancy, abortion, contraception, or birth control, STDs (including HIV/AIDS), and reproductive health care topics directly related to sexual activity.[2] Sex-related items not focused on sexual health issues (i.e.,

---

[1]One of the teen magazines, *Sassy,* was not published continuously throughout the study period, so fewer issues were included in the final sample.

[2]A copy of the coding guide is available from the first author. Any item that specifically concerned having sex was coded, as were any items concerning pregnancy, abortion, contraception, or STDs. Items concerning reproductive health issues were coded if they dealt with sexual activity. For instance, an article concerning how having a mastectomy would affect a woman's sex life would have been coded, but an article concerning new techniques in treating breast cancer would not have been coded. Similarly, an article dealing with the incidence of cervical cancer would not have been coded unless it made specific reference to the link between STDs and cervical cancer.

articles offering advice on how to improve the reader's sexual performance) were coded for mention of a variety of sexual health topics. The coders also measured the length in column inches of each coded item, including text and accompanying graphics that included text—but not design elements such as pictures. Ten percent of the sample issues were selected for blind double coding, producing an overall intercoder agreement rate of 86%.

RESULTS

The first research question was about the amount of magazine content devoted to sex-related items, and within that subset of overall magazine content, how much space was devoted to items primarily focused on sexual health topics. For purposes of this analysis, sexual health topics were defined as contraception, pregnancy, abortion, emergency contraception, HIV/AIDS, other STDs, and articles discussing reproductive health care. Figure 7.1 shows that, judging simply by the sheer amount of text in column inches, the majority of sex-related content focused on non-sexual health topics, with the exception of teens' magazines in the 1986–1989 period. In teens' magazines, the amount of space devoted to sexual health-focused content increased slightly, by about 6%, between the 1986–1989 period and 1993–1996, and the amount of space devoted to sex-related content not focused on health issues increased by 80%. In women's magazines, the increase in non-health sex-related content was not so dramatic, climbing by about 26%; however, in women's magazines, the amount of space devoted to sexual health-focused content dropped by nearly 15% during the same period.

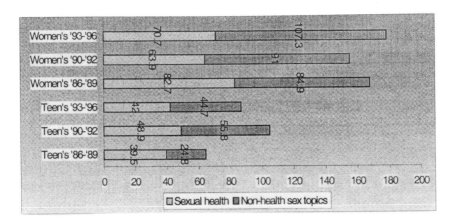

FIG. 7.1. Average column inches per issue devoted to sexual health and nonhealth sex topics.

Sexual Health Versus Sexual Success: Topic Focus

The second set of research questions asked what sex-related topics the magazines focused on, how those topics changed over the decade, and how those topics differed in women's versus teens' magazines. The results appear in Table 7.2. Again, we see that the emphasis on health issues within sex-related content declined over the decade in both women's and teens' magazines. Health-focused items were at least as common as other sex-related items in teens' and women's magazines during the 1986–1989 period, but by 1993–1996, non-health-focused topics dominated. Among the sexual health topics, pregnancy was the most common topic in women's magazines in all three eras; in teens' magazines, pregnancy received the most attention in 1986–1989 and in 1993–1996, but during 1990–1992, contraception and HIV/AIDS articles were more prevalent. Neither type of magazine included many articles focused on abortion issues, although during the middle period, these articles were the focus of almost 11% of sex-related items in teens' magazines. For both types of magazines, the focus of sex-related content changed significantly over time; teens' and women's magazines differed significantly in the distribution of topics only during the 1993–1996 period.

What Specific Sexual Health Information Is Included?

The third set of research questions asked about the specific types of information included in the sex-related content of the magazines. Not surprisingly, items that focused on contraception, pregnancy, STDs, etc., were most likely to mention specific sexual health issues (e.g., specific diseases or birth control methods, new HIV testing and treatment options). However, even items that focused on non-health sex topics, such as sexual performance, included information about sexual health; in fact, nearly 30% of non-health-focused items mentioned at least one sexual health issue. For that reason, the figures in Table 7.3 and the results discussed throughout the rest of the chapter reflect the inclusion of specific information across all coded items, not just those focused on sexual health issues.

Table 7.3 shows the percentages of all coded items that included any mention of six key sexual health topics: contraception, planned and unplanned pregnancy, abortion, STDs, and HIV/AIDS. As the table shows, in general, information related to contraception was most likely to be included in both teens' and women's magazines. There was relatively little change in the inclusion of sexual health content over the decade, although information related to planned pregnancy became less common in women's magazines. In teens' magazines, information about contraception was more likely to be included during the 1990s than during the earliest period, and

TABLE 7.2
Main Focus of Sex-Related Items in Teens' & Women's Magazines, 1986-1996

% of All Coded Items

Main Focus of Item	Teen's Magazines				Women's Magazines			
	'86-'89 (N = 42)	'90-'92 (N = 56)	'93-'96 (N = 88)	Total (N = 186)	'86-'89 (N = 249)	'90-'92 (N = 259)	'93-'96 (N = 418)	Total (N = 926)
Contraception	11.9	12.5	3.4	8.1	10.8	10.4	9.8	10.3
Pregnancy	16.7	8.9	13.6	12.9	20.1	19.3	11.5	16.0
Abortion	2.4	10.7	0.0	3.8	4.8	4.2	6.0	5.2
Emergency contraception	0.0	0.0	1.1	0.5	0.0	0.0	0.5	0.2
STDs	11.9	8.9	9.1	9.7	4.0	5.4	4.5	4.6
AIDS/HIV	2.4	12.5	8.09	8.1	8.0	7.7	6.9	7.5
Reproductive health care	4.8	1.8	8.0	5.4	6.0	2.7	2.4	3.5
All sexual health	50.1	55.3	43.2	48.4	53.7	49.7	41.6	47.2
Non-health sex topics	50.0	44.6	56.8	51.6	46.2	40.2	58.4	52.8
	Chi-square (df = 16) = 26.716, p < .05				Chi-square (df = 16) = 26.756, p < .05			

Note. Distribution of topics differed significantly between teens' and women's magazines during 1993–1996. Chi-square (df = 8) = 19.814, p < .05. Percentages may not add up to 100% due to rounding.

TABLE 7.3

Mention of Specific Sexual Health Topics Within All Sex-Related Items in Teens' & Women's Magazines, 1986–1996

% of All Coded Items Mentioning Topic

	Teens' Magazines				Women's Magazines			
Any Mention of:	'86–'89 (N = 42)	'90–'92 (N = 56)	'93–'96 (N = 88)	Total (N = 186)	'86–'89 (N = 249)	'90–'92 (N = 259)	'93–'96 (N = 418)	Total (N = 926)
Contraception	23.8*	42.9[c]	34.1[b]	34.4[d]	23.3	21.2	20.1	21.3
Planned pregnancy	2.4[c]	5.4	2.3[c]	3.2[d]	20.5***	12.7	12.0	14.5
Unplanned pregnancy	26.2[c]	30.4[d]	27.3[d]	28.0[d]	6.8	6.6	9.3	7.9
Abortion	2.4*	14.3	5.7	7.5	6.4	7.3	10.0	8.3
STDs	14.3**	39.3[d]	37.5[d]	32.8[d]	17.7	13.5	14.4	15.0
AIDS/HIV	21.4	26.8	27.3[a]	25.8[b]	18.9	20.5	17.7	18.8
Any sexual health topic	61.9	80.4[c]	64.8[a]	68.8*[b]	66.3***	62.2	54.5	59.8

Note. Chi-square shows significant difference between teens' & women's magazines for this period: [a]p < .10, [b]p < .05, [c]p < .01, [d]p < .001. Chi-square shows significant difference between periods for magazines of this type (teens' or women's): *p < .10, **p < .05, ***p < .01, ****p < .001

abortion-related information was most likely to be included during the 1990–1992 period.

There were numerous differences, however, between teens' and women's magazines' inclusion of specific sexual health information. In general, Table 7.3 shows that teens' magazines were more likely than women's magazines to include some mention of contraception, unplanned pregnancy, STDs, and HIV/AIDS. Perhaps not surprisingly, the only sexual health topic women's magazines were more likely to mention was planned pregnancy.[3]

Our analysis also provided more detailed information about the birth control methods most likely to be mentioned in the magazines. In general, condoms were the method most likely to be mentioned, particularly in the teens' magazines. In women's magazines, oral contraceptives (the Pill) were almost as likely to be mentioned as condoms, and the Pill was the most frequently mentioned method in teens' magazines from 1986 to 1989. During the later two periods, however, teens' magazines mentioned condoms nearly twice as often as any other birth control method.

The mention of specific contraceptive methods differed fairly substantially in teens' versus women's magazines. The sex-related content in teens' magazines was more likely than that in women's magazines to mention condoms (10.4% vs. 6.8%), the Pill (18.0% vs. 8.0%), spermicides (6.3% vs. 2.4%), and abstinence (3.2% vs. 0.9%), whereas women's magazines were more likely to mention IUDs (3.9% of coded items in women's magazines vs. 1.4% in teens' magazines).[4] Other references to contraception topics also varied between the two magazine types, with teens' magazines more likely than women's magazines to mention contraception in general (16.2% vs. 4.4%), the failure to use contraceptives (5.4% vs. 1.8%), the health benefits of contraception (6.3% vs. 2.6%), female responsibility for using contraception (5.4% vs. 2.1%), and where to get contraceptives (4.5% vs. 1.3%). The only specific topic women's magazines were more likely to mention was contraceptive research (2.9% of coded items vs. 0.5% of coded items in teens' magazines). As these figures illustrate, however, neither type of magazine was very likely to include much discussion of specific contraception-related topics on a regular basis. It is somewhat encouraging that in the teens' magazines, about 1 of every 6 sex-related items at least mentioned contraception

---

[3] The easiest way of explaining how distinctions were made between articles about birth control/contraception and planned pregnancy is to say that the former focused on the planning, while the later concerned the pregnancy. In other words, articles about contraception were those in which the central concern was avoiding pregnancy; items about planned pregnancy were those primarily focused on a pregnancy the woman had sought. Obviously, however, items related to planned pregnancy might include information about contraceptive methods; for instance, an item might have mentioned how long a woman needs to be off oral contraceptives before she starts trying to get pregnant.

[4] All differences were statistically significant at the $p < .05$ level.

in general. Two fairly typical examples were a pair of *YM* articles about girls who had unplanned pregnancies and each girl's decision whether to keep her baby or give it up for adoption. One mentioned that the girl and her boyfriend had been using condoms but didn't use them consistently; the other indicated that the condom the boyfriend used had failed (Gilman, 1990; Spivack, 1990). Some teens' magazine articles went further, offering teens advice about how to discuss contraception with their parents (Raffel, 1988),[5] but even in "special sections" on sex, health, and intimacy, the teens' magazines included few details about contraceptive methods (Ganske, 1991–1992; Rodriguez, Norvell, & Haze, 1995).

Women's magazine articles sometimes mentioned contraception, even in articles primarily focused on non-health sex topics. For example, in *Mademoiselle*'s May 1996 article titled "How to Enjoy Sex With the Lights On," the 7th of 10 "tips" was "Be Prepared." It not only advised readers to talk with their partners about contraception and disease prevention "long before you're both stark naked and panting like dogs," but encouraged them to think about putting on a condom or inserting a diaphragm not as an interruption of spontaneity but "as the last tantalizing step just before the really big fun starts" (Snowden, 1986, p. 161). Unfortunately, articles that did not include any mention of contraception were far more common in both teens' and women's magazines. Typical were a September 1995 *Ladies' Home Journal* article called "The Joy of Quick Sex," which offered about a page worth of text extolling the virtues of "quickies" without mentioning contraception (Ryan, 1995); similarly, a May 1996 *Cosmopolitan* article, "The Mysterious Power of Sex," ran three full pages discussing people's willingness to risk losing their spouses, children, careers, etc., for sex, without including any mention of sexual health risks, including pregnancy or STDs (Rice, 1996).

Given that pregnancy was generally the most common sexual health focus (see Table 7.2), it is somewhat surprising that the magazines mentioned none of the specific pregnancy-related topics very often, with the exception of unplanned pregnancy scares. An unplanned pregnancy scare was the most likely topic to be mentioned in teens' magazines, whereas planned pregnancy leading to a birth was most common in women's magazines. Teens' magazines were statistically more likely than women's magazines to mention an unplanned pregnancy scare (14.9% of all coded items in teens' magazines vs. 1.7% in women's magazines), pregnancy tests (2.7% vs. 1.0%), unplanned pregnancy leading to a birth (5.4% vs. 1.8%), and abortion (5.0% vs. 2.2%). Women's magazines were more likely than teens' magazines to include mention of a birth resulting from a planned pregnancy (6.4% of coded items in women's magazines vs. 1.4% of teens' magazine items), miscar-

---

[5]However, this article mentioned only one specific method—oral contraceptives.

riages of a planned pregnancy (3.4% vs. 0.9%), and the health risks of pregnancy (2.5% vs. 0.5%).

The teens' magazine articles about unplanned pregnancies included some discussion of the difficulties pregnant teens face. For instance, one *YM* article about a teen mother began with a preface warning that "only half of all teen mothers finish high school, and two-thirds of the families headed by women who had their first child before age 20 live below the poverty level." The article itself noted that because she was pregnant, "Angela" couldn't attend parties, the prom, or the senior class trip. Much of the article, however, seemed to suggest that having a baby was primarily a complicating factor for "Angela"; she graduated third in her high school class with a straight-A average, was vice president of the school's National Honor Society chapter, and received a full-tuition, four-year college scholarship, which she was able to accept because her parents took care of her baby during the week (Spivack, 1990). The contrasting story in the same issue tells of a teenage girl who gave her baby up for adoption—but acknowledges that her situation is "quite unusual" because she and the baby's father were able to choose the adoptive parents and because the adoptive parents "have made us a part of their family" (Gilman, 1990, p. 110). Another *YM* story about a teenage girl who gave up her baby for adoption provided some practical advice, defining the differences between open and closed adoptions, for example, but ended with a strong focus on the emotional pain her decision caused her (Duncan, 1988).

Abortion issues in general received very little attention in the magazines, with no specific abortion topic mentioned in more than 6% of the items within any magazine type and in any period. In general, decision making about whether to have an abortion was most likely to be mentioned; all three previously mentioned articles dealing with teens' unplanned pregnancies included discussion of their reasons for deciding against having abortions. Nonsurgical abortion methods also received some coverage.

The sex-related items in the sample, particularly in teens' magazines, were fairly likely to include mention of STDs in a nonspecific way; nearly 23% of the coded items in teens' magazines and about 6% of those in women's magazines mentioned unspecified STDs. The magazines were quite unlikely to discuss specific STDs by name, although teens' magazines seem to have become somewhat more likely to mention specific STDs (syphilis and genital warts) in the 1990s as compared with the late 1980s. *YM*'s annual "Intimacy Reports" included useful information about STDs, including descriptions of symptoms and treatment possibilities for genital warts, herpes, chlamydia, gonorrhea, and syphilis in its December 1991–January 1992 special section (Ganske, 1991–1992). The same information, substituting trichomoniasis for syphilis, appeared in its February 1995 special section (Norvell, 1995). Both special sections also included information about HIV/AIDS.

Because of the importance of the HIV/AIDS epidemic in the United States in the 1980s and 1990s, we also wanted to examine in more depth the information magazines provided about this critical STD. The results showed that the magazines did pay considerable attention to HIV/AIDS. Over the whole study period, nearly 1 in 5 items in teens' magazines mentioned sexual transmission of HIV, while about 1 of every 10 items in women's magazines did. Women's magazines, however, were more likely to include mention of HIV testing (3.9% of coded items vs. 1.4% of teens' magazine items).

Given the frequency with which teens' magazines mentioned the sexual transmission of HIV, it's somewhat surprising how infrequently they mentioned any other HIV/AIDS-related topics, particularly prevention methods. The teens' magazines did sometimes mention abstinence and the use of condoms for HIV prevention; for instance, the *YM* "Intimacy Report" from December 1991–January 1992 advised readers that, "if you're going to have sex, you've absolutely, positively got to . . . 1. Use condoms to protect yourself from AIDS and other STDs" (Ganske, 1991–1992). At best, however, prevention topics appeared about once for every 4 mentions of sexual transmission of HIV. Women's magazines also made relatively infrequent mention of any method for preventing HIV transmission and, in fact, appear to have grown less likely to mention HIV prevention as the 1990s passed.

TABLE 7.4
Mention of Specific Non-Health Sex Topics Within All Sex-Related
Items in Teens' & Women's Magazines, 1986–1996

	% of All Coded Items	
Any Mention of:	Teens' Magazines (N = 186)	Women's Magazines (N = 926)
General sexual activity	55.9[d]	44.1
Sexual decision making	32.3[d]	8.7
Virginity	16.7[d]	3.0
Female decision-making responsibility	14.5[d]	5.2
Lack of desire	2.7[d]	17.8
Sexual dysfunction	2.2[d]	7.8
Sexual attraction	5.4[d]	19.4
Extramarital affairs/cheating	4.3[c]	8.6
Sex acts & techniques	3.8[d]	19.1
Monogamy	1.6[d]	19.7
Enhancing sex appeal	1.1[d]	15.7
Sexual fantasies	1.1[d]	10.8

Note. Chi-square shows significant difference between teens' & women's magazines: [a]$p < .10$, [b]$p < .05$, [c]$p < .01$, [d]$p < .001$

Finally, the last set of research questions concerned the context in which sexual health information appeared: What non-health sex-related topics did the magazines discuss, and how did these topics change over time? The results, shown in Table 7.4, reveal that the most common topic in both teens' and women's magazines was sexual activity in general, which included any mention of sexual intercourse. Beyond that common topic, the material in the teens' and women's magazines differed quite dramatically. In women's magazines, the other most commonly mentioned topics were sexual monogamy, sexual attraction, sex acts and techniques, the lack of desire for sex, and enhancing sexual appeal. In teens' magazines, in contrast, the most common topics included sexual decision making, virginity, and female responsibility for making decisions about sex. Cross-tabulation analysis showed that, when analyzed within magazine type, there were no statistically significant changes in the inclusion of these topics over the decade.

CONCLUSIONS AND DISCUSSION

So, what have we learned about the sex-related messages teen girls and young adult women are likely to have encountered over the past decade? First, if we consider the percentage of items and amount of space focused on sexual health versus non-health sex topics, we find that readers are increasingly likely to have learned that they need to be more concerned about sex per se—for example, 21 ways to "make his thighs go up in flames"—rather than sexual health. This is especially true for readers of women's magazines. Certainly, the individual magazines vary in their inclusion of sexual health information, but taken as a group, women's magazines provide their readers with far more information about attracting sex partners and improving sexual performance than about protecting themselves from unwanted pregnancies and STDs.

It's also important to note that women's magazines have substantially increased the amount of space given to non-health sex topics, whereas space for articles focused on sexual health has decreased. In teens' magazines, the balance is not so lopsided, and the amount of space devoted to sexual health issues more nearly matches that given to other sex issues. The bad news, however, is that teens' magazines have increased the amount of space focused on non-health sex issues even more, percentage-wise, than have women's magazines; at the same time, space for sexual health-focused content has grown only slightly. This change in the balance of sex versus sexual health content suggests that these important sources of health information for teenagers and young women are de-emphasizing sexual health issues.

One has to wonder if advertisers' concerns may be playing a role in the decreasing focus on sexual health topics. After all, advice about increasing one's sexual appeal, sexual fantasies, sexual attraction, and even sexual dysfunction or "cheating" may provide a more supportive context for cosmetic, perfume, and clothing advertisements than would articles warning about the potential hazards associated with sex.

Although some items dealing primarily with sexual attraction or sexual performance also included sexual health information, most did not. *Cosmopolitan* magazine provides numerous examples of missed opportunities to incorporate sexual health information into non-health articles. For example, an April 1996 issue featured an article entitled "The Spectacular Infinite Variety of Sex," which discusses sexual encounters and sexual positions in great detail with virtually no mention of such topics as birth control or STDs (Batten, 1996). Although the teens' magazines also missed many opportunities to educate their readers about crucial sexual health concerns, they were at least more likely than the women's magazines to talk about pregnancy and STD prevention. For example, nearly 1 in 5 sex-related items in the teens' magazines mentioned the sexual transmission of HIV.

On the other hand, the results also show that sexual health issues are mentioned relatively often even in articles focused on non-health sex topics. Almost one third (30%) of sample items that were focused on other sex topics included at least some mention of a sexual health issue. As long as the sexual health information provided in these non-health-focused articles is accurate and in sufficient depth to be useful to readers, these mentions may serve as valuable reminders about sexual health concerns. For instance, some AIDS educators have noted that including positive references to condoms within the context of articles focused on sexual pleasure might help to eroticize condom use, thus increasing their acceptability.

Another point that's worth noting is that some of the topics categorized in this study as non-health sex topics could be—indeed, often are—considered to be sexual health issues. For instance, rape and sexual abuse, mentioned in 11% of the teens' magazine items and almost 8% of the women's magazine items, often are included in discussions of sexual health concerns. Items discussing sexual decision making, one of the most common topics in the teens' magazines (27.5% of all items), may well have included information about depression, self-esteem, and body image issues that are also sometimes included in the definition of sexual health (Huston, Wartella, & Donnerstein, 1998). For instance, an article on sexual decision making in the January 1993 issue of *YM* magazine ("Sexual Pressures: How to Decide What *You* Want to Do") talked about the emotional aftermath girls may face when sex "just happens" and about self-esteem conflicts that may arise when a girl feels that she is the only virgin in her peer group (Kohn, 1993). This item was coded as focusing on sex, not sexual health.

Nonetheless, as the discussion at the beginning of this chapter illustrates, adolescent girls today face significant sexual health risks, and because of those risks, they need accurate and comprehensive information about pregnancy and its consequences, contraception, abortion, and STDs, including HIV/AIDS. Some magazines are attempting to provide such information. For example, the December 1991–January 1992 issue of *YM* included an "Intimacy Report" that candidly discussed such issues as HIV/AIDS, STDs, and rape, as well as sexual decision making (Ganske, 1991–1992). Girls also may need encouragement to view those sexual health issues as at least equal in importance to sexual attractiveness and successful sexual performance. The results of this study suggest that sexual health issues may not be receiving that kind of emphasis, particularly within the pages of women's magazines.

As noted earlier, when we compare the total space and percentages of items focused on health versus non-health sex issues, the results suggest less attention to health issues in women's than in teens' magazines. Not surprisingly, the data revealed that the same was true for the likelihood of including numerous types of specific sexual health information; that is, whenever there were differences, teens' magazines were more likely than women's magazines to mention various specific sexual health topics. In general, the data suggest that the teens' magazines are more likely to provide sexual health information than are women's magazines. For instance, since January 1992, *YM* magazine has published annual special sections that include information about STDs and other sexual health concerns, along with articles about how to decide when to have sex for the first time, how to handle "morning-after angst," and how to respond to boys' sexual pressure.

Additional research will be needed to determine whether readers of women's magazines are affected by the balance of sex versus sexual health content. It seems plausible to argue that when women's magazines fail to mention sexual health concerns—either as the focus of articles or in the context of items focused on sexual attraction or sexual performance, the message to readers is that adult women need not worry about such issues, that unwanted pregnancy and STDs are primarily of concern for teenagers. As the readership statistics in Table 7.1 illustrate, girls 16 to 19 years old are far more likely to read magazines targeted to young adult women than they are to read the teen-targeted magazines. These girls also are more likely to be sexually active. Our study results suggest that older adolescent girls may find that just as they are becoming sexually active and their need for accurate, comprehensive sexual health information is increasing, the magazines they read are offering more encouragement to be sexually active but less information about protecting their sexual health.

Our data also suggest that even when the magazines do mention or focus specifically on sexual health issues, they may not cover these topics in much depth. For instance, pregnancy was the most likely of the sexual health topics to be coded as the primary focus of the items. However, the results showed that few specific pregnancy-related issues were mentioned in even 5% of the items. The implication may be that magazines' coverage of sexual health topics is more likely to appear in bits and pieces scattered throughout an issue or even across several issues, making it harder for readers to develop a complete understanding of these topics. The coverage of pregnancy also was sometimes sensationalized, as in an August 1995 issue of *YM* that included the cover teaser "Sex Shocker: I'm a Virgin, but I'm Pregnant!" (Lee, 1995).

There also is still significant room for improvement in the content of the teens' magazines. For instance, even the purportedly comprehensive sex, health, and intimacy reports now included in *YM* annually did not provide readers with much specific information about contraception. Thus, it may not be surprising that the vast majority of unintended pregnancies occur among couples who are using no contraceptive method, who choose less effective methods, or who are using a method inconsistently or incorrectly (Henry J. Kaiser Family Foundation, 1999.)

This study has provided us a closer look at the role magazines may play in adolescent girls' development of their sexual selves. More study will be needed, however, before we can truly understand how important—or unimportant—the sex-related content of magazines is to girls. As Steele and Brown (1995) noted, adolescents are not passive recipients of the messages in magazines or in any other form of media. We need to continue studying how teenage girls select and attend to the information magazines provide, how they interact with that information, comparing it with what they know about their own and others' experiences, and how—if at all—that content ultimately is woven into the fabric of girls' sense of themselves as sexual beings.

ACKNOWLEDGMENT

The authors would like to acknowledge the Henry J. Kaiser Family Foundation, which commissioned the study on which this chapter is based.

REFERENCES

Alan Guttmacher Institute. (1998). Facts in brief: Teen sex and pregnancy [Online]. Available: http://www.agi-usa.org/pubs/fb_teen_sex.html [1999, June 29].

American Social Health Association. (1995). Gallup study: Teens know more than adults about STDs, but STD knowledge among both groups is low [Online]. Available: http://sunsite.unc.edu/ASHA/press/galteen091495.html [1999, July 22].

Batten, M. (1996, April). The spectacular, infinite variety of sex. *Cosmopolitan*, 180–185.

Centers for Disease Control. (1998a, September 18). Trends in sexual risk behaviors among high school students—United States, 1991–1997. *Morbidity and Mortality Weekly Report, 47*(36), 749–752. Retrieved June 23, 1999, from the World Wide Web: http://www.cdc. ov/epo/mmwr/preview/mmwrhtml/00054814.htm.

Centers for Disease Control. (1998b, September). Young people at risk: Epidemic shifts further toward young women and minorities. *CDC Update* [No pagination]. Retrieved June 29, 1999, from the World Wide Web: http://www.cdc.gov/nchstp/hiv_aids/pubs/facts/youth.pdf.

Centers for Disease Control. (1998c, September). National data on HIV prevalence among disadvantaged youth in the 1990s. *CDC Update* [No pagination]. Retrieved June 29, 1999, from the World Wide Web: http://www.cdc.gov/nchstp/hiv_aids/pubs/facts/jobcorps.pdf.

Duncan, B. (1988, September). Not always for keeps. *YM, 36*(7), 48–51.

Endres, K. L. (1990, August 9–12). *Refocusing science news to reach a specialized audience: AIDS coverage, mobilizing information and teen magazines.* Paper presented at the annual convention of the Association for Education in Journalism and Mass Communication, Minneapolis, MN.

Ganske, M. J. (1991, December–1992, January). The intimacy report. *YM, 39*(10), 46–54, 107–108.

Gilman, L. (1990, November). I gave up my baby: One girl's agonizing story. *YM, 38*(9), 84–86.

Henry J. Kaiser Family Foundation. (1996). *The 1996 Kaiser Family Foundation survey on teens and sex: What teens today need to know, and who they listen to.* Menlo Park, CA: Author.

Henry J. Kaiser Family Foundation. (1998). Sexually transmitted diseases in America: How many cases and at what cost? [Online]. Available: http://www.kff.org/archive/repro/policy/std/std_rep.html. [1999, July 22].

Henry J. Kaiser Family Foundation. (1999). Contraception in the '90s [Online]. Available: http://www.kff.org/content/archive/1270/contra90f.htm. [1999, October 12].

Huston, A. C., Wartella, E., & Donnerstein, E. (1998, May). *Measuring the effects of sexual content in the media: A report to the Kaiser Family Foundation.* Menlo Park, CA: Henry J. Kaiser Family Foundation.

Kohn, K. (1993, January). Sexual pressures: How to decide what *you* want to do. *YM, 40*(10), 50–53.

Lee, S. (1995, August). I got pregnant and I didn't even have sex. *YM, 43*(7), 48.

Norvell, C. (1995, February). Sexually transmitted diseases: How much do you really know? *YM, 43*(1), 37.

Price, J. H., Desmond, S., & Kukulka, G. (1985). High school students' perceptions and misperceptions of AIDS. *Journal of School Health, 55*(3), 107–109.

Raffel, D. (1988, April). How to talk to your parents about contraception. *YM, 35*(3), 78–80.

Rice, R. (1996, May). The mysterious power of sex. *Cosmopolitan, 22*(5), 184–187.

Rodriguez, A., Norvell, C., & Haze, D. (1995, February). Superconfidential: Sex, health and intimacy, info for your eyes only. *YM, 43*(1), 33–39.

Ryan, G. R. (1995, September). The joy of quick sex. *Ladies' Home Journal, 112*(9), 88, 92.

Simmons Market Research Bureau, Inc. (1998). Simmons Teen-Age Research. New York: Author.

Simmons Market Research Bureau, Inc. (1995). Simmons Teen-Age Research. New York: Author

Snowden, L. (1986, May). How to enjoy sex with the lights on: 10 ways to give your inhibitions the night off. *Mademoiselle*, 158–161, 188.

Spivack, C. (1990, November). I kept my baby: One teenage mother's story. *YM, 38*(9), 87, 112.

Steele, J. R., & Brown, J. D. (1995). Adolescent room culture: Studying media in the context of everyday life. *Journal of Youth and Adolescence, 24*(5), 551–576.

Stephenson, T., & Walsh-Childers, K. (1993). Missed opportunities: Coverage of Magic Johnson and AIDS in magazines popular with teenagers. Paper presented at the annual conference of the International Communication Association, Washington, DC.

Sutton, M. J., Brown, J. D., Wilson, K. M., & Klein, J. D. (1999). Screen sex, 'zine sex and teen sex: Do television and magazines cultivate adolescent females' sexual attitudes? Paper presented at the annual conference of the Association for Education in Journalism and Mass Communication, New Orleans, LA.

Wysocki, D., & Harrison, R. (1991). AIDS and the media: A look at how periodicals influence children and teenagers in their knowledge of AIDS. *Journal of Health Education, 22*(1), 20–23.

8

Stuff You Couldn't Ask Your Parents: Teens Talking About Using Magazines for Sex Information

Debbie Treise
University of Florida

Alyse Gotthoffer
University of Miami

"YOU CAN'T POSSIBLY BE PREGNANT! I NEVER EVEN TOLD YOU ABOUT THE FACTS OF LIFE!!!"

Reprinted with special permission King Features Syndicate

In today's information age, teenagers are bombarded with information from a number of media sources. Many times they are actively looking for this information, particularly in cases involving health-related problems. Therefore, one of the more important functions of the media is to provide health information to those seeking it. The mass media can be tools for the promotion of healthy behaviors (Flora, Maibach, & Maccoby, 1989; Wallack, 1990). New media, such as the Internet, and cable television channels, such as MTV, have become popular sources of health information for teenagers (Mink, 1997). In addition, traditional media, such as entertainment television and newspapers, often cover health issues that may influence health-related knowledge and lead to healthier lifestyles (Montgomery, 1990; Signorelli, 1990).

Magazines are another important source of health information (Babakus, Remington, Lucas, & Carnell, 1991; Worsley, 1989). Readers often rely on magazines for information about health-related topics because they are perceived as credible sources (Halpern & Blackman, 1985). Women in particular have come to rely on magazines, as many report having trouble getting their doctors to give them detailed health information. In fact, some women feel that although physicians typically have a low regard for women's health issues (Fidell, 1980), magazines, as third parties, publish information about important topics such as contraception that are of interest to women, and therefore may be deemed credible sources by readers (Halpern & Blackman, 1985).

In addition to being a source of health information, magazines also have the ability to influence people's attitudes, knowledge, and beliefs about health topics. Brown and Steele (1995) found that entertainment media, including magazines, play an important role in shaping Americans' sexual beliefs, attitudes, and behaviors. Coverage of health issues by magazines also may lead to positive changes in people's health-related behaviors (Flay, 1987; O'Keefe & Reid-Nash, 1986).

Sexual and reproductive health are two of the more common and influential types of health information covered in magazines. Many magazine articles deal with contraception, sexually transmitted diseases (STDs), and sexual behaviors (Walsh-Childers, Treise, & Gotthoffer, 1997). As part of a recent national telephone survey conducted by the Henry J. Kaiser Family Foundation (1996) on men's roles in contraception, 1,000 adult men and women were asked about (a) the importance of men's and women's magazines in providing them with information about birth control, preventing STDs, and sexual health that they are not likely to get from other sources; (b) the importance of magazines as a source of information on reproductive and sexual health issues; and (c) how often they personally obtain information from magazines on these topics. Both men and women (75% of all respondents) said magazines were an important source of information on these topics. Younger adults were especially likely to cite magazines as an important resource for information about sexual health. For example, two thirds (64%) of respondents aged 18 to 24 thought men's and women's magazines provided them with information on reproductive and sexual health, and 87% said magazines were very important or somewhat important sources of information on these topics (Henry J. Kaiser Family Foundation, 1996).

Given the growing number of sexual health problems in the United States, it is important that sexual health information be disseminated. Although fewer young adults are engaging in behaviors that put them at risk for STDs (Ventura, Curtin, & Mathews, 1998), more than half of teens aged 15 to 19 have had sex (Henry J. Kaiser Family Foundation, 1996). AIDS has become the sixth leading cause of death for those between the ages of 15 and 24, and the second leading cause of death among those 25 to 44 (National Center for Health Statistics, 1995). The Centers for Disease Control also reported that among the more than 12 million people in the United States who acquire an STD each year, approximately 3 million are teenagers (Institute of Medicine, 1997).

The focus of this study was to determine what and how much teens are learning about reproductive health issues from the media, particularly magazines. What does this information mean to them? How do magazines help form and inform teens' attitudes about their own sexual identities and relationship issues? Do they learn "models" of sexual health?

Focus Groups and Question Guide

We conducted seven focus groups ranging in size from 8 to 12 participants. A total of 83 participants (32 males, 51 females), 13 to 24 years old, were recruited from three cities: Atlanta, Georgia, and Sarasota and Gainesville, Florida. Groups were divided by gender and age, separating younger teens (ages 13 to 18) from older young adults (19 to 24). Participants were chosen to reflect a mix of ethnic backgrounds, ages, incomes, and size of home city. They were recruited from private and public schools, theater groups, church groups, and inner-city recreation centers. Each focus group member was screened to assure media attentiveness, and, in particular, magazine readership.

The sessions lasted from 35 to 90 minutes each. Sessions were conducted in conference rooms and classrooms. Focus group moderators, professors and graduate students from a large southeastern university, began with introductions: a brief explanation of the purpose of the focus group, the moderator's role, and participant "rules."

Moderators used a standard interview guide that served as a semistructured "conversation starter" to ensure that the topic areas regarding what teens are learning about reproductive health issues were addressed.

Participants were encouraged to speak as freely as they wished and to guide the direction of the sessions toward what they felt was important to define their media interactions. Each focus group began with a general discussion of media use overall and progressed through use of magazines for health and reproductive health information.

Analysis Techniques

The sessions were videotaped, transcribed by professional transcribers, and coded by the first author of this chapter and a graduate student trained in qualitative methods. Transcripts were coded according to the method of analytic induction and comparative analysis (Glaser & Strauss, 1967) to find common patterns. Analytic induction involves scanning the focus group transcripts for themes or categories emerging across the data, developing a working scheme after examination of initial cases, then modifying and refining it on the basis of subsequent cases. Our emphasis was on construction rather than enumeration. To construct analytic categories, the coders reviewed each transcript line by line. Coders agreed on the final analytic coding scheme following independent analysis. As a validity check, the categories and their definitions were provided to a small number of the participants from each age group. No misinterpretations were reported.

FINDINGS

Broad categories emerged central to this study, including: overall media use, use of magazines for health information, information gained about health topics addressed in magazines, suggestions for potential improvements in article packaging, presentation style and source credibility, and suggestions for possible topics to be covered by magazines. (Because the focus of the study was print media, only those media, including both print and online versions of magazines, have been reported here; however, focus group members frequently discussed other types of media.)

Use of Magazines

Both male and female participants attended to a variety of media, including magazines, television, newspapers, books, radio, movies, and the Internet. Across all groups, magazines, television, and the Internet were cited as the media to which respondents attended the most. Overall, participants reported being heavy readers of the following magazines: *Cosmopolitan, Glamour, Seventeen, Elle, YM, Essence, Mirabella, Sassy, Teen, Vogue, GQ, Men's Health, Men's Fitness, Sports Illustrated, Vibe, Ebony,* and *Esquire.*

Young female participants listed the *Teen* and *Seventeen* chat rooms as sources of various types of information. Females overwhelmingly read magazines, whereas males appeared to attend more to the electronic media. Interestingly however, female-targeted magazines enjoyed a high secondary readership among our male focus group participants. Participants in three of the male focus groups said they read women's magazines to learn about women and to provide entertainment and conversation. One participant in the 14- to 18-year-old group said:

> . . . we were sitting around flipping through, I don't know which, and it was "How to make . . ." beauty tips like, "How to make your breasts look larger," "How to make your breasts look smaller," "How to make you look taller," "How to make you look shorter," "How to make your hair blond," "How to make your hair brown," and literally went through and made every single physical attribute a girl could possibly have sound bad. And basically, everyone reads those, right? [group agreement]

In the 19- to 24-year-old male group, one session member said, "It's good for conversation. It's good to have in the back of your mind." Similarly, another member of the same group said:

> I was reading an article in *YM* about how to pick up guys. Step One, look at a guy and smile . . . all these cheesy steps. It was so entertaining, but so off the wall. Some of it really does work, but some of it was like, whatever.

Learning From Magazines

Although many participants thought that sexuality and relationship issues are covered far more often than sexual health topics, all participants in the focus groups reported seeing numerous articles in magazines dealing with reproductive health issues. The most commonly cited topics were AIDS, HIV, condom use, breast cancer, birth control, pregnancy, prostate cancer, and, to a lesser extent, STDs. One participant in a female 19- to 24-year-old group said that she got information from new studies:

> You always find a new study. They always have a little thing in there about that. And articles that have you check yourself for breast cancer. You know, people go right to the advice columns for health. You know, they have interesting tips. Little information things.

Several female and male groups cited recent special issues or special sections in women's magazines like *Seventeen* that have addressed serious reproductive health issues in a thorough and forthright manner. Both males and females praised them and found them both informative and credible.

Referring to one of these articles, one female in the 13- to 18-year-old group explained, "It was like, 'Wow, this is great.' It had condoms, it had the IUD." Another female in the same group echoed, "I was really into it. I mean, like wow! This is really interesting. And then on the flip side, they had all the different diseases and what happens." And finally, another participant said,

> I just thought that was great! They were being so honest, and they were like, "You know, this is what happens, this is how you can treat it, and this is what you could have done to prevent it." And I thought that was an excellent article.

Many participants felt that they were learning from the life stories of everyday teens as presented in magazines. As one female in the 13- to 18-year-old session said, "I think that one good thing that magazines do when you read them is that they have put fear into the youth of America as far as AIDS. And I'd rather be afraid than dead, you know?"

Source of Confidential Sexual Health Information

Several females said they believe that magazine articles serve an important function for women who want information about reproductive health but do not have a family member or friend to speak with, or who want confidentiality. They may have problems and questions they want answered but "don't really want to ask anyone else." One female in the 19- to 24-year-old group said,

> I think sometimes you go to them because maybe you want it [information] confidentially. Like maybe personal health issues or something. But I think if you really, really needed to solve a problem, you would go to a doctor or a clinic of some sort.

Another female in the same group said that when she was in middle school she read magazines; "stuff you couldn't go to your parents about, you turn to a magazine article for the facts that it really answers."

Similarly, a female in the 13- to 15-year-old group said that magazine information on sexual health issues is helpful because: "I mean, if you don't know anything about it, it's, well, reading it is very interesting. I mean you can learn a lot from what they have to say instead of being embarrassed to ask your parents." The question-and-answer sections of magazines fulfill a similar confidante role for other members of the same group. One participant said, "Like if someone else had that problem and maybe they were too scared to write in or you never really, like, thought about it. You read about their problem, and you get the answer for them, and it helps you."

Catalyst for Discussions With Doctors

Almost all groups mentioned that they have used both magazine content and advertising to get reproductive health information. Women in several groups mentioned finding useful magazine articles about birth control and medication, and bringing those articles to the attention of their physicians. One woman cross-checked birth control advice given by her doctor against a birth control advertisement and found some risk-related information that the doctor had neglected to tell her.

Although most said they did not specifically look for health information, they said they read the articles if they "spark interest." However, some mentioned that because of the threats that young people face today, they just may look. For example, one male in the 19- to 24-year-old group said:

> The world we live in right now, the younger generation, I mean, we're into to-tally different kinds of diseases now. Like when you were our age, you didn't have to worry about a lot of stuff we have to worry about now. It's almost like another sexual revolution again right now. And you've got all this stuff to worry about. So, of course, every day you're going to see about how to pre-vent stuff from happening.

Realism

Many of the younger females said that to be more useful to them, magazine articles need to be more realistic so that they can relate to them. They had difficulty relating to the couple portrayed in the "perfect relationship" and to the "perfect teen who has the perfect, normal teenage life, with a boy-friend and tons of friends and popularity and all these clothes and stuff like that." Another female in the 13- to 18-year-old session added that it is diffi-cult for her when magazine articles

> assume that we all get straight As and are on the honor roll. What about those who are struggling with their grades? They assume you already know where you stand, you know where you're going with your future, and a lot of us don't.

In other words, the information about sexual health and reproductive health not only needs to be presented in a realistic manner, but it must also be relevant to their lives, to their age, or to a current issue in their lives (i.e., weight loss, pregnancy prevention, family illness). As one male in the 19- to 24-year-old focus group said:

> If it's something that relates to you, or somebody that you know, then it'll catch your eye. My mom has rheumatoid arthritis, so if I see an article on that,

I'll stop and read that. And, you know, things that relate to things that are personally relevant, I think, are the things that you stop on.

Packaging/Presentation Style

Participants discussed several physical layout techniques that attract them to a particular health article. Males and females in the 19- to 24-year-old groups wanted their information simple, short, and easy to read. A female in the 19- to 24-year-old group said that information is most readable when magazines

> make it more understandable for the readers. This is what could happen to you. This is the type of diseases that are out there. Here's some of the symptoms . . . what it does, what could happen to you. This could make you die.

Several in these same groups noted liking pictures, eye-catching headlines to attract them, and "little boxes of facts . . . that are quick to look at. You know, like, been there, done that."

A female in a 19- to 24-year-old focus group related, "That's why I like magazines. I like to get straight to the point. If an article is too long, I'd just rather go and talk to a doctor. It's more fast-paced." Similarly, another participant in the same group said:

> It's like when you read, you just want it cut and dried. This is what happened. This is how I'm going to cure it or whatever. I hate to get into all the medical technologies, such and such does whatever. I just want it short and concise. Tell me what I want so I can flip to the fashion articles.

In contrast, younger teens wanted more in-depth coverage than older participants. Many said they thought the articles they find are sometimes too superficial, and relationship issues are "cutesy" and "fluffy." Additionally, they said the issues are "presented weakly" and dealt with "politely" so that readers will not be offended and will be enticed to return to the magazine. Although these participants believed the information is factual, they also believed that it is edited to appear politically correct. For example, one 13- to 18-year-old focus group member said,

> I find the sexual topics they choose to write about will be very brief, very to the point—not offensively to the point. It's just okay—cut and dry. That's going on. Next subject. You know, written that way. And that's when I feel they should delve into it a lot more.

The question-and-answer sections were cited as an area where editors often equivocate so as not to insult readers. For example, one participant said, "I think it's very factual. I just think sometimes they're not as detailed as they could be. Like they'd like to just rush over a subject nicely and politely and not offensively, and that to me is why it's not satisfactory."

The presentation styles of articles also either encouraged or deterred teens from reading. Both the male and female groups did not enjoy an impersonal, "preaching" tone. Instead, the participants across all age-groups wanted to be able to sympathize with or relate to a person or a story; they said articles were more readable if they captured emotion or could be tied to a lived experience. A female from the 13- to 15-year-old group said that she enjoyed reading a "real-life story" because "usually they have a part on how you can prevent it from happening to you, how to get help. You can learn a lot about things happening to you."

Similarly, a male in the 14- to 18-year-old group said:

> I think we might be getting too many statistics, and we just need, like, a more personal attack. Like, I know I've had a friend that had been really affected by, like, an aunt that died by AIDS and he was just devastated. I know that what he has told me, he's never going to have unprotected sex. And I think that really works more than shoving statistics in our throat. If something really happens to you, if someone close to you dies, it's more effective than all the statistics.

Source Credibility

Almost every focus group raised the issue of source credibility. Of interest is the fact that, for health issues, mainstream women's magazines were seen as less credible than professional sources such as medical doctors. Many times our participants were unsure whether facts were "backed by some company," who is "putting out the reports," "who's funding the study."

Additionally, our participants did not find reports about health issues "as believable as in a scientific journal" because writers may not have proper qualifications. One male in the 19- to 24-year-old group related,

> The average health care reporter, I would wager, if you were to test them, compared to the average person on the street, they wouldn't know any more about health than the average person. And that's obviously going to lead to some problems.

Although not many of our female focus group participants read health magazines, they said they found them more credible than the mainstream women's magazines.

Reflecting a certain skepticism, a female in a 19- to 24-year-old focus group session said, "Even when the article shows it was written by a doctor, you can never be absolutely 100 percent sure that the doctor wrote the article or actually was quoted saying that." Clearly then, an opportunity exists for magazines to enhance credibility by incorporating and stressing medical sources with credentials in the area of the issue being covered.

Topic Suggestions

There were a number of topics participants felt should be covered. For example, many of the participants felt that the media placed too much emphasis on certain "glamour issues," like AIDS, breast cancer, and prostate cancer, to the exclusion of other relevant topics. While discussing the prevalence of coverage of HIV, one male from the 14- to 18-year-old focus group said, "All they ever talk about is HIV. Do they even realize how many more [STDs] there are out there? They just figure it's the biggest. If you protect yourself from HIV, you pretty much protect yourself from everything else."

In other words, participants wanted to see a broader range of topics covered. A male in the 13- to 15-year-old group said, "I wish there was more information about more things. Like there might be a certain STD that you don't know about. If you know about it, you can prevent it. But if you don't know about it, you can't prevent it."

Another participant in the 13- to 18-year-old group suggested that she would like "more articles about how to go about talking to your parents. And I'd like to see more articles for parents about how to talk to your kids."

Both male and female participants suggested the need for increased coverage of abstinence issues. For several female groups, remaining a virgin was a difficult choice in the peer-pressure world of adolescence, and media compounded the problem through heavy coverage of sex. Male participants also felt that abstinence issues needed to be covered more. One male in the 14- to 18-year-old group said:

> I have a problem with media and magazines. . . . they focus on the fact that people are getting AIDS, HIV, they're getting chlamydia, they're getting all the other ones, but they don't tell you how to keep from getting that. You know, they have the condoms, but they don't really preach about what really keeps you from getting that, which is abstinence. And they need to focus more on that.

Another topic females in particular wanted to see addressed in magazines was personal empowerment. They suggested less emphasis on sex, the need for sexual relationships, and the "pleasing-your-man syndrome." Many female participants believed that articles targeted to men begin from the premise of independence, but those directed to women mostly focus on "how to make your man happier." Instead, many of the participants wanted to see more articles empowering females to look to themselves as a source of fulfillment and satisfaction. In a 13- to 18-year-old session, one female suggested:

> ... there are a lot of girls who can't get boyfriends and there are a lot of guys who can't get girlfriends. There should be articles in there about you don't need to, you can go out with your friends. . . . there need to be other things like, you know, that's not the most important thing in your life right now. You have school ahead of you, sports, there is all this stuff that you can do and that should be the most important thing in your life. And that's what magazines do, they make a relationship the most important thing in your life.

Similarly, another female in the same group said that instead of stories devoted to pleasing the guy and "improving yourself" so that you will "make men wild," magazines need to be "doing stories on how to find, like find you and how it appears to you and how to enjoy yourself and how to enjoy life and stuff like that."

Young male and female participants were interested in more information on how to protect themselves during sexual encounters. What appeared to be missing for them, much like the empowerment articles, was information on how to deal with the issues surrounding condom negotiations. As one female suggested, what is needed is "how to protect yourself when you're having sex. [There is] a lot of how to wear condoms, but what if a guy doesn't wear one? I mean, you're gonna lose him. So you're gonna have unprotected sex."

Although the media were both damned and praised for their coverage of reproductive health issues, one young woman in the 13–18 focus group session presented an alternative view:

> It's easy to point fingers at media, I think. But there's also personal responsibility. Why should we blame magazines and TV and movies and books for not giving us exactly what we want when they are a fine source of information. They're not lying about anything, but they're not giving us exactly what we want to hear. Well, that's why we need our parents, or that's when we need educators, teachers . . . things like that to help us.

DISCUSSION

"Clearly, no knowledge is more crucial than knowledge about health. Without it, no other life goal can be successfully achieved" (Allensworth, 1993, p. 14).

Participants in this study clearly wanted sexual health information and wished for magazines to continue to provide this knowledge. The focus groups revealed that many participants did use magazines for acquiring sexual health knowledge and as a source for forming beliefs and attitudes about sexuality in relationships. Although many teens used the information they read in magazines to gauge their sexual health, norms, and expectations, many also resisted the manner in which the information is presented.

These teens were concerned with the depth and accuracy of articles and advertisements about sexual health. They discussed writer expertise, article layout, and magazine credibility as possible barriers to using magazines for information. Magazines are an important sexual health education tool, particularly for younger teens who wanted more in-depth information in the articles.

The rising number of sexual health problems in the United States, coupled with participants' reliance on magazines for information, presents many opportunities for magazine editors. Even though many people use magazines as information sources, the results of this study suggest a number of areas where magazine editors could improve their coverage of sexual health issues.

Include In-depth, Detailed Coverage
of Sexual Health Issues

Sexual topics often are sensitive. In fact, many times they are so sensitive that they are not discussed or taught; therefore, many teens look to magazines for that information. Research has shown that sex education actually increases healthy sexual behaviors and leads to a delay in first sexual intercourse (Education, 1993). However, groups such as the Moral Majority have continued to increase their efforts to deter sexual health education in schools, under the assumption that if young people do not learn about these behaviors, they will be less likely to engage in them (Whitehead, 1994).

This has a number of implications for young people, who are at high risk for STDs, AIDS, and pregnancy. Many current sex education programs actually include less material on topics such as contraception than they did a generation ago (Hopkins, 1993). Although most schools have sex education programs, many restrict their education to the teaching of abstinence. And although this certainly is the safest alternative to these ailments, it is not the most realistic, as large numbers of teens continue to engage in sexual activity (Alterman, 1996).

Although the younger participants in this study agreed that abstinence should be stressed, they also pointed out that because teenagers are having sex, they need information about preventative measures other than just abstinence. Those in the 13- to 15-year-old focus groups agreed that although teaching abstinence is important and necessary, this does not mean that topics such as STDs, birth control, and contraception should be left out.

Include Articles About How Parents and Teens Can Talk to Each Other About Sexual Health

Many young people do not get sexual information at home because parents often do not feel comfortable discussing sexual issues (Gordon, 1996). Similarly, the younger participants in our study said that many times they had trouble going to their parents for sexual information either because their parents were uncomfortable talking about sexual matters with them or because they were too embarrassed to talk to their parents. Some suggested they would benefit from articles about how to talk to parents about sexual health, as well as articles for parents about how to talk to their children.

Provide More Detail About Contraception and Disease

Some participants argued that although contraception and disease are covered, often they are glossed over so as not to be "offensive." However, if teens are relying on magazines as sources of sexual health information, then editors may want to reconsider how they provide this information for them.

Include Articles Written by Reliable Sources and Include Statistics

Participants in the 19- to 24-year-old focus groups questioned the expertise of the writers of sexual health articles. Many said that they wonder where the writers get their information and whether vital pieces of information are left out due to the writers' lack of knowledge. Some argued that just because the magazine identifies an article's author as a doctor, there is no guarantee that this is so. Articles written by doctors and other reliable sources, as well as statistics and information from well-known sexual health organizations, could serve as credible educational tools and would increase readers' confidence in the magazine.

Convey Information That Is Accurate and Complete

Some participants were concerned about who the magazines' gatekeepers are and what influence they exert over the content of sexual health articles. They were suspicious that some articles are written so as not to offend advertisers or other sponsoring organizations. Therefore, many did not completely trust the information in magazines. Indeed, research has shown that sponsors and advertisers can exert a powerful influence over editorial content (Baker, 1997; Cranberg, 1993). One study found that magazines containing cigarette advertising were less likely to report the hazards of smoking

(White & Whalen, 1986). Given that, it is not unreasonable for readers to assume that magazines accepting ads for birth control methods, for example, may not report the potential harm these methods can pose.

Include Articles Written for the "Typical" Reader—Not the "Perfect" Reader

Teens are evaluating, interacting with, and internalizing the information as it applies to their lives. They asserted that many of articles talk about "the perfect teen" rather than average teens like themselves. To make sexual health relevant, these articles need to contain relevant situations for the reader. Positive behavior change can be expected only if the target can relate to the problem being addressed (Rosenstock, 1974).

Change the Focus of the Stories to Include Real-Life Situations

Many participants said they often empathize with the people in the stories, making the situation or problem more real to them. If the reader can relate to the character and his or her problem, this may increase perceived susceptibility to the particular ailment or disease described, which may, in turn, result in healthier behaviors (Becker, 1974; Rosenstock, 1974).

Provide a More Visually Appealing Story

Stories that are copy heavy and tedious to read are more likely to be ignored in favor of articles that highlight or bullet important information. Young adults in particular want all of the necessary information presented in a straightforward manner. For them, time is a factor, and they prefer articles in an easy-to-read format.

Provide Useful Information on a Broader Range of Topics

Focus group participants complained that frequently articles about sexual health are superficial and filled with "cutesy" layouts, rather than helpful information. They said magazines need to focus on presenting them with truthful, detailed stories about sexual health and birth control, so they can use this information in their decision making. For teens, the layout of the story is secondary to useful information.

Participants felt it is necessary to cover a broader range of topics, not just AIDS, which they perceived to be the most commonly covered topic. For example, they want to learn about the symptoms and prevention of other prevalent STDs, such as herpes and chlamydia. As one participant said, "If you know about it, you can prevent it. But if you don't know about it, you can't prevent it."

Include Articles Related to Personal Fulfillment, Self-Confidence, and Independence

Some of the older female participants suggested that magazines need to include articles about personal empowerment and teaching women to focus on themselves, not on men. This sentiment was echoed by the younger teens as well, who suggested that magazines focus too much on getting a boyfriend and not enough on being independent. They added that most magazine articles center on pleasing a man, rather than on pleasing yourself. Magazines clearly have an opportunity to educate their readers on these important, neglected issues.

Although participants felt magazines could improve in a number of areas, some also said they are pleased with the information magazines currently provide. A number of participants said they find useful information both in editorial content and in advertisements for reproductive health products. Direct-to-consumer advertising of prescription drugs has continued to increase in magazines, giving consumers more information about health products than ever before (Carpi, 1997). Advertisements for products such as birth control methods contain a great deal of information about risks, benefits, and alternative methods (Treise, Gotthoffer, & Walsh-Childers, 1997). Thus, magazines may be doing a good job of making this information available to readers through advertisements as well as through accompanying articles.

In essence, this study suggests a valuable formula for magazine editors. As providers of sexual health information, there is enormous potential for magazines to educate readers about their sexual health. The results of this study suggest that the need for sexual health information varies with age. Teenagers prefer detailed, accurate stories to which they can relate. Many of them do not receive sexual health information in school or from their parents, so they rely on magazines to tell them what they need to know. Therefore, magazines directed toward this age-group need to continue covering issues such as teen pregnancy, STDs, and birth control, and should consider doing so in greater depth.

This study provides a closer look at how teens interpret, use, evaluate, and interact with the sexual health information presented in magazines. As a mass media tool, magazines have the power to provide much-needed information to a number of target groups and may have the ability to contribute to the reduction of unhealthy sexual behaviors.

REFERENCES

Allensworth, D. D. (1993). Health education, state of the art: Working together for the future. *Journal of School Health, 63,* 14–20.

Alterman, E. (1996). Neutering America: Repression of sex information. *Nation, 262,* 6–7.

Babakus, E., Remington, S. J., Lucas, G. H., & Carnell, C. G. (1991). Issues in the practice of cosmetic surgery: Consumers' use of information and perceptions of service quality. *Journal of Health Care Marketing, 11,* 12.

Baker, R. (1997, September/October). The squeeze: Some major advertisers step up the pressure on magazines to alter their content—Will editors bend? *Columbia Journalism Review, 36,* 30–36.

Becker, M. H. (1974). The Health Belief Model and personal health behavior. *Health Education Monographs, 2*(1), 324.

Brown, J. D., & Steele, J. R. (1995). *Sex and the mass media.* Menlo Park, CA: Kaiser Family Foundation.

Carpi, J. (1997, July 14). Could drug ads be bad for your health? *Investor's Business Daily,* p. A1.

Cranberg, G. (1993, May 15). Newspapers face more advertiser pressure than they report. *Editor & Publisher, 126,* 52–53.

Education: More sex in class, please. (1993, November 7). *Observer,* 24.

Fidell, L. S. (1980). Sex role stereotypes and the American physician. *Psychology of Women Quarterly, 4,* 313.

Flay, B. R. (1987). Evaluation of the development, dissemination, and effectiveness of mass media health programming. *Health Education Research, 2,* 123.

Flora, J. A., Maibach, E. W., & Maccoby, N. (1989). The role of media across four levels of health promotion intervention. *Annual Review of Public Health, 10,* 181.

Glaser, B., & Strauss, A. (1967). *The discovery of grounded theory.* Chicago: Aldine.

Gordon, S. (1996). What kids need to know: Most parents and school systems fail to provide teenagers with relevant sex education. *Psychology Today, 20,* 22.

Halpern, D. F., & Blackman, S. L. (1985). Magazine versus physicians: The influence of information source on intentions to use oral contraceptives. *Women & Health, 10,* 9.

The Henry J. Kaiser Family Foundation. (1996). *The 1996 Kaiser Family Foundation survey on teens and sex: What they say teens need to know, and who they listen to.* Menlo Park, CA: Author.

Hopkins, E. (1993). What kids really learn in sex ed. *Parents, 68,* 46–49.

Institute of Medicine. (1997). *The hidden epidemic.* Washington, DC: National Academy Press.

Mink, E. (1997, October 10). Teens & freedom: MTV on "right" track. *New York Daily News,* p. 114.

Montgomery, K. C. (1990). Promoting health through entertainment television. In C. Atkin & L. Wallack (Eds.), *Mass communication and public health* (pp. 114–128). Newbury Park, CA: Sage.

National Center for Health Statistics. (1995). *Advance report of final mortality statistics, 1995.* Hyattsville, MD: U.S. Department of Health & Human Services, Public Health Services, CDC.

O'Keefe, G., & Reid-Nash, K. (1986). *The uses and effects of public service announcements.* Paper presented to the National Partnership to Prevent Alcohol and Drug Abuse, Washington, DC.

Rosenstock, I. M. (1974). The Health Belief Model and preventive health behavior. *Health Education Monographs, 2*(4), 354.

Signorelli, N. (1990). Television and health: Images and impact. In C. Atkin & L. Wallack (Eds.), *Mass communication and public health* (pp. 96–113). Newbury Park, CA: Sage.

Treise, D., Gotthoffer, A., & Walsh-Childers, K. (1997). Ten years of reproductive health advertising in women's magazines. In D. D. Muehling (Ed.), *Proceedings of the 1997 American Academy of Advertising Conference* (pp. 194–201). CDC Press.

Ventura, S., Curtin, S., & Mathews, T. (1998). *Teenage births in the United States: National and state trends, 1990–1996.* Hyattsville, MD: U.S. Department of Health & Human Services, CDC.

Wallack, L. (1990). Improving health promotion: Media advocacy and social marketing approaches. In C. Atkin & L. Wallack (Eds.), *Mass communication and public health* (pp. 147–163). Newbury Park, CA: Sage.

Walsh-Childers, K., Treise, D., & Gotthoffer, A. (1997). Sexual health coverage in women's, men's, teen, and other specialty magazines: A current-year and ten-year retrospective content analysis. Henry J. Kaiser Family Foundation. Menlo Park, CA.

White, L., & Whalen, E. (1986). How well do American magazines cover the health hazards of smoking? *ACSH News and Views, 7*, 8.

Whitehead, B. D. (1994). The failure of sex education. *Atlantic, 274*, 55–70.

Worsley, A. (1989). Perceived reliability of sources of health information. *Health Education Research, 49*, 367.

Girls in Print:
Figuring Out What
It Means to Be a Girl

Jennifer Wray
Ohio University

Jeanne R. Steele
University of St. Thomas

Be sexy, but not a slut. Stand up for your self, but don't be a bitch. Be thin, but don't have an eating disorder. Play sports, but don't be too aggressive or competitive. Be smart, but not a nerd. Believe in yourself, but don't be conceited. Speak up, but don't be too loud or have a big mouth. Be original, but not weird. These are some of the stupid standards people expect from girls and women.

They've made this perfect girl that we all strive to be. But we don't have to fulfill anyone's sick idealized dream. You DO have the freedom to be what you want to be.

—Marjorie, 15 (From "What it means to be a girl," *Some Misplaced Joan of Arc,* http://www.angelfire.com/sk/misplaced)

In 1997, *Seventeen* magazine boasted a circulation of more than 2.4 million young women and a pass-along readership of more than 8 million, capturing more than 53% of the teen magazine market. Among teen girl magazines, *Seventeen* was and still is the leader. It is the oldest and most widely circulated of the "teenzines" (Evans, Rutberg, Sather, & Turner, 1991, p. 100). Because *Seventeen* touches the lives of so many adolescents, it is important to consider the kinds of social messages and values young women may derive from the magazine. If one can believe the magazine's own publicity, "*Seventeen* has always been more than simply a magazine. It has been a rite of passage for young women in America for over fifty years, guiding them on an exuberant tour of self-discovery and helping them to express themselves in creative and positive ways" (*Seventeen* media kit, 1997). *Seventeen*'s tools for self-discovery, according to its media kit, are "the latest trends and most critical issues affecting its readers, including personal relationships, style and beauty, guys, college, cars, music and pop culture."

Despite the magazine's persuasive rhetoric, a small but vociferous group of young women take issue with *Seventeen*'s and other mainstream teen magazines' perspectives on what it means to be a girl. These resisters are the publishers of "zines," self-published, underground publications written for a variety of reasons, none of which have anything to do with making a profit.

In this chapter, we compare what the archetype of teenzines, *Seventeen*, has to say about being a teenaged girl with what "zinesters" say. This is accomplished through a qualitative content analysis of 16 issues of *Seventeen*—September 1997 through December 1998—and 30-plus zines. Content per se, however, is not the sole focus. Rather, much of the chapter is dedicated to giving voice to the motivations and attitudes of the zine publishers we contacted. Another important voice is that of author Jennifer Wray. At 20, she is a member of the age-group targeted by the glossy teen girl magazines. And, as a student, she provides a counterbalance to the "ontological privilege" (Currie, 1997) accorded to typically White, middle-class academics like coauthor Jeanne Steele, her professor. As coauthors, we were interested in exploring what teens think about (in Wray's words) *Seventeen*'s "unholy trinity of fashion, beauty, and overemphasis on heterosexual relationships." And we wanted to know whether zines offer teen girls an alternative way of looking at themselves as sexual human beings.

Whereas *Seventeen* is highly commercial and enforces the norms of heterosexuality and reliance on "looking good" for the opposite sex, with all that the label implies, zines are more open to alternative life experiences. The driving force behind *Seventeen* is profit and maintaining the status quo; the driving force behind zines is creative self-expression. Zines are personal publications. Often they are dedicated to topics that appeal to specific groups, from pop culture enthusiasts to straightedge vegans (people who do not use drugs or consume any animal products or by-products). Zinesters write about their passions, not about subjects designed to capture a particular demographic group for advertisers. The noncommercial aspect of zines means that the writer/publisher does not cater to anyone's needs but her own. Despite the blatant bias of most zines, Elissa Nelson (1997) suggests that they may actually provide a wider range of perspectives than commercial teen magazines, since "no one using their voice—i.e., publishing a zine—can be rendered invisible by incorrect representation." Like Nelson, we love "the honesty that comes with the rejection of any idea of journalistic integrity, unbiased perspective, reporter's distance." These qualities do not seem to be of much importance to the publishers of teen magazines.

Another quality inherent in zines is the sense of community they create. Writes Angela Richardson (1996): ". . . zines have facilitated the networking of many young feminists across the country" (http://www.library.wisc.edu/libraries/WomensStudies/fc/fcrichrd.htm, 1996). Although mainstream media have given zines some news coverage, they generally are discovered through word of mouth, friends, or a review in another zine. There is little sense of hierarchy in zines, with readers often contributing as much as the creator (Nelson, 1997). Writers often offer their zines free in exchange for a copy of a reader's zine. If a reader does not have a zine to trade, the cost is typically very low, from the cost of postage to a couple of dollars.

Originally created by science fiction fans in the early 1930s, zines became more widespread in the 1970s when, according to Vale (1996), "empowered by the 'DO IT YOURSELF' (DIY) philosophy of the punk rock revolt . . . thousands of dissatisfied, savvy malcontents [we]re expressing their authentic thoughts and feelings via the cheapest print medium available: xeroxed zines" (p. 4). The spread of easily accessible photocopiers, the introduction of computers into schools and homes, and, most recently, widespread access to the Internet made publishing accessible to people with few resources, adolescent girls among them.

Many of the zines produced by young women today are the products of a movement called Riot Grrrls, founded in 1991 by a group of feminist punks in Olympia, Washington, and Washington, D.C. (Altculture, 1999). The group protested the male-dominated structure of both the punk scene and society at large. They subverted the notion of how a "girl" should look by adopting aspects of "little-girl" looks, but with a twist. Some would write words like "rape" or "slut" on themselves with permanent markers to confront passersby with what they perceived to be mainstream society's bigotry (Chideya, 1992). Riot Grrrl bands also proved that they could rock just as hard and just as loud as their male counterparts.

Although short-lived, the Riot Grrrl phenomenon had a profound impact on zine making. The group formed the nucleus for a supportive network of like-minded young women, and zines provided an easily accessible medium for them to communicate with one another.

The content and perspectives of zines remain true to the spirit of punk, addressing issues that are not typically covered by mainstream media. The punk movement encouraged people to create and perform, even if they had no conventional talent. Similarly, zine writers typically are not professionals at what they do, and often their work is imperfect, with typographical errors and misspellings.

If most zines are money-losing propositions created by people who have little formal training in writing, what motivates women to make them? Through our research, we discovered that often writers create zines because they do not see anything in mainstream media that addresses their lives. Traditionally, women have had limited access to the money and the means to control media. For young women who do not see themselves reflected in the pages of *Seventeen* or other mainstream magazines, zines offer a way to affirm and legitimate their experiences. Zines allow women to express what they see as the truths about their lives, in contrast to mainstream magazines, which often misrepresent what it is to be a woman. The multiplicity of voices in the world of zines allows the recounting of a variety of experiences and perspectives.

THE STUDY

The study was undertaken at Ohio University as an Honors Tutorial College study project during spring quarter 1999. Because the time frame was short, we decided on a research design that was simple yet capable of generating rich data. Our goal was to compare *Seventeen*'s messages about desirable behavior for young women with zines' editorial content on the same topic. Although messages about sexuality were our primary interest, we took the stance that a girl's sexual self could not be severed from her social self, or psychological self, or physical self. In other words, sexuality must be considered in the context of the whole person.

Seventeen was selected as the magazine to be studied, not only because it is the largest and oldest of the teenzines but also because we were already familiar with its contents and could borrow a complete set of issues from the local public library. Sixteen issues—from September 1997 through December 1998—were considered. In addition to pragmatic considerations, we justified our sample because, of all the mainstream teen girl magazines (e.g., *Savvy*, *Sassy*, *Teen*, *YM*), *Seventeen* has been studied more thoroughly and more frequently than any other (Carpenter, 1998; Currie, 1997; Duke & Kreshel, 1998; Durham, 1998; Evans et al., 1991; Peirce, 1990).

Finding a reasonably representative sample of zines proved more complicated. Seeking female zinesters over the Internet sounded like a quick way to draw a convenience sample; however, we quickly learned that using keywords like "girl*," "teen*," and "zine*" yielded a multitude of pornographic Web sites but few zines. (The asterisk assured a search for every version of these words. For example, the identifier "teen*" would search "teen," "teens," "teenager," and "teenagers.") Through trial and error, two criteria for finding teen girl zines were identified: The participating teen had to identify her work as a zine and she had to identify herself as an adolescent girl. Because identities can readily be disguised online—for commercial or other reasons—we tried to ensure that "real" girls were linked to all zines referenced. This was accomplished by communicating directly with the publishers of identified zines.

"gURLpages" (http://www.gurlpages.com), a web domain owned by the search engine Lycos and sponsored by dELIA'S clothing catalogue, contained a listing called "Browse gURLpages," which yielded many helpful sites. The gURLpages were created by young women who took advantage of dELIA's invitation to create personal home pages on the Internet free of charge. Though it does not specifically say that it is a women-only entity, the name of the Lycos' site implies as much. The gURLpages site was helpful not only for its index of zines, but also for its message board, where anyone can post a question or a comment. Interested parties can respond in both a public forum, by posting a message on the site, and privately, by replying through e-mail. Wray posted a message inviting participation in the study on the gURLpages' bulletin board and bulletin boards on other sites—Pander Zine Distro (http://members.aol.com/GopanderGO) and Chainsaw Records (http://www.chainsaw.com)—frequented by teens. Her post asked for e-mail responses from girls who had created zines and were interested in talking about them.

Zines that met our criteria were also found through web rings. Web rings are links that people place on their Web sites to connect visitors to other sites that share a common theme or philosophy. One general zine web ring as well as a teen zine web ring, two Riot Grrrl web rings, and several other pro-grrrl rings were found. Not all of the Web sites had online versions of zines, however. Some of them simply listed contact information for ordering paper zines. About 20 requests for paper zines were sent out, but only five print zines were received in the mail. The low return rate may have resulted from the fact that many zines fold after a few issues, and several years had passed since some of the lists were posted. This is likely an indication of the transitory aspect of zines, both online and in print.

Zine editors were also found through word of mouth. Once identified, zine editors were e-mailed a list of questions and a request to pass on the questions to anyone they thought might be interested in the study. This snowball recruitment method elicited about six responses. Two young women who did not have immediate access to e-mail printed hard copies of the questions and returned their responses by mail. Within about 6 weeks, 33 respondents, aged 11 to 20, were involved in the study. After the girls responded to the first round of questions, which were a mixture of demographic and general questions about their sexual experience and feelings/motivations about zines, Wray followed up with more in-depth probes about the girls' attitudes toward zines and teen magazines. The girls tended to respond more freely and with more comments to these follow-up questions than to those in the first round, perhaps because they viewed their e-mail correspondence as a conversation with a newfound friend.

Unfortunately, like mainstream magazines, zines are still written primarily by and for members of the White middle class. Despite the wide net cast, only two study respondents were non-White. One was African American, the other Hispanic. This underrepresentation of minorities may be due to zines' connection with punk, a movement that also was primarily White and middle class. Literacy and access to technology also may have been factors in the low minority response.

When approached, the zinesters had a lot to say. Kara, 19, said that commanding a piece of the media via zines is "empowering to girls like myself who are unimpressed with the way the system works." For Kara, zine making is a way to resist a media community that "caters to the ignorant." Instead of allowing the media to speak for young women, these young women have created their own media to speak for them, one that accurately voices their opinions and ideals.

The girls we communicated with had basically the same reasons for starting a zine. Fifteen-year-old Claudia summed up the motivation of many of the respondents:

> I guess I was just sick of sitting back and watching things happen. I wanted to make something that someone could see, and could cause someone to really think about their life and their self. I wanted to make a difference. I wanted to change the world (yes, I'm still naive enough to think I can change the world). And, since I live in a little suburban hellhole, the most global thing I could think of was the [I]nternet, where anyone, even certified idiots like myself, can voice whatever works they have. So I taught myself HTML and put things that really mattered on my pages, things that were REAL to me. And I love my page to bits and pieces, even though it's not the greatest.

When asked what they believed to be the best thing about zines, a number of girls expressed resistance to the consumer culture favored by most mainstream magazines, saying that a lack of a profit motive on the part of the creator was a good quality. "[Zines are] not driven by profit. They're pure, for lack of a better word," wrote Rachel, 18, who also said she liked the proactive, not commercially driven aspect of zines. Zines offer "[u]nbiased opinions on real issues, ad-free reading material, an impetuous [sic] to action," she said. Kate, 18, said she felt that the relative ease of creating zines was the best aspect, because, she wrote, "They're DIY. They allow anyone a medium to express whatever they want. They give the people who make them a sense of accomplishment, of having their voices heard."

The personal nature of a zine is its biggest achievement, others said. Readers feel close connections to the writers of zines because, generally, zine stories are written in an informal, first-person voice. *Seventeen* treats teen girls as if they are a homogeneous collection with the same life experiences; zine writers are more likely to acknowledge differences. The personal nature of zines allows individuals to write about their unique (or sometimes quite typical) life experiences. No matter how "weird" a girl may feel, she can find a zine that speaks to her. Zines give young women who are going through similar life experiences a venue in which to communicate with one another. Often, the writing in zines can be more powerful than that in commercially driven magazines because, "[there is an] actual person speaking behind them. Not just some 30-something that thinks she knows what it's like to be a teen girl. With zines the person writing them is writing from experience," said Colleen, 13.

Sasha, 16, wrote that the originality of zine topics made zines superior to mainstream magazines: "... [T]he articles aren't the same thing over and over like traditional magazines," she argued, facetiously citing imagined articles in *People* magazine (The most intriguing people of all time!) and *Seventeen* (10 Best Makeovers!).

BEING A *SEVENTEEN*-STYLE GIRL

In the case of *Seventeen*, you *can* tell a book (or a magazine) by its cover. The magazine's covers promise young girls that if they purchase *Seventeen*, they can be perfect and truly happy. With cover blurbs like "True crush to true love: make it happen" (September 1998) and "How to get the perfect haircut" (August, 1998), who can blame teenage girls for using *Seventeen* as a guidebook? Its cover lines suggest it has all the answers for whatever a teen girl desires.

Though *Seventeen* is popular with many young women, a majority of the girls interviewed, even those who read or had subscriptions to the magazine, felt that it did not address the life of a teenage girl realistically. Wrote Claudia, "I read them [teen magazines] sometimes when I'm bored but the utterly mindless portrayal of teenage girls in this society kinda gets to me. I am not one of those girls. I never will be. I am me, and that's what keeps me going." Anya, 16, the only African American respondent, who once had subscriptions to both *Seventeen* and *YM*, agreed, writing, ". . . mass media does not aim anything at me specifically (it's always to Blacks, or teens, or teen females, but never all three)." She went on to describe teen magazines as being "horrible, but in a funny way. I'll read them in the grocery store if I need a laugh. . . ." Anya was not the only one to read teen magazines with a sense of irony. Jessica, 17, wrote, "My sister used to subscribe to them all, so I had access. They were pretty humorous [in an ironic sense] but sad. I still pick them up in amazement that they haven't changed a bit."

Emily, 16, also said that she read *Seventeen* and other teen magazines. Wrote Emily, "[I read them] to use their negative messages [and] turn them into positives in my personal zine." Often girls will clip images or text from magazines and then respond to them on the pages of their zines. For example, girls will take photographs from the magazines and use them to question the use of thin models in the magazines. They can scan in the images (in the case of online zines) or cut and paste them (in the case of print zines) and manipulate them in their zines.

Seventeen can seem like a lifesaver for girls trying to navigate the turbulent seas of adolescence but unaware of any other options. Krissie wrote that she was once a reader because, "When I was younger I was drawn to the flashy covers and promises of foolproof 'how to get a boyfriend' tips, quizzes to reveal whether or not you're a good friend, or anorexic, or a square, or whatever."

Seventeen remains popular, the girls wrote, because many people are not aware of alternatives other than different (but remarkably similar) mainstream teen magazines.

Another aspect of *Seventeen* that the girls found problematic was that although the magazine is called "*Seventeen*," in reality its readers tend to be much younger than 17. Wrote Sara, 16:

> [*Seventeen* is] marketed at (and read by) the typical teenage girl who doesn't own her sense of self. Who doesn't know who she is or who she truly CAN BE. This is why most teen magazines are so dangerous—they get girls who will listen to them telling them that the most important thing right now is to get a boyfriend and make him happy.

Sara's 14-year-old sister, Beth, agreed: "[Typical readers are] girls who are adolescent and are having a hard time defining their emotions, and themselves, and are therefore insecure, so it is easier to manipulate them."

Sara and Beth were not the only girls who believed that *Seventeen*'s typical readers were younger than 17. Said Sasha,

Actually, I think that the magazine is more marketed toward the younger set, like 11- or 12-year-old girls, 'cause they look up to teenage girls. [The advertisements in the magazine are] for Dream Phone and Girl Talk Date Line, board games made by Parker Brothers and Golden, respectively, and stuff like that. You see teenage girls about 15–17 playing with this stuff [in the ads], when in reality the ages of the girls who buy these things is more like 10–12.

Krissie said that she felt the magazine was geared to appeal to middle-class White girls in middle school or high school.

In a piece called "How NOT to make a magazine, otherwise titled, How to be like all the other girl/woman magazines," Christy Brown (1999), 20, criticizes the media for the fashion spreads inside the pages of teen and adult women's magazines. Writes Christy, "Starve 3–10 already anorexic models for a few weeks." "Buy out any magazine that teaches girls to be assertive, confident, and happy."

Girls Are Obsessed With Guys

In the 16 issues of *Seventeen* in our sample, teasers about "guys" and heterosexual relationships were given prime placement on the covers of the magazine. With few exceptions, such "sell lines" consistently appeared on the upper left-hand side of the page, a place that typically draws readers' eyes first and consequently is dedicated to selling the magazine. The magazine also attracts readers to sell lines about guys by using the largest size type on the page. Also, "guy" cover blurbs often were highlighted by the use of contrasting (not black) color. Teaser topics ranged from "550 guys on first moves, secret crushes, & the worst thing a girl could do" (October 1997) to "10 reasons guys dump you (that have nothing to do with you)" (June 1998) to "Violent boyfriends: how to protect yourself" (August 1998).

When they buy *Seventeen*, girls buy into a belief system that says having a successful romantic relationship should take ultimate priority in their lives. Girls can achieve such a relationship, they are told, by buying the "right" products, looking the "right" way, and acting in the "right" manner. Right behavior follows the conventional norms governing male–female relationships. Duke and Kreshel's work (1998; along with our own research) indicates that girls do have the ability to interpret and resist the messages that *Seventeen* sends. Yet it is unrealistic to believe that girls do not, in some way, internalize the negative messages they receive, no matter how hard they try to resist.

Embarrassing oneself in front of a "crush" (colloquial for love interest) is the ultimate humiliation for a girl, according to *Seventeen*, as evidenced by the large number of such stories in "Trauma-rama," a section devoted to "tale[s] of embarrassment and horror" (*Seventeen*, February 1988, p. 20). Although not explicitly labeled as such, "Trauma-rama" works as a gendered behavior guide. Young women share their mistakes so that other young women can learn from them. Young women who are aggressive, who approach their crushes, usually take a fall in one way or another (many times literally). Girls are taught to be passive, not aggressive. The "Trauma-rama" section reinforces the idea that a young woman is easily discredited. Everyone is watching the girl, waiting for her to do something embarrassing.

To illustrate: One girl wrote that

> It was the first day of school and I was feeling so great that I found the nerve to talk to my crush. . . . But I got so nervous that I missed the first step completely, and then proceeded to slide all the way down the stairs on my butt. My crush just laughed and went off to class. (*Seventeen*, September 1997, p. 40)

Clearly, the girl was humiliated by her fall, but she offered no judgment about the boy's insensitivity. In a similar vein, another girl wrote about an incident that occurred when she was buying pretzels at the food court in the mall and spied her crush in line in front of her. "I tried to act calm and collected," she wrote, "and I even talked to him like I was cool. I even gave him my phone number. But then as I walked away, I slipped on the floor. . . . My crush laughed hysterically, and I felt completely humiliated" (*Seventeen*, June 1998, p. 18). Another girl wrote that when she embarrassed herself, "The worst part was that the guy I'd had a crush on since sixth grade, who was sitting in the next row, started laughing. It was the most embarrassing day of my life" (September, 1997, p. 40). So, in *Seventeen*, girls are embarrassed and boys laugh in a teenage echoing of what feminists have identified in content analyses of women's magazines as "ideological constructions that work to define women's understandings of their experiences in ways that guarantee the reproduction of patriarchal definitions of the social world" (Currie, 1997, p. 455).

Typically criticized, along with other teen and women's magazines, for being a vehicle of "women's subordination" to men (Currie, 1997, p. 456), *Seventeen* in recent years has attempted to give its readers a more progressive (read "feminist") view of sex and relationships. But for the most part, its attempts fail. For example, in the September 1997 issue, Jennifer Braunschweiger advises teens: "It's way more misery and heartache to have a rotten boyfriend than no boyfriend at all." Yet in the same piece she also writes: "The player [a womanizer] is so cute, so charming and friendly, it's no wonder you spend your every waking minute thinking about him" (p. 132). Only when a boyfriend is "rotten" is a girl better off without one. To the writer, it is acceptable and normal to be obsessed with a guy. Because young girls look to *Seventeen* for guidance (Durham, 1998), they will learn that there is (and should be) nothing more important in a girl's life than thinking about her love interest, even if he sometimes turns out to be a jerk. It's no surprise that having a guy is so important, for as Braunschweiger writes, ". . . everyone else thinks you're cool since he's into you" (*Seventeen*, September 1997, p. 132). She tells readers that a girl's social standing is determined by her sexual relationships.

On another occasion, *Seventeen* offered readers "75 reasons why life without a boyfriend rocks" (February 1998, pp. 44–45). The list imagined a reader who let her boyfriend control her life. *Seventeen* suggested that without a boyfriend, "You never need to worry that your platforms make you too tall" or "You can go from hippie chick to body-pierced punk girl without worrying about what he thinks." Staff writer Forman told girls that, "Life is stressful enough without some guy pressuring you to go further than you want to." Meant to be funny, the list incorporated a traditional subtext (e.g., being without a boyfriend is not a desirable position to be in). Ten of the 75 reasons why it is good to be single involved flirting or making some sort of sexual contact with other guys. Although *Seventeen* occasionally suggests that it is okay to be single, the magazine's overarching theme is that the only good reason for getting out of a relationship with one man is to find a new one.

The boy-obsessiveness of *Seventeen* can be found in a multitude of similar articles. "*Seventeen* survey: 550 guys tell all" helps readers understand what makes young men tick. "Crush cures" recommends that the best way to deal with an unrequited crush is to "Transfer your affections to a more worthy suitor" (November 1997, p. 64).

Although *Seventeen* is intended to appeal to young women, the majority of zinesters in this study gave a resounding "No" when asked if teen magazines portray women positively. Both Sara and Colleen said that they had problems with *Seventeen*'s emphasis on dating as a high priority for girls. Wrote Sara:

> Teen magazines offer an image that womyn [sic] are supposed to be "beautiful," sweet, thin, underestimate themselves, fake their personalities just so they can "get the guy," when truly, the only guy (or girl) worth having is the one who will accept you for yourself.

Colleen wrote:

> [*Seventeen* portrays women positively] to an extent. . . . [However,] you don't need a guy. If that's what it takes to be the quintessential teen girl, then count me out. I'll date when I'm good and ready. Not because some teen magazine says that 13 is a great age to start or whatever it may say.

Seventeen gives girls a voice about controversial matters in a column called "Whatever," which allows young women to vent their frustrations about different topics. For example, in the September 1997 issue, a girl identified only as H. C. B. wrote in to ask, "How come when guys are bossy, they are leaders, but when girls are bossy, they're bitches?" (p. 130). While this question lent itself to opening a forum for debate and challenging the status quo, the magazine provided no response. Despite some signs that the magazine is trying to be less subservient to normative femininity (Duke & Kreshel, 1998), it nevertheless gives ink to the same ideas over and over. Guys fear commitment, are sexually aggressive, and mysterious. Girls are romantic and worried about their appearance. They are primarily concerned with guys and what guys think of them. *Seventeen* teaches girls that by buying the right products and behaving the right way, a girl will be able to get the guy she wants.

Girls Are Heterosexual

A glaring silence in *Seventeen* is its lack of attention to people who are not heterosexual. In the 16 issues of the magazine studied, the issue of same-sex attraction was mentioned only twice, once in an advice column, and once in a section called "Voice," which purports to tell the stories of true events in the lives of ordinary young women. In a "Voice" article titled "Close Friends," Noelle Howey (1997) talked about two sexual experiences she had as a young girl. To lure readers into the story, *Seventeen* placed a quote pulled from the text of the story in the center of the page in big bold letters. It read: "My mom explained to me that lots of girls experimented with other girls, and it was totally normal." The words "lots of girls experimented" were printed in boldface type and the words "totally normal" were printed in orange type, graphically emphasizing the normalcy of sexual experimentation. Howey told readers that as a fourth grader, she and her then best friend used to "play lips together kissing" (p. 80), and then when she was 13, she "made out" with another best friend.

Howey's story provided the magazine with an excellent opportunity to address the spectrum of sexuality that characterizes people's sexual orientations—bisexuality and lesbianism included. However, *Seventeen* avoided taking such a potentially controversial stance. Instead, Howey—whose story undoubtedly was edited to fit the magazine's editorial concept—alluded to future heterosexual relationships for the girls, never once suggesting that there could realistically be an alternative sexual lifestyle. *Seventeen* further weakened the story's potential for changing homophobic attitudes toward lesbianism and bisexuality by using a story that had obviously occurred in the not-so-recent past. The author's mention of Duran Duran, a group popular in the early 1980s, was a dead giveaway.

Rachel saw *Seventeen* as being decidedly heterosexist. She wrote:

Occasionally in the dentist's office I'll pick one up if I see some mention to queer issues, which is almost never because queer issues are virtually ignored by mainstream youth media. (And to think people wonder about high suicide rates, homelessness rates, and drug/alcohol abuse by queer youth. . . . Alienation, perhaps?)

Along similar lines, the young women expressed a reluctance to commit to heterosexuality, especially if they had little sexual experience. Said Erin, 15, "I don't agree with classifying sexuality, because people can switch around their preferences all the time and they shouldn't be stuck in a category. I guess I'm heterosexual, maybe crossing over a bit to bisexual." Of the 33 girls in our sample, 3 were, as Susan referred to herself, "just plain queer"; 16 were heterosexual; 6 felt that they fell somewhere between heterosexual and bisexual; and 8 were bisexual. Liz, 17, categorized herself as "omnisexual, but a practising [sic] asexual."

The girls' openness toward sexuality and gender was reflected in their zines.

Teresa Molter, in her zine, "*go teen go*," showed an astute ability to identify what is wrong with the mainstream media. She wrote:

> What needs to die: Objectification of teenage girls in mass culture, in this case, teen magazines. The idea that all teen girls need to:
> a) be thin/skinny/go on diets (In order to please boys, fit into clothing made for ten-year-olds, be supermodels, sell their bodies, etc.),
> b) have a boyfriend/be attached to a boy/need a boyfriend in order to feel validated by other teens, society, parents, etc.

Few people would argue with Teresa's belief that "Love is good." But she moves beyond that notion by making a more radical assertion, saying "[L]ove does not have to be strictly and only boy/girl. Love is what you feel! Experimentation is fun. Sex isn't all it's hyped up to be, and remember that you have to love yourself before you can truly love someone else." (http://gurlpages.com/goteengo/)

Girls Are Monogamous

In her zine, *Salza #6* (www.gurlpages.com/zines/zoonbaby/Salza6.html), Cleopatra Jones, 19, publishes an account of sexuality that would never appear in the pages of *Seventeen*. The author, Peanut Butta, writes:

> This year it's become painfully clear to me what damage American society can do to a young grrrl . . . In exploring my own and seeing my friends explore their own sexual capacities this past year, I feel confused as to what the "normal" sexual encounter should be like. I've derived from society that a "nor-

mal" sex life happens like this: Have a steady boyfriend around age 16, experiment a bit. Then, as you get older—have a few more boyfriends, mess around some more—maybe even lose your virginity, but ultimately grow up, marry a man, and stay true to him. But that's not the way that things have been happening at all. It seems to me like "normal" girls shouldn't be interested in porno, sex, kink, but they are. Maybe the nice ones won't admit it, but we're all CURIOUS.

In *Seventeen*, girls routinely write in seeking advice for their relationship problems. In the "Diary of a cheater," however, zinester Peanut Butta [a pseudonymous name the writer chose] doesn't look for advice but rather a forum for sharing her own experience: "Anyone who's ever cheated knows there is guilt, but deep down, there is a feeling of liberation. That is why I do it." (http:www.gurlpages.com/zines/zoonbaby/cheater.html) This is not a girl sharing a sob story with a magazine. This is a girl who is not ashamed of resisting the heterosexual norm.

Leslie, 20, also explores alternative views of sex and relationships in her zine, *Vertiginous Pulp*. A majority of the zine is concerned with a love triangle consisting of Leslie, her boyfriend, Mike, and an unnamed ex-boyfriend. Writes Leslie:

> There is always so much confusion behind friendship. So many definitions behind what it means to be "just friends" and what it means to be "dating." The definition is kept between the two lovers, friends, or whatever. We come to those terms for ourselves, not those around us. . . . Friends do whatever they want, whatever makes them happy, so long as others aren't being hurt. . . . It can be as simple as "I love you."

Leslie struggles to come to terms with both of the young men involved, never really resolving the matter.

Girls Are Appearance-Conscious Consumers

The girls saw dual purposes in *Seventeen*. The magazine, they said, works both as a social control and as a way to encourage consumerist, beauty-centric behavior. In *toxic.snapple* (http:www.toxic.snapple.org), Amelia P. has included a piece called "Why I hate TV." She derides mass culture for dictating what is the proper behavior and appearance for a woman. Writes Amelia:

> . . . women are taught from birth to want to be pretty. From frilly pink dresses to the legions of teen fashion magazines, the message is crammed down their throats for so long that nobody even thinks to question it. It becomes a non-issue, an accepted way of thinking.

It is difficult to imagine *Seventeen* castigating an appearance-conscious society in a like manner.

Wrote Sara, "[*Seventeen*'s goal is to] sell a sense of security to teenage [sic] girls. So that they know their 'places' in society, so that they don't have to feel the need to rebel against the system." The system was seen by teens in the study as promoting traditional beauty standards (being thin, being White) and sex roles (heterosexual and monogamous). Kate saw *Seventeen*'s purpose as enforcing the status quo:

> Though some of them do have some positive articles now and then about self-esteem and health concerns, etc., they're just contradicted by the photos on the following pages of beautiful, skinny, blemish-free women that all look so happy . . . which is the ideal that most readers of those mags try to attain. The other main purpose: buy buy buy.

Sasha also saw the purpose of *Seventeen* as being "[t]o sell products. Every other page is like, 'Let's see how Julie looks after her makeover!' And they go into detail to tell their readers what products are used and stuff. 'For her eyes, we used L'Oreal eye shadow #5.'" Rachel addressed the same idea even more succinctly. *Seventeen*'s purpose, she said, is "Profit, duh."

The teens attributed their peers' attraction to *Seventeen* primarily to the influence of consumerism on society. Writes 20-year-old Nikki:

> It really frustrates me that teen magazines are so popular. I think their popularity comes from a vicious circle. They make young girls feel like they "need" certain things or need to be a certain way and then tell them how to become that way. The girls become so self-conscious that they keep turning to magazines for more info.

Kate wrote that she felt that *Seventeen* remains popular because:

> [M]ost teens are trained to be materialistic consumers, and magazines like *Seventeen*, *Teen*, *YM*, etc., are just guidebooks to all the latest fashions, accessories, and makeup they can run out and buy. They also encourage teenage girls to jump on every new trend, which I personally think leaves them with little individuality or identity as far as lifestyle goes.

Seventeen's own literature confirms the importance of consumerism to the magazine. In a 1997 promotional piece sent to potential advertisers, the magazine wrote, "[P]artner with *Seventeen* and make sure your brand is reaching these powerful consumers as they are developing their identities and establishing their own personal loyalties. . . ." For *Seventeen* and its parent corporation, K-III Magazine Publishing Corporation, girl power apparently means buying power. *Seventeen* teaches girls that successful relationships can be achieved through good looks and appropriate (normative) behavior, as well as by consuming advertised products. In a 1997 press release, the magazine brags about having a high percentage of editorial matter, yet its own numbers said that 56% of the magazine was devoted to advertising.

BEING A WOMAN THROUGH ZINE-COLORED GLASSES

Zines, like traditional magazines, cater primarily to White, middle-class teens; however, they do allow for more diversity in representing what it means to be a woman. When posed with the question, "What does it mean to be a woman?" some of the girls shied away from answering, finding the issue too abstract. Others preferred to avoid categorization and definition. Still others, however, saw strength in womanhood. Said Elizabeth, 15: "To be a woman, you are real to yourself and you never give up—you are strong, outspoken and alert." Fifteen-year-old Jane also saw womanhood as power. She said, "I think it means a lot of things. I don't feel I'm limited—in fact, I think I feel even less limited than some males because I can express my thoughts and emotions more, and I don't feel compelled to 'be cool.' "

In 15-year-old Marjorie's zine, she tackles a subject that is generally relegated to the "Sex & Body" section of *Seventeen*, her first period. Writes Marjorie:

> The day I got my rag was the best day of my life. . . . I felt in control that day; a young woman able to make her own choices. . . . I loved everything about it— from the sight of it to the smell of it, everything.

In the piece called "Scarlet Perfection," Marjorie has taken an event that is often considered dirty and embarrassing and made it powerful.

IF ZINESTERS EDITED *SEVENTEEN*

When asked how *Seventeen* and its cohorts in the teenzine industry could be improved, the girls had a number of suggestions. Said Rachel:

> I would take out the advice columns that tell you to make a fool out of yourself to attract boys. (Like this one column that told girls to fall flat on their faces to appear helpless and attract boys—"Damsels in distress or pathetic teenyboppers? You decide.")

Sasha echoed Amelia's words, saying, "[*Seventeen*] would be for all types of girls and less focused on image, how you look, vanity, or getting boyfriends and garbage like that." Jen, 14, suggested that *Seventeen* should both shift its focus away from an emphasis on trying to achieve a heterosexual ideal and not enforce gender distinctions:

> I would make it more accessible to lesbians and bi[sexual] girls, more accessible to guys, gay or not, no more how to get a date quizzez [sic], no more how to know if he really likes you shit, just honesty, friendship, and opinions. A place to vent, to be accepted, not a place to be shamed and boy-obsessed.

Mandy saw the ideal *Seventeen* as a potential forum for activism. She wrote:

> I'd get rid of all the "Oh listen to this embarrassing thing that happened to me in class" articles, and put instead articles on proactive stances against racism, sexism, classism, and all of the other awful "isms" out there, plus ways to help out in your community, etc.

The girls expressed mixed feelings when asked if zines should stay underground. Opinions were divided almost evenly; however, the general sentiment seemed to be that it would be acceptable for zines to become more widely known by other teens if their content did not change. Wrote Sasha: "Anyone should be able to write a zine if they have something good to write about. There will always be zines that are more 'underground' than others, and zines that come out of different scenes and different walks of life." Kate agreed that zines should be available to more people, writing:

> . . . a lot of important messages that zines have to offer are often squashed because the people who really need to hear them don't have access. . . . I think it's nice to have this underground place, but it would help society more if it WEREN'T so underground.

Maybe one solution to the dilemma of mainstream versus underground is for *Seventeen* to take some of its cues from underground publications. Surely the magazine's writers, editors, and publishers should be able to obtain copies of zines, whether they be in print or online. Perhaps this would encourage *Seventeen* to understand zinesters rather than simply co-opt their style. By reading zines and seeing what girls have to say, the creators of *Seventeen* might come to a better understanding of the lives of young women.

During the study, Rachel said that *Seventeen* is and will remain popular because, "there will always be vain, airheaded teenybopper girls about." But what if the growing numbers of girls creating zines could convince *Seventeen* that its old-fashioned and out-dated way of addressing girls is, frankly, out of style? There is no doubt that the perennially popular magazine wields a great deal of power. Perhaps *Seventeen* could use its influence

to encourage girls to take a more proactive outlook. The magazine has resources (a large budget, a dedicated, well-educated staff, and access to millions of readers) to touch the lives of millions of impressionable young
women in a more positive, open-minded way. Although change will not
come overnight, it can come. *Seventeen* may not ever be the magazine that
zinesters wish for, but hopes for improvement should not be seen as mere
wishful thinking.

REFERENCES

Altculture (1999). *Riot grrrls*. [Article]. Retrieved December 12, 200, from the World Wide Web:
    http://www/altculture.com/aentries/r/riotxgrrrl.html.
Brown, C. (1999). *How NOT to make a magazine, otherwise titled, How to be like all the other
    girl/woman magazines*. Author. Retrieved May, 1999 from the World Wide Web: http://www/
    chickpages.com/zinescene/nekochan.
Carpenter, L. M. (1998). From girls into women: Scripts for sexuality and romance in *Seventeen*
    magazine, 1974–1994. *The Journal of Sex Research, 35*(2), 158–168.
Chideya, F. (1992, Nov. 23). Revolution, girl style. *Newsweek*, p. 84.
Currie, D. H. (1997). Decoding femininity: Advertisements and their teenage readers. *Gender &
    Society, 11*(4), 453–477.
Duke, L. L., & Kreshel, P. J. (1998). Negotiating femininity: Girls in early adolescence read teen
    magazines. *Journal of Communication Inquiry, 22*(1), 48–71.
Durham, M. G. (1998). Dilemmas of desire: Representations of adolescent sexuality in two teen
    magazines. *Youth & Society, 29*(3), 369–389.
Evans, E. D., Rutberg, J., Sather, C., & Turner, C. (1991). Content analysis of contemporary teen
    magazines for adolescent females. *Youth & Society, 23*(1), 99–120.
Forman, G. (1998). 75 reasons why life without a boyfriend rocks. *Seventeen*, Feb. 1998, pp. 44–45.
Howey, N. (1997). Close friends. *Seventeen*, Nov. 1997, p. 80.
Nelson, E. (1997). What makes it a zine? http://members.aol.com/erickalyn/elissa.html.
Peirce, K. (1990). A feminist theoretical perspective on the socialization of teenage girls through
    Seventeen magazine. *Sex Roles, 23*(9/10), 491–500.
Richardson, A. (1996). Come on, join the conversation!: 'Zines as a medium for feminist dialogue
    and community building *Feminist Collections, 17*(3–4), pp. 10–14. Retrieved December 12,
    2000, from the World Wide Web: http://www.library.wisc.edu/libraries/Womens Studies/
    fc/fcrichrd.htm.
Seventeen media kit (1997). New York: K-III Magazine Publishing Corp.
Vale, V. (1996). *Zines!* Vol. 1. San Francisco: Author.

III

MOVIES, MUSIC,
THE INTERNET

CHAPTER

10

Romancing the Script: Identifying the Romantic Agenda in Top-Grossing Movies

Carol J. Pardun
University of North Carolina–Chapel Hill

Zits

Reprinted with special permission King Features Syndicate

THE POWER OF FILM

> *When only fourteen years of age, I fell in love with one of my classmates; I
> can remember that after seeing Rudolph Valentino in 'The Sheik of Araby,'
> I would try to make love to my girl as he did to the heroine, but I guess I
> was a miserable failure.*
>
> —from Herbert Blumer's 1933 diary,
> quoted in Jowett and Linton (1980)

Decades later, teens still swoon over love scenes (try talking to a love-
struck teen about why she loved *Titanic*) and they still emulate what they
see in the movies ("Yeah, Baby" is the appropriate *Austin Powers* response).
Movies have captured the imagination of viewers in ways available to no
other medium. As Berger (1997) has said: "Audiences, through the willing
suspension of disbelief, become emotionally affected by these images,
sounds, and music, and also often identify with characters in films and
learn something about themselves and about life in the process" (p. 147).

As the quote at the beginning of this chapter shows, this is not a recent
phenomenon. Early in the 20th century, the viewing public eagerly accepted
the unique experience of sitting in a movie theater, to such an extent that
by 1923, fifty million viewers went to the movies each week (Jowett & Linton, 1980). Most would agree that ever since, Americans have maintained
their love affair with the Big Screen even though today they often are
watching movies on their television sets.

Hoffner and Cantor (1990) argue that "the information viewers receive
about characters is scripted, designed specifically to produce a particular
impression in a relatively efficient manner" (p. 65). Bachen and Illouz (1996)
have said that movies (as well as television and advertising) may be an especially significant source of information because of their redundant and
formulaic characters. In other words, the characters, plots, and scenes
within movies provide frames for the movie viewer to categorize patterns
of images. If this is the case, it is important to investigate what messages
movies provide for viewers. The focus in this chapter, then, is on romantic
interactions in movies—surely not the only important script that movies
present, but one that can leave important impressions on an impressionable movie market: teenagers. Although the characters on screen can influence both teens and adults, the intentional and "larger-than-life" saliency of
the characters may have a bigger impact on adolescents who are still forming their worldviews.

Teens are the largest demographic segment of moviegoers (Strasburger,
1995). As early as 1979, nearly half of all moviegoers were less than 21 years
of age (Jowett & Linton, 1980). We've all read newspaper stories about 14-
year-old girls who have viewed *Titanic* dozens of times, or 13-year-old boys

who skipped school to wait in line for hours, hoping for tickets to the opening show of *Star Wars: The Phantom Menace.* Surprisingly, however, little systematic research has been conducted on teens and movies.

UNDERSTANDING SCRIPTS

Researchers have long been interested in understanding the messages that the media portray and have used various means to frame their understanding. It is clear from earlier research that the teen years are when we learn about the relationship between sex, romance, and love. Bachen and Illouz (1996) found that 94% of the young people in their study looked to television and 90% to movies for love stories. In contrast, only one third said they looked to their mothers and only 17% looked to their fathers to learn about romantic love. Peirce (1993) has argued that teen girls look to magazines to understand the love "script."

Jeffres (1997) has shown that the less people know about an issue, the more likely they are to rely on the media for interpretation of that issue. Therefore, since teens find it difficult to talk to authoritative figures about sex, romance, and love, they may be particularly cognizant of those images in the media, as they look for understanding—and interpretation.

Fiske and Hartley (1978) argued early on that in order to understand the impact of images on a particular audience you must first know what the images are. Although they were primarily concerned with television, their arguments are applicable to other media as well. They have said that the media "reflects, symbolically, the structure of values and relationships beneath the surface" (p. 24). Furthermore, they looked at content analysis as a way of bridging the gap between reality and "reality" as shown in the media.

Others have understood the viewer's interpretation of this gap as framing. Goffman's (1974) study of frame analysis conceptualized the viewer as understanding images through a limited selection of frames. He has argued that we can think of frames as a set of rules, or a way of helping us know how to interpret an image. In this chapter, the focus is on describing the "rules" for romance as seen in top-grossing movies as a way to understand the message of romance that would penetrate a media-impressionable audience's frame for understanding. A few researchers have attempted to categorize the rules for romance (although not within the movie genre). But we also can learn them by watching the interactions in "media life." Surprisingly, few have systematically tried to understand these scripts as portrayed in the movies—that larger-than-life media form that teens spend hours attending to and from which they learn their own set of rules about how to make sense of the romantic game.

ROMANCE IN THE MEDIA

Much of the attempt to understand the messages portrayed in movies has
been a matter of counting images (often focusing on stereotypes, violence,
or overt sexual conduct) using quantitative content analysis. For example,
Signorielli (1997) found that more than one third of the female characters in
movies were motivated by the desire for a romantic relationship and two
thirds of those characters talked about romance (p. 11). Brown, Greenberg,
& Buerkel-Rothfuss (1993) summarized several movie content studies, finding that every R-rated film included at least one nude scene and that R-rated
movies contained more sexually violent scenes than X-rated movies.
Strasburger (1995) found that in the most popular movies there were 32
times more unmarried sexual encounters than episodes involving husband
and wife. Taken together, a picture evolves of the typical moviegoer viewing overt sexual scenes, most often between unmarried couples. These
studies are an important contribution to the literature, but still needed is a
systematic way to code for interactions among characters if we are to understand the rules or "scripts."

As adults who already have a general knowledge of sexual scripting, we
understand that to get to the point of coitus, other things typically must
happen first. But teens, who are hesitant to ask adults about the scripts, do
not necessarily know the appropriate rules for the scripts. How are those
"other things" before coitus portrayed on film? Are teens being exposed to
the kinds of images that will allow them to see how the sex act is connected
to other acts? In other words, do movies provide romantic scripts as well as
the more obvious—and recognizable—sexual scripts?

Typically, those other acts are some kind of romantic interlude that includes events or a context that sets the stage for the more obvious sexual
advances. Researchers are beginning to explore events surrounding overt
sexual messages as portrayed in the movies. For example, Bachen and
Illouz (1996) interviewed 183 children, ages 8 to 17, in an attempt to understand what children consider romantic in the media. The children believed
that romantic love was indicated when it was represented with clear romantic codes, such as hugging and kissing, and when the scene deviated
from daily life, such as showing a couple at the beach (p. 293). The work of
Bachen and Illouz is an important first step in understanding what is portrayed on screen from a teen's perspective, but it is necessary not only to
record what viewers think is important, but to record and categorize the
images to which they are responding.

Herbert Blumer's research (cited in Bachen & Illouz, 1996), posited that
movies play "an important role in helping adolescents to mentally visualize
and anticipate future behavior through day-dreaming activities" (p. 282). So,

what is the romantic landscape provided for the adolescent moviegoer today? What romantic scripts do adolescents see?

METHOD

It is surprisingly difficult to identify specific movies that attract a large teenage market. Occasionally, a blockbuster like *Titanic* focuses the attention of masses of teens. Other movies created specifically for the teen market (such as *10 Things I Hate About You* or the surprise 1999 summer hit *The Blair Witch Project*) also attract attention. But teens view more than teen-specific movies or heavily promoted films. Unfortunately, no publicly available list of teens' top movies exist. Therefore, I analyzed the 15 movies listed by the Simmons Market Research Bureau as movies that teens viewed in large numbers during 1995, because this was the most recent available list and coincided with the data "Children Now" Kaiser study discussed elsewhere in this book. Some of the 15 movies, such as *Clueless*, focused on teen relationships, but others, such as *Independence Day*, did not. The movies used in my study are listed in Table 10.1.

The movies were coded for incidents involving all interactions (whether romantic or not) between males and females, using a qualitative approach called *grounded theory* as developed by Strauss and Corbin (1990). Using this approach, the researcher views the films with no previous expectations other than a general understanding of "looking for romance," and al-

TABLE 10.1
Movies Included in Analysis

- *Clueless*, PG-13, for sex-related dialogue and teen use of alcohol and drugs
- *Batman Forever*, PG-13, for strong stylized action
- *Dangerous Minds*, R, for language
- *Casper*, PG, for mild language and thematic elements
- *Pocahontas*, G
- *Ace Ventura, When Nature Calls,* PG-13, for crude humor

- *Jumanji*, PG, for menacing fantasy action and some mild language
- *Apollo 13*, PG, for language and emotional intensity
- *Father of the Bride—Part II*, PG, for some mild language and thematic elements
- *Toy Story*, G
- *Nine Months*, PG-13, for crude humor
- *Mr. Holland's Opus*, PG, for mild language
- *Now and Then*, PG-13, for adolescent sex discussions
- *Happy Gilmore*, PG-13, for language and some comic sexuality
- *Congo*, PG-13, for jungle adventure terror and action and brief strong language

Note. Ratings explanations taken from the IMDB Internet movie database, us.imdb.com.

lows the data to "speak for itself." Previous studies (Ward, 1995) have created the coding list first and then looked for the previously defined sexual or romantic themes. Strauss and Corbin's (1990) approach flips the process and groups characteristics with the goal of eventually describing the themes. Strauss and Corbin describe their method this way:

> A grounded theory is one that is inductively derived from the study of phenomenon it represents. That is, it is discovered, developed, and provisionally verified through systematic data collection and analysis of data pertaining to that phenomenon. Therefore, data collection, analysis, and theory stand in reciprocal relationship with each other. One does not begin with a theory, then prove it. Rather, one begins with an area of study and what is relevant to that area is allowed to emerge. (p. 23)

In other words, rather than trying to see if the sample of movies contains what researchers have already defined as romantic interaction, the grounded theory method involves the researcher searching through the data, looking for ways for the data to reveal insights on the meaning of romantic interactions. This method is done by a triple-level analysis: open coding, axial coding, and selective coding.

Level One Analysis—Open Coding

Strauss and Corbin (1990) describe open coding as categorization of the data by comparing for similarities and differences of the data. By examining the data line by line, an initial attempt to organize the data in a logical manner is attempted. It is important to remember that the categories that emerge in the first stage are merely preliminary categories that may change on further analysis.

Level Two Analysis—Axial Coding

During the second level of coding, the data are examined a second time in light of the emerging categories created during the open-coding phase. The goal is to link appropriate subcategories with shared traits from other categories, paying particular attention to action-oriented verbs that often provide the interactional links.

Third Level of Analysis—Selective Coding

The goal of the selective-coding level is to decide what the core concept or concepts of the data are. In essence, all the analysis from the first two levels of coding are boiled down to one or two key conceptual findings about the data.

Analysis was begun by identifying every encounter (whether romantic or not) between two people of opposite sex. (It was beyond the scope of this study to attempt to identify same-sex relationships.) This resulted in 309 total encounters for all movies in the sample. Each incident was recorded and described as accurately as possible on a separate index card. At this point, no attempt was made to explain what any of the encounters meant, but rather to simply describe the situation. For example, in the movie *Independence Day*, an incident occurring 30 minutes into the movie was recorded as:

> *"Teen boy and girl embracing in van. He puts moves on her to get some action— 'this could be our last night on earth.' They start to kiss, are interrupted."*

RESULTS

Level I—Open Coding

After all 309 incidents were recorded, the first level of coding began. This was done by organizing the 309 index cards into various piles with other index cards that described incidents containing similar ideas or phrases. As discussed earlier, this was done without creating categories prior to investigating the data. In other words, the first card was examined and a category created that could describe that card; it was then placed in the first pile. For example, in the incident described above, a category of "Foreplay That Could Lead to Intercourse" was created. The card was then placed in that pile. A second card was then selected, compared with the first to see if it fit in the first category; if not, a second category was created to include that second card. This procedure was continued for all 309 incident cards. Although it would have been possible to end up with 309 categories, patterns quickly emerged, resulting finally in 30 initial categories. These categories are listed in Table 10.2. After this open-level coding, several initial observations were made:

1. Very few of the incidents contained any kind of direct reference to sexual intercourse. In light of other writers' comments about the amount of sex in contemporary movies, this was somewhat unexpected. For example, there was only one incident of a couple in the act of making love (the couple was married), one incident that took place shortly after intercourse, and two incidents that involved one person asking another to have sex and being refused.

2. There is a plethora of conversation—rather than action—about romantic relationships in the movies. One third (33%) of all coded incidents involved talking rather than action. Although many of these conversations fo-

TABLE 10.2
Categories Created After Level 1—Open Coding

• Everyday Married Life	• Flirtation
• Sexual Jokes	• Unrequited Love
• Nudity	• Foreplay
• Jealousy	• Couple Breaking Up
• Sacrificial Action	• Dancing
• Opposite Sex Teaches Partner a Lesson	• Kissing
• Deception	• Romantic Touching (holding hands, hugging)
• Danger	• Exciting News
• Everyday Male–Female Conversation	
• Intercourse	
• After Intercourse	
• Opposite Sex Unable to Do Something	
• One Partner Invites Sex	
• Romantic Couple Arguing	
• Dreams	
• Discussion of the Future	
• Reflection of the Past	
• Third Party Discussion of Romantic Partner	
• Peaceful Togetherness	
• Romantic Talk	
• Romantic Look	
• Declaring Love	

cused on romance, nearly half (44%) of the incidents were arguments between romantically linked partners.

3. Much of the romantic encounters took place off screen. Kissing (38 incidents), touching (64 incidents), and arguing (45 incidents) were the most common encounters coded in these movies. However, third-party discussions, where two people talked about the relationships of other people, were also quite common, with 23 such incidents coded. For example, in the movie *Pocahontas*, Pocahontas's father talks to her about a warrior who has asked to marry her. Pocahontas tells her father the warrior is too serious; her father argues that he would be a good provider. The potential groom is offscreen during the encounter. This incident was coded as "Third-Party Encounters."

Level 2—Axial Coding

After all incidents were placed in appropriate initial categories, axial coding began. For this stage, all first-level categories were examined to see if, by moving into a more abstract level of thinking, some categories could be combined. For example, at the first level, three separate categories focused on something other than the present situation ("Reflection on Past," "Discussion of Future," and "Dreams."). An episode from *Twister* helps to clarify the kind of incident that was recorded as "Reflection on Past":

> *She tries to pick up fallen sensors from ground and he drags her away. He confronts her, tells her that she's obsessed and has to stop **living in the past** and to look at what she has in front of her.*

An episode from *Father of the Bride—Part II* illustrates the initial "Discussion of Future" category: *"Wife talks to husband about fear of having menopause. They discuss **the changes that await** them. Nina talks about worrying that George **might want** a new wife."*

A "Dream" incident was coded in *Pocahontas*: *"Governor Radcliffe **imagines** finding gold in the New World and his reception back at Court afterwards. In his **daydream**, the ladies of the court all kiss his hand and swoon over him."*

These three first-level categories were placed in a new category described as "Being Uncomfortable with the Present," because each of the incidents in the three level-one categories hinged on dissatisfaction with the current situation the character found himself or herself in.

The remaining 27 categories were reanalyzed in this way. The "Couple Breaking Up" category was collapsed with the "Romantic Couple Arguing" category to form a broader category, "Romantic Friction." "Foreplay," (1 incident), "One Partner Invites Sex," (2 incidents), "Intercourse" (1 incident), and "After Intercourse" (1 incident) were combined into the new category "Circling Around Intercourse." It should be noted that even with this more expansive definition, only 5 incidents (less than 2% of the total sample) were closely related to the actual act of intercourse.

The first-level categories "Opposite Sex Unable to Do Something," "Sacrificial Action," and "Danger" all seemed to share a common theme of "Power/Powerless." An example from each initial category helps to elucidate this category:

- From *Jumanji*, category of "Danger"
  Girl screams; boy screams; girl gets pulled into game [against her will]; boy follows.
- From *Batman Forever*, category of "Sacrificial Action"
  Chase (who has been kidnapped) tells her captor that "Batman will save me."
- From *Independence Day*, category of "Opposite Sex Unable to Do Something"

Father is talking to son who is drunk and despairing, tells him that every-
one loses faith sometimes. Dad admits he hasn't spoken to God since wife
died.

At this point, it could be noted that some of these described incidents could also be listed in other categories. The *Independence Day* incident could have been placed in the "Third-party Discussion of Romantic Partner" category. However, in such cases, a decision was made about the overriding theme of the incident. In this case, it was decided that he was not talking about his wife as a romantic partner as much as he was talking about his powerlessness, being unable to keep his wife from dying.

"Sexual Jokes," "Unrequited Love," "Deception," and "Jealousy" were collapsed into the new category called "Negative Romance," because the common thread among these categories was some encounter between a male and a female that was unpleasant.

An interesting category emerged when combining "Peaceful Togetherness," (*husband and wife smiling, whispering together,* from *Apollo 13*), "Male–Female Conversation," (*husband and wife talking about baby,* from *Mr. Holland's Opus*), and "Exciting News" (*announcing pregnancy, everyone jumping up and down,* from *Father of the Bride—Part II*) categories. All of these incidents included in any of these categories focused on the day-to-day existence of a male/female relationship. The vast majority of these incidents involved a husband and a wife, but a few involved boyfriends and girlfriends. Even the "Exciting News" category described events typically part of meandering through life. Therefore, this category was renamed "Monotonous Monogamy." In addition, after reexamining the "Nude" category, it was noticed that the only incidents of nudity were of a wife alone in the shower; therefore, they were collapsed into the "Monotonous Monogamy" category. Slightly more than 10% of all episodes (37) coded in this study were categorized as "Monotonous Monogamy."

"Kissing," "Flirtation," "Dancing," "Romantic Touching," and "Romantic Looking" were reclassified into the category called "Non-Progressive Romance," because in each incidence there was no indication that the couple would continue the physical connection or that it would eventually proceed to something further along sexually. Nearly half (45.6%) of the incidents coded (141) were placed in this category. It should be noted that although some of these episodes involved a husband and wife, the majority (73%) involved nonmarried couples.

"Third Party" and "Declares Love" maintained their uniqueness in the second level of analysis and were, therefore, left intact to the third level of coding. The reconceptualized categories are presented in Table 10.3.

After reanalyzing the categories, several observations can be made concerning how relationships are depicted in movies:

TABLE 10.3
Categories Reorganized During Level 2 Analysis

- Romantic Friction
  - Romantic couple arguing
  - Couple breaking up
- Third-Party Romance Talk
  - Third party discussion of romantic partner
- Love Declaration
  - Romantic talk
  - Declaring love
- Power–Powerless Interactions
  - Sacrificial action
  - Opposite sex teaches partner a lesson
  - Danger
  - Opposite sex unable to do something
- Circling Around Sex
  - Intercourse
  - After intercourse
  - One partner invites sex
  - Foreplay
- Discomfort With the Present
  - Dreams
  - Discussion of future
  - Reflection of the past

- Nonprogressive Romance
  - Romantic look
  - Dancing
  - Kissing
  - Romantic touching (holding hands, hugging)
  - Flirtation
- Monotonous Monogamy
  - Everyday married life
  - Nudity
  - Peaceful togetherness
  - Exciting news
  - Everyday male–female conversation (when involving married couples)
- Negative Romance
  - Sexual jokes
  - Jealousy
  - Deception
  - Unrequited love

1. The depiction of marriage is less than compelling in movies—whether the movie focuses on the marriage relationship or not. For example, in the movie *Father of the Bride—Part II*, the viewer understands that Nina and George are a committed married couple. However, when compiling all the incidents of interaction between Nina and George, the majority of the interactions focus on the mundane functions of marriage rather than the excitement and joy of commitment. Most of the interactions revolve around arguing and cooking.

2. Engaging in pre-intercourse behavior is normal behavior for teenagers in movies—whether the movie is about romance or not. More than one third of the incidents analyzed focused on some form of romantic interaction without any indication that sexual intercourse might occur. For example, in *Casper*, there is a touching scene where Casper's wish is granted and he becomes human for the night. He goes to a party and approaches Kat. They dance and embrace. There is little indication that this might lead elsewhere.

3. Even though all coded 309 incidents showed some kind of interaction between men and women, for the most part they demonstrated difficulty in communication. We've already discussed the frequency of arguing in the coded incidents. This seems particularly poignant given that so few incidents involved one character declaring some form of love. There were only 16 incidents of any kind of love declaration, and of those, only 4 used the word *love*. In only 2 of those incidents (one from *Happy Gilmore* and one from *Independence Day*) does one character speak directly to the other character using the phrase "I love you." In neither of these cases are the couples who declare love married. More common was telling someone else about a couple's love. For example, in *Pocahontas*, as the Indians prepare to execute John Smith, Pocahontas throws her body on top of his, saying that they'll have to kill her first and that she loves him. She does not, however, speak to Smith.

Third Level of Analysis—Selective Coding

As discussed earlier, the goal of the selective coding process is to make a decision about the core concept of the data. This is the most difficult analysis because the researcher has to leave some data behind and decide what the theme or story of the research project should be. This is not to say that the theme that emerges is the only story, but throughout the previous two levels of analysis, some persistent themes tend to become more noticeable than others. At this point, finding a metaphor or two that can encompass the concepts portrayed in the data becomes helpful. As Lakoff and Johnson (1980) have said, all of life can be broken down into metaphors, and they argue that "The essence of metaphor is understanding and experiencing one kind of thing in terms of another" (p. 5). For this study of teens and romantic messages, two metaphors could be applied: one for sex and one for romance.

The Mystery of Sex

A theme running through several categories at the first two levels of coding was the difficulty in articulating a sexual relationship. It's somewhat remarkable that given the attention of previous research to the ubiquity of sexual content, the movies in this sample seem devoid of overt sexual scenes. It's almost as if the moviemakers have decided that sex relations are too hard to explain and best left to the imagination of the viewer. For example, in the movie *Pocahontas*, it's "Grandmother Willow" (a talking willow tree) who gives the heroine guidance about love and marriage. Pocahontas is told to "wait for the spirits"—they will tell her. However, we never really learn much about what awaits the Indian princess. In *Apollo 13*, a wife looks longingly at her husband in their bedroom—but no words of love are exchanged between the two. In *Independence Day*, Captain Steve Hiller is clearly embarrassed—and doesn't want to talk about it—when an army buddy discovers he is planning to propose marriage.

The Innocence of Romance

After looking at all 309 incidents from several different angles, it became more apparent that the romantic images portrayed in these movies are disconnected from sexual episodes. Although this may be good news for some people (i.e., if you are a parent, you don't have to worry about your teen seeing writhing bodies on the big screen), it also means that viewers don't see that extended romantic encounters can lead to more serious sexual relationships, or that mature couples experience romance as well. The data seem to imply that romance is for the young alone—not necessarily the young at heart.

If it is understood that movies help determine the romantic frame for adolescents, then the adult community needs to understand that teens may be experiencing a major disconnect about the manner in which relationships work in real life. If, indeed, what teens see in movies sets the agenda of how they will view everyday relations, then some concerns may arise. Obviously, this is not to say that all teens will experience movies this way; nor is this to say that teens should not attend movies (or that they should see couples having sex so they know "how it works"). It is possible, however, to say that perhaps the messages teens take away from movies may create more confusion than illumination.

Thinking of the recorded incidents in terms of mystery or innocence, three overall concluding ideas bear further study:

1. Just because overt sex is absent from a movie, that doesn't mean that the message teens receive is healthy, neutral, or appropriate. As earlier studies have taught us, the media can have powerful impact on audiences. This may be equally true with movies and teenagers. Although it is remarkable that when examined closely, very little overt sexual action was shown in teens' movies, the potential downside is that teens will not see the potential negative consequences of inappropriate sexual behavior or the benefits of appropriate behavior.

2. For the teen, romance exists without context. Romantic interludes in the movies in this sample focus on young couples, often couples who don't know each other well and who have no plans for the future. Tender moments seem to exist "just because." There were as many romantic moments among couples who hardly knew each other as among those who knew each other well. But across the board, romance didn't seem to have any kind of meaning or link to further actions.

3. In the movies, teens don't see any connection between romance and marriage—or even long-term relationships. For all the touching, cooing, and gazing occurring among young couples in the movies, there is not much of that same tenderness among married couples. And even in movies such as *Independence Day*, which shows a husband who is committed to his wife (although they are apart, except for a few minutes, in the movie), the real romance occurs between an ex-husband and his ex-wife. There is a nice scene in which a previously romantically involved couple do choose to marry in the face of trouble; but even then it is emphasized that this is no ordinary couple (she works as a stripper and has a son from a previous relationship). And although this couple seem in love with each other, they never declare their love to each other.

CONCLUSION

After examining 309 specific encounters between men and women in movies that teens have seen in record numbers, we can conclude that the romantic script portrayed in movies is that romance is an innocent phenomenon, which has no relevance to the "real life" facing young people. Once romance progresses to something serious, it becomes a mystery. It is difficult to explain (as evidenced by the lack of love declarations in these movies); it just happens. Then, "somehow," you just end up married, and that's when the mundane begins.

It is risky to make sweeping generalizations about the romantic script of movies based on only 15 films. But it does at least give us a beginning construct. A next step would be to use these constructs to see how they apply in other movies that teens view. For example, how are married couples portrayed in movies like *Titanic*? Does the romance end when the couple marries in *Notting Hill*? Are the word-savvy characters of *You've Got Mail* able to declare their love to each other? Do any of these movies show how romance is one slice of a bigger pie?

In any event, romantic messages are more subtle—and potentially more problematic—than overt sexual scenes. It's important that we continue to try to understand how teens make sense of what they encounter on the big screen—and then to understand how they connect that to their own lives.

REFERENCES

Bachen, C. M., & Illouz, E. (1996). Imagining romance: Young people's cultural models of romance and love. *Critical Studies in Mass Communication, 13*, 279–308.

Berger, A. A. (1997). *Narratives in popular culture, media, and everyday life.* Thousand Oaks, CA: Sage.

Brown, J. D., Greenberg, B. S., & Buerkel-Rothfuss, N. L. (1993). Mass media, sex, and sexuality. *Adolescent Medicine: State of the Art Reviews, 4*(3), 511–525.

Hoffner, C., & Cantor, J. (1990). Perceiving and responding to mass media characters. In J. Bryant & D. Zillmann (Eds.), *Responding to the screen: Reception and reaction processes* (pp. 63–101). Hillsdale, NJ: Lawrence Erlbaum Associates.

Jeffres, L. W. (1997). *Mass media effects* (2nd ed.). Prospect Heights, IL: Waveland Press.

Jowett, G., & Linton, J. M. (1980). *Movies as mass communication.* Beverly Hills, CA: Sage.

Lakoff, G., & Johnson, M. (1980). *Metaphors we live by.* Chicago: The University of Chicago Press.

Peirce, K. (1993). Socialization of teenage girls through teen-magazine fiction: The making of a new woman or an old lady? *Sex Roles, 29*(1/2), 59–67.

Signorielli, N. (1997). A content analysis: Reflections of girls in the media. *Children Now and the Kaiser Family Foundation.*

Strasburger, V. C. (1995). *Adolescents and the media: Medical and psychological impact.* Thousand Oaks, CA: Sage.

Strauss, A. L., & Corbin, J. (1990). *Basics of qualitative research: Grounded theory. Procedures and techniques.* London: Sage.

Ward, M. L. (1995). Talking about sex: Common themes about sexuality in the prime-time television programs children and adolescents view most. *Journal of Youth and Adolescence, 24*(5), 595–615.

11

Teens and Movies: Something to Do, Plenty to Learn

Jeanne R. Steele
University of St. Thomas

The month was January; the year, 1995. A movie called *Higher Learning* opened on the Wednesday preceding the Martin Luther King holiday weekend. Described by the *Boston Globe* as a "combustible new campus drama" by *Boyz 'n the Hood* director John Singleton (Carr, 1995), the movie sparked mixed reviews, gunfire, and fist fights. In a suburb of Washington, D.C., a 21-year-old was fatally shot in an apparent drive-by shooting after leaving an afternoon screening of the film. In Canton, Ohio, teens started brawling at the Canton Centre Mall following a sold-out Saturday night showing. It took 20 police officers to break up the ruckus. In Michigan and Illinois, there was more of the same (Evans & Busch, 1995).

Without these headline-making incidents, a majority of adults probably never would have heard of *Higher Learning*. Teens, however, flocked to the film. It grossed $17 million during its first 6 days at the box office and finished the holiday weekend second only to *Legends of the Fall*, starring teen heartthrob Brad Pitt (Natale, 1995). Although teens' volatile response to *Higher Learning* may be atypical, the importance—power, even—of movies in adolescents' lives became clear during a qualitative study I conducted in 1995.

Why are movies so important during the teenage years? Because movies take teens to places they may never have been before and introduce them to situations they may not yet have experienced. In one study of 10- to 15-year-olds, movies and television were ranked ahead of friends, school, mothers, the Internet, fathers, and magazines (in that order) as sources from which the young people learned "a lot" (Angell, Gordon, & Begun, 1999, p. 67). In addition to being important sources of information, movies serve as catalysts for teens to talk and think about issues infrequently addressed in other forums. And movies help teens see where they fit in the world. "We never look at just one thing," Berger (1977) tells us in *Ways of Seeing*. "We are always looking at the relation between things and ourselves" (9).

I first learned about *Higher Learning* when conducting a series of focus groups with teens during January and February 1995. It was the most popular of all the films mentioned as favorites on a media-use questionnaire I asked focus-group participants to fill out. Of the 51 teens, 11 (4 Black, 7 White) named it as one of the best movies they had seen in recent months. This chapter does not focus solely on *Higher Learning*, however, but rather on movies in general and the role they play in teens' use of media.

The Adolescents' Media Practice Model (Steele, 1999; Steele & Brown, 1995) grounds this discussion. It asserts that the diversity of teens' lived experience and their involvement in the complex task of identity formation are keys to understanding the role movies play in their lives (see Introduction, pp.). Teens' sense of who they are—what they know and believe—shapes their encounters with movies, and those encounters in turn shape their sense of themselves. Developmental stage, the sociocultural influences of race, class, and gender, and the socializing influences of family, friends, and school also figure prominently in adolescents' media practice.

In their original agenda-setting study, McCombs and Shaw (1972) called attention to the news media's ability to tell people what issues to think about. Subsequent research expanded on that notion and suggested that the news media, as agenda setters, not only tell people what public issues to think about but also how to think about them (Shaw & Martin, 1992). This study suggests that for adolescents, who have little interest in reading newspapers or watching the nightly news (Stepp, 1996), movies are often agenda setters. Movies caused some teens in the study to question taken-for-granted attitudes about issues like race, sex, and violence, but they helped other teens to reinforce preexisting notions and behavior patterns. Although the study's primary focus was the interface between media and teenage sexuality, study teens' interests were hard to corral—reminding me that sex is far from the only thing on their minds and that media practice encompasses all media, not just one medium in isolation. Often, during focused group discussions, talk about movies switched seamlessly to talk about television or music. Similarly, it was hard to keep the teens focused on sexuality when their favorite movies centered on violence or race or drugs. Consequently, this chapter emphasizes teens' movie practices, within the broader context of media practice. It does so by illustrating the Adolescents' Media Practice Model, showing how its key components—selection, interaction, and application—come into play when teens talk about media.

METHOD

My study considered a broad question: Where do the mass media (not just movies, but also television, radio, and magazines) fit among other primary influences in teens' lives as they forge their sexual identities and refine their attitudes, values, and beliefs about love, sex, and relationships? The study was designed like a funnel—wide at the top (in terms of numbers of participants and areas of inquiry) to generate a broad understanding of teens' media practices, and narrower in focus at the bottom to explore emerging themes in greater depth.

The first phase consisted of eight focused group discussions in which 51 teens participated. A subset of these teens, 1 to 3 from each focus group, kept written or tape-recorded media journals ($N = 13$) and then participated in a "room tour"[1] or in-depth interview ($N = 14$).[2] (Table 11.1 provides a more detailed description of these breakdowns.)

---

[1]"Room touring" is a research technique devised to encourage teens to talk about the cultural artifacts, many of them drawn from the media, housed in their bedrooms (Brown, Dykers, Steele, & White, 1994). The method involves giving teens a handheld tape recorder and inviting them to conduct a tour of their rooms. Talking about the mementos, trophies, photos, posters, and other material objects many teens display in their bedrooms opens the door to the meanings they associate with them.

[2]One teen participated in an in-depth interview but did not complete a media journal.

TABLE 11.1
Sample Composition

Crowd/Peer Group	Participated in Focus Group	Kept Journal	Room Tour or Interview
Drexel Middle School (N = 6)			
male, Black	Shawn, 13		
male, Black	Jawaun, 13		
male, White	Jamie, 13	√	√
male, White	Matt, 13	√	√
male, White	McKay, 13		
male, White	Karl, 13	√	√
Anderson Middle School (N = 7)			
(females, White)	Elizabeth, 13	√	
	Susan, 13	√	
	Cassie, 14		
	Sophie, 13		
	Julie, 13		
	Neena, 13		
	Lindsey, 14	√	√
Spencer Community Center (N = 8)			
(females, Black)	Shamiah, 11	√	√
	Amber, 13		
	Trevy, 14		
	Cherie, 11		
	Tanya, 13		
	Angel, 14		
	Andrea, 11		
	Charise, 12		
Spencer Community Center (N = 5)			
(males, Black)	Smittie, 14		
	Tyrone, 14		
	Arizona, 14		
	Leon, 12	√ (incomplete)	
	Darius, 13		
City Space 1 (N = 9)			
female, White	Leigh, 14		
female, White	Leah, 14		
female, White	Nancy, 16		
male, White	Rob, 17		
male, White	Weston, 16		
male, White	Jeremy, 15		
male, White	Peter, 18	√	√
male, other	Alex, 16		
male, Hispanic	Josh, 18		

(Continued)

TABLE 11.1 *(Continued)*

Crowd/Peer Group	Participated in Focus Group	Kept Journal	Room Tour or Interview
City Space 2 (*N* = 7)			
male, White	David, 19		
male, White	Eric, 16		
male, White	Sean, 17		
male, White	Marvin, 18	√ (inc.)	√
male, White	Michah, 17		
female, White	Meredith, 18	√	√
female, White	Cat, 18	√	√
Teen Mothers (*N* = 6)			
female, White	Stacey, 14		
female, Black	Jade, 16	√	√
female, Black	Precious, 15		
female, Black	Tiffany, 17		
female, Black	Alycia, 17		
female, Black	Tenita, 16	√	√
Riverside High School (*N* = 3)			
female, Black	Desiray, 15	√	√
male, White	Jonathan, 18		√
male, White	Andrew, 18		√

Beginning the inquiry with focus groups made it possible to tap into the wide array of ideas about the media that emerged as the teens interacted with one another and the discussion moderator. My goal was to get teens talking about the relationship between the mass media and sexuality in an informal, relaxed setting that would simulate their everyday talk and clarify the socially constructed meanings about love, sex, and relationships that they shared (Lunt & Livingstone, 1994). The teens' self-account media journals and my subsequent in-depth interviews with them afforded additional vantage points from which to explore the dialogic tension between group loyalties and individual attitudes, values, and beliefs. The topic of movies figured prominently in the mix.

PARTICIPANTS

Three objectives guided my recruitment strategy:

1. To involve both younger and older teens so that developmental differences could be considered. Grade in school was used as an admittedly rough cut between younger teens (enrolled in middle school) and

older teens (enrolled in high school). Nevertheless, only one year over-
lapped: 14-year-olds attended either middle school or high school.

2. To oversample teens who, as previous research suggested, were more
    likely to engage in risky sexual behavior (e.g., intercourse at a young
    age, unprotected sex, or sex with multiple partners).

3. To include teens who frequently are underrepresented in studies of ad-
    olescent sexuality because of recruitment and retention problems and
    the challenges of getting parental consent.

In keeping with these objectives, I recruited focus-group teens through
naturally occurring groups of friends at Anderson and Drexel middle
schools, Riverside High School, and organizations that worked with the
populations of interest. (To maintain the confidentiality of study participants, the names of schools and other recruitment sites are pseudonyms,
and so are the names of individual teens.) These organizations included a
countywide adolescent parenting program designed to help teenage mothers complete high school without getting pregnant again (Teen Mothers); a
recreation center serving a predominantly Black neighborhood (Spencer);
and a downtown teen center (City Space), which catered to young people
looking for a place to hang out and be with friends after school and on
weekends. Most of the teens lived in a southeastern town of about 40,000; a
few lived in adjoining communities.

PROCEDURE

Focus Groups

The focus groups were held at times and in places deemed convenient and
nonthreatening (e.g., the opposite of "uncool") to the teens. Sites that quali-
fied included a community center and a teen center, the public library, and
a meeting room at a local college. When they arrived, the teens filled out
two brief questionnaires: one containing demographic questions and the
other detailing what media they liked best and how much time they spent
with various types of media. Normally, the discussions began with some informal talk about media preferences; then two music videos—Blackstone's
"I Don't Want to Say Goodbye" and TLC's "Creep"—were shown to jump-
start the discussion about sexual media content and to provide an across-
groups window on interaction, one of the integral steps in media practice.
Discussion moderators followed a loosely structured discussion guide to
ensure consistency across groups, but they were encouraged to pursue related topics as they arose. Actual discussion times ranged from about 60 to
90 minutes. Snacks were served and the journal-keeping/room tour phases

of the study were explained toward the end of each session. Each teenager received $15 in cash for participating in a focus group.

Media Journals

Each journal keeper (N = 13) was supplied with a small tape recorder or boom box and two audiotapes, as well as a "journal kit" that included a notebook, colored pen, scissors, and glue stick to encourage active participation. I personally delivered these kits to the teens' homes. Journal keepers were asked to spend 15 minutes a day for 7 days recording or writing down commentary about what they saw and heard in the media and how it related to what they had learned about love, sex, and relationships at home, in school, and from their friends. Daily prompts were designed to keep journal keepers focused on the topic of sexuality, but the teens also were instructed to "feel free to discuss other things related to the media and how they fit in your life." A $20 incentive was offered for keeping a journal.

Movies were the suggested topic for the third day of journal-keeping. The journal prompt read:

> Movie day. What's the best movie you've seen in the past couple of months? Give the name. Tell me about the story. Who were the stars? What did you like best about it? Least? Who is your favorite actor? Why? Actress? Why? What do you like about them? What kinds of movies—like action, comedy, romance, cop shows—do you like best? Of the movies that are out now, which ones do you want to see? What's the best movie you've seen in the past year? Give the name. Describe the story line and why you liked it. Give your views about sex in the movies. Do movies paint a realistic picture of love, sex, and relationships?

Room Tours/In-depth Interviews (N = 14)

The final stage of data gathering involved talking in greater depth with teens about what they had said or had written in their journals and accompanying them on self-narrated tours of their bedrooms. The room tours (Steele & Brown, 1995) gave teens an opportunity to talk about the significance of their "favorite things" (Wallendorf & Arnould, 1988). The teens were asked to pay particular attention to room decorations and memorabilia that pointed to their sense of who they were, what they valued, and the kind of life they wanted to lead. Participants who preferred to be interviewed elsewhere were given that option. Several of the high school teens opted to meet and talk at a local coffee shop where they liked to hang out. Teens were paid an additional $20 for participating in a room interview or an in-depth interview somewhere else.

SELECTION

Teens spend more time listening to music and watching television than they spend watching movies. Nevertheless, there is something intrinsic to movies that makes this form of mass media particularly enticing and powerful for teens. "There is a huge viewership," reports the *New York Times Magazine*, "spearheaded by teen-age girls, who will pretty much see or watch anything as long as the actors and actresses look like teen-agers too" (Hirschberg, 1999, p. 44). And where the girls go, so will the boys. Since the 1950s, the lucrative teen market has accounted for at least one third of all admissions to American movie theaters (Rickey, 1998; Squire, 1983).

Although the *Times* is correct about the size of the audience (the largest teenage audience in history thanks to the baby boomers' proclivity to have children), my data contradict the notion that teenagers will watch anything. Teens are selective, often deciding which movies to watch based on previews painstakingly produced to appeal to their tastes. Even though teens in the study realized—as Arizona, 14, observed in the Spencer Community Center focus group—that promoters "just take a good clip out of the movie that has someone havin' sex and stretch it on the preview to make people think that somethin' good goin' to happen," they still let themselves be sold by the promise of the preview. Jawaun, 13, a student at Drexel Middle School, said:

> If it's a movie that I've seen the previews and really want to see, I'll try to see it in a movie theater. Like I want to see *Higher Learning*, but, if I don't have time to go see it or something, I'll just wait until it comes out on video.

What teens find appealing in previews and films varies along ethnic, gender, and age lines. As other researchers have found with television shows (Appiah, 1997) and advertising (Whittler, 1991), Black teens in the study showed a marked preference for movies featuring Black actors and story lines rich in Black cultural cues. Six Black teens but no White teens listed as one of their favorite films *Jason's Lyric*, a love story about a lower-middle-class Black man whose efforts to stay away from crime and drugs are rebuffed at every turn. And five White teens but no Black teens named as their favorite *Surviving the Game*, an improbable, high-stakes action film that chronicles the "hunt" of a Black, homeless man forced to run for his life by a group of White men intent on killing him for sport. Although the film featured Black rapper Ice T as the hunted man, the story line was more culturally embedded in White values, rituals, symbols, traditions, and material objects—the cues Appiah (1999) associates with cultural embeddedness—than in Black culture. Set in the Pacific Northwest, the movie's plot was so fantastic that it may not have appealed to Black youths who, studies suggest, rely heavily on the media for information about the way the world really is for Blacks and the Black community (Greenberg & Brand, 1994).

Black teens, males and females, also talked about spending more time with media, movies included. During the Riverside High School focus group, Desiray, 15, Black, said her family watched movie videos "about every night." However, Jonathan, 18, White, said he hardly ever went to movies because they cost too much. "I don't really rent them much, either. A lot of times I guess I don't watch them that much just because they're long. I just kind of feel like I'm wasting time if I watch one."

Tyrone, 14, Black, in contrast to Jonathan, bragged about watching TV and movies late into the night. "Two o'clock, four o'clock in the mornin'," he asserted, were his favorite viewing times. When the moderator asked what kinds of things he watched at that time of night, Smittie, also 14, chimed in: "Sex shows!" But the moderator told him to "Let [Tyrone] talk!" So Tyrone continued:

Tyrone:	Some of 'em, yeah, some good movies like *Demolition Man*.
Moderator:	You got cable?
Tyrone:	Yup!
Mod.:	And sometimes you watch, what'd he say, sex shows? What's a sex show like? What kinds of things are in a sex show?
Tyrone:	People in bed!

Distracted by a disturbance outside, Tyrone lost the floor to Darius, 13, whose interest in sex shows was somewhat different from Tyrone's and Smittie's. Although Tyrone and Smittie had been talking about televised movies, Darius, a year younger than them, started talking about a show he had seen on reality TV. For him, sex show meant a video of a live birth.

Darius:	I'll be watchin' shows like that ...
Mod.:	What shows?
Darius:	Like early, sometimes, they be havin' like people havin' pregnancy, and I be watchin' that.
Mod.:	What do you mean by "having pregnancy"?
Darius:	Well, they be havin' pregnancy ...
Smittie:	TLC ... The Learning Channel and you can't break away ...
Darius:	I be watchin' that sometimes!
Mod.:	And what do you learn? What do you get from that?
Darius:	How the baby is born!
Mod.:	OK. I mean, so they just show you like the baby bein' delivered, or ... ?

Darius: Yes, sometimes they show . . .

Leon: Yeah, comin' out . . .

Darius: Nah, they show . . . I seen one where they, um, this woman couldn't have it out, and so she had to have 'em cut her stomach to get it out!

Gender and age differences also were apparent in the teens' movie rankings. The drawing power of teen idols exerted an especially strong pull on the female middle school students. Not only did the younger teen girls like to talk about their current favorites, they also liked to bring their likenesses, in the form of life size posters and handmade, cut-and-paste collages, right into their bedrooms. For example, Lindsey, 14, had a poster of Leonardo DiCaprio, star of the phenomenally successful *Titanic*, over her bed so that he would be the last person she saw before going to sleep and the first when she woke up. When the Anderson girls were asked to talk about their favorite movies and the kinds of relationships they saw in movies, *A River Runs Through It*, starring Brad Pitt, was the first movie mentioned. Thirteen-year-old Cassie's observation that "There isn't anything much cuter than Brad Pitt in that movie!" was like the starter's gun at a road race. The girls were off, vying for a chance to rave about Brad Pitt's charms.

Several of the middle school White boys listed *Forrest Gump* as a favorite, and they also liked the slapstick humor of Jim Carrey's *Ace Ventura* and *Dumb and Dumber*. *The Mask*, another comedy featuring Carrey, was also listed as a favorite by four of the middle school teens. None of these movies showed up as best shows for high school-aged teens, suggesting that the story lines were less appealing to a more mature audience. For early adolescents, however, actor Carrey got it just right: the dumber, the better. In his journal, Karl, 13, a White seventh grader, explained the appeal of dumb humor this way:

> Anyway, um, I really like this movie [*Dumb and Dumber*]. I thought it was very funny. There were several dumb humor parts, and that's the kind of humor I like. I find it very easy to watch this because there are very sarcastic parts and they did some stupid things. I thought the movie was hysterical. The plot was pretty good, too.

Violent television shows and movies featuring lots of "good-lookin' women" were also popular with the younger males. Comments like "I mean I goin' watch that show 'cuz people get beat up and stuff" and "I like *Cape Boxer* and stuff . . . jus' all it is is fightin' " were typical. Older teens in the study showed more variation in the movies they liked, perhaps because they were surer of their own tastes and less influenced by their friends' preferences. Action and violence (*Natural Born Killers*, *Reservoir Dogs*, and *Pulp Fiction*) were popular with them, too, but they also talked about enjoying art films (*Victenstein*), science fiction (*Star Wars*), and "hippie" films (*Easy Rider, Flashback*).

Because of the small size of my sample, it is impossible to generalize from these data; nevertheless, certain themes emerged with remarkable consistency. They suggest these tentative assertions about what teens look for in movies:

- Males want action and sex; girls want romance and information about how to be in the world.
- Younger teens want to sample life through slapstick comedy; older teens prefer more sophisticated humor and intrigue.
- Teens gravitate toward movies that feature people their own age or older. The tendency is to "buy up."
- Black teens prefer movies that feature Blacks.

INTERACTION

Director John Huston underscored the power and magic of the big screen by making it the subject of his camera in the 1985 movie version of *Annie*. What can equal the excitement and sense of anticipation moviegoers share with Annie as she walks down the aisle of Radio City Music Hall, transfixed by the prospect of experiencing her first movie? Just as the glitz and glamour of the Rockettes was able to transport Annie out of her everyday "hard-luck world," so, too, do movies allow teenagers to vicariously sample emotions and experiences that may stand in stark contrast to the realities of their everyday lives. Through music, moving images, and sound, movies have the ability to focus teens' attention and allow them to experience life unfettered by the usual constraints of time and space.

Going to the movies or watching movies on video at a friend's home are decidedly social activities for teens. Rarely, it seems, would they watch a video alone. In the research literature, parasocial interaction (Antecol, 1997) and involvement come closest to the concept of interaction as posited in the Adolescents' Media Practice model, but these constructs fail to capture the activity seen in this study. For the teens in this study, the entire viewing experience—where and under what conditions they watch a movie and with whom, as well as postviewing activities like rehashing particularly scary or sexy scenes with friends—are integral to interaction.

Learning and change, the data suggest, occur not just while experiencing a movie but also after. This broader understanding of interaction accounts for both individual-level and group-level engagement with movies, and individual- and group-level applications or effects. Understood as activity, or practice, interaction includes: sensory attention (watching or listening) to the medium or message; involvement (emotional, psychological, and physical) with the medium or message; and cognitive processing (comprehension and interpretation) of the media message—a meaning-making activity that can continue for days, weeks, and even months after the viewing moment.

Movies, it was found, are interlocutors or participants in a dialectic give and take between what teens know about themselves and society and what they still have to learn. In a sense, movies (and videos and television shows, too) are like third parties that engage teens in conversations they cannot imagine having with their parents, teachers, or even friends. Matt, 14, explained in his tape-recorded journal that he hadn't learned much about love, sex, and relationships from his parents because talking about such things was "not exactly a dinner table discussion, unfortunately." Movies, on the other hand, are great educators, Matt said. In response to the journal prompt about movies, he wrote about *Forrest Gump*: "It was just a great movie . . . which really showed a lot of teenagers who saw it what I think love really should be about and I think that was good."

Forrest Gump also taught Matt about AIDS:

> And he always had a crush on her, and he ended up having her baby. He had, they had kids together. Umm, she died of AIDS, which was realistic. It's getting more and more realistic every day, and it kind of showed both parts of the relationship—the sex spectrum, umm, the part that we all love . . . and Jenny having AIDS, which is a bad part because if you are not careful you are going to get it, which is one reason kids need to be educated. Us teenagers need to be educated on, umm, this sort of thing.

Thinking about his own life and the future he envisioned for himself, Matt again said he thought *Forrest Gump* was a great movie.

> It was simple. It showed us how complicated we make our lives and what a great life Forrest had even though he really didn't try hard. He just lived every day and had fun. He did what he felt like and he got rich off of it and had a great life.

Teens also can learn asocial behavior from movies. For instance, Smittie, 14, understood the message of the Blackstone video to be: If your girl is cheating on you, then you should cheat on her to make her jealous.

> Smittie: 'Cause, like, like the way the whole video was set up, you know, he was cheatin' on her, so she went out and found another person . . . and that's what most people do in real life, you know. They think someone be cheatin' on them, you know, and they just go find them another mate, ya know?

Mod.:   So do you think the video helped that, or stopped it, or . . .

Smittie: It helps because it gives people more ideas, 'cause like, some
             people that watch it could be cheatin' . . . could be bein'
             cheated on right then, by they husbands or by they wives,
             and they look at the video, and the video gives them an idea
             of what to do!

Although the characters in the video were not married, Smittie makes the
leap to husband and wife—filling in the spaces between video cues with a
sexual script he can relate to.

Smittie's interpretation of the video was not the only interpretation, however. Tyrone, 14, another member of the Spencer Community Center boys'
group, thought that the girl in the video "just didn't want it no more 'cause
he was havin' an affair with somebody else." A third boy, Arizona, 14, de-
manded of Smittie: "Hey, look. If you got a girlfriend and she's cheatin' on
you, you ain't gonna break up with her?"

Smittie retorted: "We're gonna talk first, Holmes! We gonna talk. . . . And
if she keeps cheatin', you gonna wanna find you another sister out there.
Yeah, yeah, yeah." Regardless of the meanings they found, the boys ultimately agreed that no matter how they interpreted the video, it suggested
ways to think about things and ways to act. Arizona summed up the group
consensus: "I don't think it's really about jealousy, but . . . videos give you a
influence on a whole lot of things! And more than likely, most people gonna
do what they see on TV anyway."

Even though he thought most people "do what they see on TV anyway,"
Arizona, like most of the study teens, particularly the older ones, still
thought television shows were fake and unreal. Talking about the TV sitcom
Married with Children, a high school male observed: "That's the only reason
it's funny. It's because it's on TV and you know it's not real and it's not happening when the TV turns off. . . . It's a fantasy you get to play with in your
mind. That's all." The teens' reaction to movies was more nuanced, but the
Black teens—especially the boys—acknowledged taking them very seriously.
Smittie was convinced that movies tell the truth: "Ya know what you see in
movies like really happened, ya know?" And Charise, 12, drew a parallel between her friend's real-life experience and a movie she had seen.

> Sally, she came to me. We been in class, and she said her boyfriend had hit her,
> and she was like, I know. . . . It was just like a movie 'cuz she was sayin' she
> know what she should do, but she don't want to and all this other stuff, 'cuz she
> love him and all that stuff. She say he hit her hard, but she said he didn't mean
> it like that and all that other stuff and she just let it go by!

Recounting the story about her friend gave Charise an opportunity to share
her own attitudes about abuse with her friends:

Like a bad relationship to me is when a boy is seein' other girls on the side, and the girl's seein' boys on the side and she usin' him for his money, and he usin' her for her money and other stuff like sex or somethin'. I think a really terrible relationship, which I will never let myself get into, is where a girl is so in love with a boy she believes she can't live without him. And if he hit her, she be like, "He only do it 'cause he love me." 'Cause I say no, love ain't about all that hittin' and stuff. And I wish a man would put his hands on me like I be seein' on TV, 'cuz he wish he hadn't of done it!

The Anderson girls' animated talk about *A River Runs Through It* demonstrated how movie story lines and teen stars can teach and elicit thoughtful responses to historical prejudices.

Cassie: Okay. See, Norman, he's the brother that's got the good relationship and all, and he just does like things, and then Paul, that's Brad Pitt! ["Ooh, ooh," from other members of the group.] He like, he was dating this Indian girl, and they went to this club and they were like, "No Indians allowed." He was like, "Excuse me? She's like everybody else," and so he like stood up for her and was really nice and all . . .

Whereas adults rely on the news media to present the "truth" about the world in which we live, teens often look to movies. During the Drexel boys' group discussion, Shawn, 13, explained that teens pay attention to media content that deals with issues they could encounter in their own lives:

But you know, you know there's people out there killin' people and junk like that, and you know they say somethin' like, they gonna show somebody gettin' murdered, a kid, you know, you gonna watch that! Say like, you a gangster right, and you see a show that has somethin' to do with drive-bys and junk, you goin' watch it 'cause, you know it relates to your life. You gonna watch the stuff that you can relate it with your life!

With these words, Shawn deftly captured the meaning of *resonance*, a theory that suggests that the potential for media effects is greater when media story lines are congruent with life experiences (Snyder, 1995). If a movie presents a view of life that teens find plausible, then its impact is amplified. As Grossberg, Wartella, and Whitney (1998) observe: "[E]ntertainment producers must aim for the appearance of reality, so that the audience will willfully suspend its disbelief and thus be entertained" (p. 336).

Teens' relationship to movies is complex. They know that much of what they see is made for the movies, i.e., the women are beautiful, no one gets pregnant, and the good guys almost always prevail in the end. Still, they credit movies with influencing people's behavior. Arizona made this observation during the Spencer boys' discussion:

> Yeah, all these movies . . . it's like givin' you an influence that you sayin' like, you don't have to have safe sex, you know, 'cuz like, you see somebody havin' sex on the movie. They don't take time on the movie to put on the condom and stuff like that, you know? They just DO it! And it make people think, you say, like, "Well, if they can just do it and not get no kinda diseases, then I can do it and not get no kinda diseases!" And that's the influence that people get, but they end up gettin' a disease, you know?

Older teens were more skeptical than younger teens about the reality factor in movies. Keen on movies with drug-related story lines, movies like *Easy Rider* and *Pulp Fiction*, the City Space teens drew a line between cool and real.

Peter:　　They like make sex like bluntly, you know, simple, and there's no realistic problem like pregnancy or any sexual problems, sexual diseases or anything! You never see a movie where like two people just like blow up some plane and they run to their apartment hiding from the FBI or something and they like strip all their clothes off and put on condoms and have sex, you know (laughs). . . . I mean that would ruin the scene, you know! . . . Anyway, they never do that because that's unrealistic, and that's not what people want to see anyway!

Mod.:　　So you just kind of decide that it's not real and so you just . . .

Peter:　　I mean it's cool, but it's not real!

Warmed up by their discussion of *A River Runs Through It*, the White girls from Anderson Middle School next launched into the retelling of *Higher Learning*. The movie generated excitement among the teens because it incorporated many of the qualities previously mentioned: Most of the actors were teenagers; the setting was a college campus that could have been anywhere in the United States; the culturally embedded cues—music, talk, dress, wall decorations—were familiar to both Black and White youth; the adults in the film played secondary and fairly stereotypical roles; and the story line, although criticized by film critics for being overwrought, could have happened.

Focusing on three freshmen—two White and one Black—trying to adjust to college life at the fictitious Columbus University, *Higher Learning* tackled a multitude of weighty issues. "It explores, among other things, racism both casual and blatant, ethnic polarization, date rape, neo-Nazis, bisexual experimentation, and the pressures society puts on black men in general and black athletes in particular," according to Kenneth Turan (1995, p. F1), film critic for the *Los Angeles Times*. Another critic observed, "You can accuse John Singleton's combustible new campus drama, *Higher Learning*, of sprawl, but you can't accuse it of irrelevance" (Carr, 1995, p. 68).

Five of the seven girls participating in the focus group had seen the movie. After a brief discussion about whether telling the ending would spoil the movie for the two who hadn't seen it, they decided it wouldn't and the narrative began. Right away, race was put on the agenda for discussion.

Cassie:	It's not, well, it's kind of violent. See it's about race and stuff, and . . . 'cuz it's like this school . . . like Columbia College or something like that, and there's all these Black people . . . and then there's some White people and how like they're all preju-diced against each other. And the Black people, they always have parties but they don't have loud music and stuff, but the cops will, um, still come and bust up their party, and then like across the street the White people will be having a party and they [the cops] won't do anything! [Group all commenting at once]
Mod.:	Elizabeth, you said it was the best movie you had ever seen! What did you think of the racism?
Elizabeth:	I mean, it wasn't, I guess I've seen better movies, but it was re-ally good because like it showed everybody's point of view! I mean, it showed why the neo-Nazis felt like they did. . . . I don't agree with that at all . . . but I mean they showed every point of view that you could have!
Lindsey:	They had all these cops in there [the movie theater], though . . .
Cassie:	They were afraid like a fight would break out so they had like six cops!

Although the group intellectually endorsed the idea of "everybody's point of view" being represented in the movie, the girls' reaction to being in a theater with a police contingent at the rear was visceral. It underscored how important the viewing context can be, not just on teens' interaction with movies but also potentially on their incorporation of or resistance to movie content. The moderator probed:

Mod.:	In the movie theater?
Cassie:	In the movie theater! and then all like, they took up the back aisle and then when you walk out, there's like a wall right there, and like you go up a big thing [ramp] like that.

Mod.:	Susan's turn!
Susan:	Well, this is kind of like *Higher Learning*, um, I read in the newspaper a while ago that when *Schindler's List* was out, people were watching the movie and these guys got kicked out of the movie theater becuz, um, during the part where they were sending the Jews to the crematorium, like putting them in the gas chamber things, people started cheering, they were like skinheads! and started like cheering, and you know, how like . . .
Sophie:	Gosh, if I saw people cheering in that movie, I would have stood up and hit 'em, too!
Susan:	I think that movies like that provoke feeling, you know, more feeling than people think they do!

The exchange about *Higher Learning* continued for several more minutes, with one girl after another expressing strongly held views. Although sexuality per se was not on their minds, the girls' talk is a good example of how interaction can coincide with the viewing experience or continue long afterward. Primed by her friends' reaction to *Higher Learning*, Susan recalls an article she had read about *Schindler's List*. Her mention of the movie evokes an emotional response from Sophie, who in turn remembers her experience of *Schindler's List*. The exchange also illustrates the role of movies as agenda setters; in this case, *Higher Learning* precipitated a discussion about race and underscored its importance for these White girls, who for the first time in their lives experienced what it felt like to be a numerical minority.

The conversation jumped from the story line of the movie, to Sophie's and Lindsey's reaction to being among the few White people in the theater, to the girls' experience of race at school.

Elizabeth:	Um, this is kind of off the subject but like, I was going to say how in the movie, they have like, I don't mean to be racist at all, but in the movie all the Black couples that they had, um, like the Black people they weren't racist against White people! But I mean, if you were to spend a day at our school you could see that it's not true at all!
Mod.:	What's not true at all?
Lindsey:	I think I know about three Black people in our whole school that are nice and they'll be like, "Hey, how you doin'." The rest of them will be like. . . . I don't know. They just . . . they hang around and they'll only be with their own race, and then they call us racist against them?!

Neena: Yeah!

Cassie: But like if we try to be nice to them, they're like, "What you thinkin'. I'm not hangin' out wit you!" 'cuz we're just not together.

The conversation continued in this vein, with Lindsey saying it bothered her that the women in the row behind her had brought a young child to the movie. Several other girls joined in, expressing various reasons (drinking, homicide, suicide, cussing) why the movie was inappropriate for a child. Then Susan, whose earlier comments about *Schindler's List* suggested that she paid more than casual attention to the media, chimed in with a pronouncement that

> [R]acism goes both ways. . . . 'Cuz I definitely think that in a lot of places, that like Black people are unfairly, you know, prejudged and stuff like that, but definitely at our school and like other places here and stuff, I mean, they judge us, too! And it's not only that White people are the prejudiced ones . . .

The girls' discussion heated up even more when they turned to the topic of a date rape portrayed in the movie. One of several subthemes that were superficially explored on screen, the rape was a White-on-White crime. The victim was a young woman who had been organizing a peace festival designed to ease racial tensions at the fictitious Columbus University. In less than subtle ways (there's plenty of blood and violence), the movie illustrated how closely the power differentials of race, class, and sex/gender systems are intertwined in daily practice. Grappling with these issues among friends, the girls engaged in what Snow and Anderson (1987) call "identity talk," a means by which they could sort out, interrogate, and firm up their beliefs about race, class, and sex/gender.

APPLICATION

Because media practice is a seamless process, it is difficult to discern the precise moment when interaction becomes application. In their animated discussion about *Higher Learning*, the Anderson girls moved back and forth between interpretation (an activity associated with interaction in the Media Practice Model) and incorporation or reaffirmation of existing attitudes (activities associated with application). As they talked, the group seemed to incorporate new positions or reaffirmed already held positions into the belief structures that formed the core of their personal and social identities regarding race. The movie played a central role in their identity talk, serving as a mediating means (Wertsch, 1991) or bridge between the real world of social relations and what they knew or believed about that world.

Black teens in the study addressed different aspects of *Higher Learning* than the White teens. All but one of the young women in the Teen Mothers focus group were Black, single, and trying to make it through high school while taking care of their babies. All came from low-income homes. As a group, they seized on the film's somewhat undeveloped references to sexual experimentation and lesbianism as the takeoff points for expressing disgust about girls kissing girls.

Mod.:	So what do you think about her homosexual ... we'll call it fantasies 'cause we really don't know. What do you'all think about that?
Two girls in unison:	Um. . . . Nasty!
Mod.:	Do you'all have any friends in your school who are homosexual?
Tiffany:	I've seen some White people (Alycia laughs) who are kissin' in the hallways. They were two White girls and they was kissin' with tongue! (Alycia laughs again.)
Mod.:	Really. So what do you all think about that?
Jade:	I think it's nasty. They got groups and everything for that.
Mod.:	You think it's nasty? You don't think they should have groups?
Jade:	I mean they can have groups if they want to, you know what I'm sayin'? As long as they don't try to recruit me! (laughter)

With her "they can have groups if they want to, you know what I'm sayin'?" Jade, 16, extended a tacit invitation to the other teen mothers to firm up their view of lesbians as "outsiders." She did this from the comfort of being an "insider" within the teen moms' community. Sophie, Lindsey, and the other Anderson girls did the same thing with their condemnation of the way Black students at their school behaved. Neena's comment pretty well sums up the group's perception: "Yeah, how come they can call themselves niggers and stuff, but if anybody like says anything like that they like get so mad." "[G]roup insiders," Hill Collins (1991) tells us, "have similar world views. . . . In brief, insiders have undergone similar experiences, possess a common history, and share the assumptions about knowledge that characterize 'thinking as usual' " (p. 54). Rather than challenging the girls to question their homophobia or understand the pain and confusion experienced by victims of date rape, the film's depiction of Kristen Connor's (Kristy Swanson) post-rape behavior caused only disdain among young women whose beliefs about such occurrences were strongly held.

Desiray, a 15-year-old Black teen mother who participated in the Riverside High School group, pasted an advertisement for *Higher Learning* in her journal and wrote this cryptic account below it:[3]

> I like this clipping because it talk about black and white needing to try to get along and plus it is a very good movie it is about black and whites it was a black and white men lieving with each other and the white dude pulls a gun out on the black dude and calls him a nigger and a monkey. Then some scenes later the white dude his name is Remey he kills the black dude named Malik's girlfriend and Malik goes after him and starts to beat and kick him in the head. Then the campus police come and start to beat Malik because he was beating Remey. After that Remey starts running from the campus police. The police corner him up against the door. He can't get the door opened because it is locked. Remey says he is sorry that he killed Malik's girlfriend. The police says its alright but to Remey its not. So Remey pulls out a gun sticks it in his mouth and blows his brains out. That was the end of the movie.

Later, during a one-on-one interview on the steps of her mother's house, we talked about what she wrote. Despite the time that had elapsed since she saw the movie, Desiray remained fascinated by Remy (Michael Rapaport), the West Coast outcast who became a skinhead. A notable difference in Desiray's oral retelling of the movie was the emphasis on White police, White power:

> Then, his roommate came in and asked him why was he [Remy] like this. Why was he tearing up his stuff? Why couldn't he tear up his own part [of the dorm room they shared]? And then he got mad and then Malik came in there and said just cool down. He threw him down on the bed and then, um, he, the skinhead, pulled out a gun and put it to his head and said, "Don't move! Don't move!" And then after that, um, he was trying to run after him but the White police, they was on his side, so they didn't let him run after him. And then the other guys encouraged him to join the White power or something. And, then, there was this little festival going on and then the policemen had got one of the boys and in a walkie-talkie he was telling him, "White power, get 'em." And then he shot his girlfriend and then he went up there and he was screaming and shaking and he ran after him and was beating him up and everything. He said, "You're nothing. You're a monkey. Look at me! I've got White power."

Judging from her account, Desiray is one of many Black teens, and Black adults as well, who expect the worst from predominantly White police forces. *Higher Learning* served to reinforce what she already believed, giving Desiray one more reason to incorporate in her psyche a distrust and

---

[3]This and other journal excerpts were typed as they appeared.

fear of the police—a predisposition coiled for discharge should she ever feel threatened by a White policeman.

Another aspect of application is resistance, a use or effect of media interaction that opposes mainstream norms. Suggested throughout the study, resistance particularly stood out in the City Scape teens' focus group discussions. Enamored by movies from the 1970s, the teens responded with enthusiasm to movies like *Easy Rider* that suggested a break with what they perceived to be society's norms. "That was so great," one of them observed. "It was just like these hippies on Harleys." "Yah," said another teen. "It's like when the hippies first started coming out and they go around the country and people are like, 'Get out of here!' You know, it's a really good movie!" "Yeah," weighed in another. "Filthy hippies!"

Teens in the City Space group I moderated said they usually watched videos because they couldn't afford the $5.50 or $6.00 it cost them to see a movie in a theater. Besides, one of them pointed out, "It's better to watch them with people! So, you can like enjoy it together, or make fun of it together!" Someone else chimed in,

Yeah. When you watch a movie with your friends, you can always talk about it. If you're by yourself, you don't want to like sit there. I mean, it's funner when you can just talk about what's going on instead of just being there, just concentrating!

"Me and Meredith rented a movie yesterday," Marvin volunteered. Meredith picked up his cue:

It was insane. It was completely insane. It was called *Wild in the Streets*. This guy doses the town's water supply and took over becuz all the ... everyone over 30 drank the water, and then he put everyone over 30 in camps. He told everyone else to not drink it. And they were all trippin' really hard.

Agreed that *Wild in the Streets* was an insane movie, the group turned its attention to *Flashback*, another movie based on a drug theme. Like members of the other focus groups, these teens—many of whom used drugs themselves—used movies they had seen to reaffirm their standing within the group. In this case, the coin of passage was acceptance of a drug culture they thought was cool. Their talk also showed how movies serve to reinforce gender stereotypes: Harleys are for boys; taking care of the world is for girls.

Sean: ... There's this picture, [again referring to *Easy Rider*], and I really want to do it some day, where you're just ridin' across the desert with this phat Harley, with beaucoup cash, just goin' ...

David:	That wouldn't be too hard . . .
Micah:	It wouldn't be too hard? Anybody have $20,000 for a Harley?
Sean:	Oh, no. They paid for it in the beginning. They went down to Mexico.
Eric:	Some friends of mine used to have Harleys. [Really?] This is a long time ago, but in Europe we used to spend a lot of time on the road.
Cat:	You're from Europe?
Eric:	Am I? No. [Oh, okay.] But I got to study over there for a little while.

By challenging Eric on the particulars of his account, Cat interrupts his show of masculinity and turns the conversation toward a fantasy she and Meredith, the only other female in the group, can participate in more readily.

Cat:	Well, when Eric takes over the world, Amsterdam and Switzerland are yours, isn't that right?
Marvin:	Yeah, when I make Eric world emperor, he's gonna give me Switzerland and Amsterdam.
Meredith:	You know what we should do? We should get [unintelligible] and lower the voting age to 14 and enlist a band and then we should take over the world . . .

Disillusioned with life as they had experienced it, these teens played with fantasies of a world in which they were in charge, and they lambasted the media for failing to "tell it like it is." Although their talk moved back and forth between movies and television shows, their friends in the other City Space focus group emphatically condemned the media, too.[4]

Youth 1:	Well, if you think about it, this country's real fucked up in a way that. . . . Like you watch TV. You watch *L.A. Law* and all that shit, and everyone is getting divorced, man. . . . Oh, yeah, my fifth wife, you know, and all this shit, man! There's no, absolutely no . . .
Youth 2:	Morals!
Youth 3:	. . . Respect for marital. . . . There's no morals. There isn't, man!

---

[4]I did not moderate this group, so I was unable to accurately identify who was speaking when just by listening to the tape.

Youth 1:   That's why, dude, that's why in this country, man, like the youngsters date. Dude, they're youngsters, man! There's no like relationships. You pick some chick and she picks some guy, and you guys just like fuck around for two weeks and then you break up. "Oh, yeah. I broke up with my last boyfriend. Now I'm going with . . ." All this shit, man! I mean, I come from Iran, right? And I was there 'til I was 8 years old. But at least I like saw how it was there, and there people just like chilled until they were like 18, and then, maybe, they'd be with two different people and they'd . . . they'd just not do anything with anybody until they decided that this was the right person. I'm not saying it should be like that, but it's like insane here! That's why like 50 percent of Americans are divorced right now! It is because people our age are just like going insane, like fucking everything. (Laughter) What the hell! It's crazy!

Youth 4:   Especially with AIDS, man. I mean . . . that disease scares the hell out of me!

Youth 2:   I know, I mean in the sixties, there was no AIDS!

Youth 1:   Yeah, not in America! So it was like all right. Free love, man! So you got to pass it around. (Laughter)

Mod.:   So, then what's the idea about . . . what's the idea that pervades about what is a relationship?

Youth 3:   Well, shit. There's no like definition of it. . . . There's no standards anymore. Just it's all like up in the air!

DISCUSSION

The words of these young people underscore their yearning for answers they can trust, their desire for "ways to be" in a world that often does not make sense to them. Teens look to movies (and television, too) to understand reality, to understand the world they have inherited. Poised, if not pushed, to break out of the safety net of childhood, they embrace movies as stories about the way the world is, the way they should act as adults. Their discussions illustrate that many of them see movies as good, if not trustworthy ("cool but not real"), sources of information about the way life is. Movies underscore the dilemmas they expect to encounter as adults.

Although they understand, at some level, that movies are commodities produced to make money for "the man," they nevertheless accord a truth factor to what they experience in the dark of theaters or on TV. Because the movie industry has singled them out as willing consumers, an audience worth millions, teens have access to entertainment fare produced just for them. The stars, the story lines, the settings of movies targeted at teens hit them where they are most vulnerable. And they respond—viscerally, emotionally.

In keeping with their life stages and lived experience, teens incorporate or resist the messages embedded in movies. Given their intense desire to fit in, to find a place or group with whom they can share the angst of growing up, teens gravitate to movies that resonate with their sense of who they are and who they want to be with. But despite their ability to reinforce the status quo, movies also afford teens an opportunity to question the givens of society's unwritten rules about gender and race relations. Even when amateurishly produced, movies hold the potential for opening up new vistas, new ways of looking at taken-for-granted assumptions about the world. And in this respect, they can be powerful agenda setters. They place before teens subjects that might otherwise be taboo—giving them an opportunity to question the norms of society.

Repeatedly, the teens in these focus groups observed that they had rarely, if ever, talked about the more controversial topics that came up in their discussions of movies: racial issues, questions related to sexual preferences, AIDS. Movies raised these issues in ways that were less circumscribed than their treatment in textbooks or sex education classes. Hungry to understand or know how they themselves felt about such things, the teens were invigorated by the opportunity to discuss their ideas. They said they rarely talked about such topics with their parents or with adults involved in school- and community-sanctioned extracurricular activities.

So where should we go with the knowledge that movies play an important role in teens' lives, that they open up windows on a better world, or at least on a world that questions the status quo? My conclusion is that adults need to spend more time watching the movies teens watch and more time talking with teens about the movies they like best. Movies are agenda setters for teens. They tell teens what issues and values are important in society, and they suggest ways to think about them. Asked what advice she would give parents, counselors, and teachers, Tenita, a 16-year-old teen mother, responded: "They should know what's goin' on! They should pay attention to their kids when they have somethin' to tell them. Just listen to them when they talk to 'em." It is possible that if we engaged teens in conversation about "their" movies, we might find new ways of thinking about the way things are, and we all—adults and teens together—might see our way clear to thinking about what it would take to make a better world.

ACKNOWLEDGMENTS

This research was supported by a grant from the University of North Carolina at Chapel Hill's Center for Health Behaviors in Vulnerable Youth, which was in turn supported by a grant from the National Institute of Mental Health, National Institutes of Health (Grant No. P20 MH 49875).

REFERENCES

Angell, E., Gordon, D., & Begun, B. (1999, October 19). It's their world: A guide to who's hot. *Newsweek*, pp. 66–67.

Antecol, M. (1997, August). *Learning from television: Parasocial interaction and affective learning.* A paper presented to the Communication Theory and Methodology Division at the annual Association for Education in Journalism and Mass Communication (AEJMC) convention in Chicago.

Appiah, O. (1997, August). *Racial differences in responding to occupational portrayals by models on television.* A paper presented at the AEJMC annual convention in Chicago.

Appiah, O. (1999, August). *Black, white, Hispanic, and Asian-American adolescents' responses to culturally embedded ads.* A paper presented at the AEJMC annual convention in New Orleans, LA.

Berger, J. (1977). *Ways of seeing.* New York: Penguin.

Brown, J. D., Dykers, C. R., Steele, J. R., & White, A. B. (1994). Teenage room culture: Where media and identities intersect. *Communication Research, 21*, 813–827.

Carr, J. (1995, January 11). The moral passion of 'Higher Learning.' *The Boston Globe*, p. 68.

Evans, G., & Busch, A. M. (1995, January 19). Violence hits theaters screening 'Learning'. *Daily Variety*, p. 1.

Film-maker sues director Singleton. (1995, July 31). *The (Montreal) Gazette*, p. E4/break.

Greenberg, B. S., & Brand, J. E. (1994). Minorities and the mass media: 1970s to 1990s. In J. Bryant & D. Zillmann (Eds.), *Media effects: Advances in theory and research* (pp. 273–314). Hillsdale, NJ: Lawrence Erlbaum Associates.

Grossberg, L., Wartella, E., & Whitney, D. C. (1998). *Media making: Mass media in a popular culture.* Thousand Oaks, CA: Sage.

Hill Collins, P. (1991). Learning from the outsider within: The sociological significance of black feminist thought. In J. E. Hartman & E. Messer-Davidow (Eds.), *(En)gendering knowledge: Feminists in academe* (pp. 40–65). Knoxville: University of Tennessee Press.

Hirschberg, L. (1999, September 5). Desperate to seem 16. *The New York Times Magazine*, 42–49/break/74–79.

Lippmann, W. (1922). *Public opinion.* New York: Macmillan.

Lunt, P. K., & Livingstone, S. M. (1994). *Talk on television: Audience participation on public debate.* New York: Routledge.

McCombs, M. E., & Shaw, D. L. (1972). The agenda-setting function of the mass media. *Public Opinion Quarterly, 36*, 176–187.

Natale, R. (1995, January 17). Holiday spurs record-setting movie weekend. *The Los Angeles Times*, p. F1.

Rickey, C. (1998, March 26). Teen-agers are the big spenders at the box office. *The St. Louis Post-Dispatch*, p. G3.

Shaw, D., & Martin, S. E. (1992). The function of mass media agenda setting. *Journalism Quarterly, 69*, 902–920.

Snow, D. A., & Anderson, L. (1987). Identity work among the homeless: The verbal construction and avowal of personal identities. *American Journal of Sociology, 92*, 1336–1371.

Snyder, S. (1995). Movie portrayals of juvenile delinquency: Part I. Epidemiology and criminology. *Adolescence, 30*(117), 53–64.

Squire, J. E. (1983). *The movie business book.* Englewood Cliffs, NJ: Prentice-Hall.

Steele, J. R. (1999). Teenage sexuality and media practice: Factoring in the influences of family, friends, and school. *The Journal of Sex Research, 36,* 331–341.

Steele, J. R., & Brown, J. D. (1995). Adolescent room culture: Studying media in the context of everyday life. *Journal of Youth and Adolescence, 24,* 551–576.

Stepp, C. S. (1996, November). The X factor. *American Journalism Review,* 34–38.

Turan, K. (1995, January 11). 'Higher learning' at Singleton U. *The Los Angeles Times,* p. F1.

Wallendorf, M., & Arnould, E. J. (1988). "My favorite things:" A cross-cultural inquiry into object attachment, possessiveness, and social linkage. *Journal of Consumer Research, 14,* 531–547.

Wertsch, J. V. (1991). *Voices of the mind: A sociocultural approach to mediated action.* Cambridge, MA: Harvard University Press.

Whittler, T. E. (1991). The effects of actors' race in commercial advertising: Review and extension. *Journal of Advertising, 20*(1), 54–60.

The Sounds of Sex: Sex in Teens' Music and Music Videos

Jeffrey Jensen Arnett
University of Maryland

Reprinted with special permission King Features Syndicate

Popular music and sex have gone together like a horse and carriage ever since the days of the horse and carriage. Early in the 20th century, jazz and blues were noted (and vehemently criticized) for the sexual intensity of both their music and lyrics. ("You can't keep a good man down," Mamie Smith sang in an early blues song, and her meaning was not lost on her listeners.) In the 1950s, jazz and blues gave way to rock and roll, and the explosive sexuality of Elvis, Little Richard, and others. From the 1960s to the present, sexual themes have increasingly permeated popular music (Christenson & Roberts, 1998), in genres ranging from ballads to rock to rap. The portrayal of sexuality in popular music has become less subtle, more explicit; by the 1980s, George Michael was singing "I Want Your Sex," and we had moved a long way from the subtlety and playfulness of jazz and blues.

Popular music has always been most popular among the young, who are attracted to the sexual intensity of both the music and the lyrics. Today's teens spend a considerable amount of their time immersed in popular music. In fact, listening to music is their top activity outside of school (Horatio Alger Foundation, 1996). In one survey, 92% of teens (aged 14 to 17) said they had listened to music on the radio during the previous day; 88% had listened to recorded music (Chadwick & Heaton, 1996). Integrating a variety of studies, Christenson and Roberts (1998) concluded that during their high school years, American teens listen to music about 3 to 4 hours per day, on average (compared to 2 to 3 hours per day for TV watching). Music is frequently a secondary activity, a background to some other primary activity, often one that has sexual overtones: dancing, parties, going to nightclubs or other social events (Lull, 1987). But teens listen to music in many other contexts as well. For example, over half of teens listen to music while doing homework (Roberts & Hendricksen, 1990).

In this chapter we begin by looking at portrayals of sexuality in songs and music videos popular among teens. Then we present a theoretical framework for understanding teens' uses of sexually themed songs and videos. Finally, we suggest directions for future research, advocating a more teen-centered approach.

SEXUALITY IN SONGS

Themes of the songs most popular with teens are diverse, ranging from social and political issues to loneliness and alienation. However, for many decades the most common themes in popular songs have been related to sexuality: love, romance, gender, and sex itself (Christenson & Roberts, 1998). Various content analyses have shown that from the 1940s to the present, between 70% to 90% of popular songs have contained themes related to sexuality. In one analysis, Edwards (1994) classified the lyrics in popular songs from 1980 to 1989, using the top 20 singles from each year. (Because songs in genres such as heavy metal and rap tend to be purchased in albums rather than as singles, these genres are underrepresented in this analysis as in most other content analyses). Phrases in songs with themes related to sexuality were classified as optimistic or pessimistic and as physical or emotional. Eighty-five percent of the songs were found to have references to sexuality, and sexuality was the dominant theme in 72%. Sixty-seven percent of the songs had one or more optimistic phrases, but 77% had one or more pessimistic phrases. Phrases were evenly balanced between physical and emotional aspects of sexuality. Lyrics rarely reflected any hesitancy about entering into a sexual relationship, despite the threat of AIDS and other sexually transmitted diseases (STDs). As Edwards (1994) dryly noted, "there was more concern about broken hearts than about disease or pregnancy" (p. 243).

Although songs with themes of sexuality have been consistently popular with teens over the decades, there has been a steady increase since the 1950s in the explicitness of the sexual lyrics in popular songs (Christenson & Roberts, 1998; Strasburger, 1995). Content analyses indicate that there has been a trend toward emphasizing the more physical aspects of sexuality, and less emphasis on its emotional aspects. However, casual sex tends to be portrayed as resulting in unhappiness (Edwards, 1994; Leming, 1987). Emotional themes remain frequent in current songs. Both males and females are often portrayed in popular songs as fools for love—needy, vulnerable, anxious, sad. "Show me how you want it to be," Britney Spears pleads in a recent example of this, her "Baby One More Time"; "My loneliness is killing me."

Although emotional neediness is more commonly attributed to females than males in popular songs (Seidman, 1992), this appears to have become less true over time. In a content analysis of songs from 1945 to 1976, Cooper (1985) found that over this period females in popular songs were portrayed less often as dependent and submissive, more often as powerful. However, as they became more powerful they also became portrayed more often as threatening, evil—dangerous seductresses. A recent example of this can be found in Ricky Martin's "Livin' la Vida Loca:" "Once you get a taste of her you'll never be the same/She will make you go insane."

SEXUALITY IN MUSIC VIDEOS

Music videos have become highly popular among teens since the early 1980s, especially among younger teens (Christenson & Roberts, 1998). Teens watch music videos for about 15 to 30 minutes per day, on average. Although this is much lower than the 3 to 4 hours a day typical among teens for music listening more generally, watching videos tends to be a primary rather than a secondary activity. The proportion of music videos with sexual imagery varies by genre, from about 50% of pop and rap videos to just 8% of heavy metal videos (Tapper, Thorson, & Black, 1994).

One of the most striking features of music videos is the sharp demarcation of gender roles, especially in relation to sexuality. One analysis of 1,000 music video characters found that males are more often depicted as adventurous, aggressive, and dominant; females, in contrast, are more often depicted as affectionate, fearful, and nurturing. Another analysis, comparing videos in different musical genres, found that rap videos were especially likely to be sexist, with females depicted as sexual objects (Utterbach, Ljungdahl, Storm, Williams, & Kreutter, 1995).

Although music videos are fairly diverse in themes and scenes, if there is a such thing as a typical music video it features one or more men performing while beautiful, scantily clad young women dance and writhe lasciviously. Often the men dance, too, but the women always have fewer clothes on. The women are mostly just props; not characters, not even people, really. They appear for a fraction of a second, long enough to shake their butts a couple of times, then the camera moves on.

A prime example of this is in the recent video for Ricky Martin's "Livin' la Vida Loca." Throughout the video, the mostly naked women shake and dance sexily. Ricky dances too, but he never shows any skin. This double standard reaches absurd proportions in "La Vida Loca." The song contains the line "She'll make you take your clothes off and go dancing in the rain," but when this line is sung, Ricky is depicted dancing in the rain with all his clothes on, while a circle of women dancing around him strip theirs off.

Why doesn't Ricky take at least some of his clothes off? Why are women depicted in so much more sexually alluring ways than men in music videos? For the same reason that there are more strip clubs featuring naked female dancers than naked male dancers, and more pornographic magazines featuring naked females than naked males: Because it is more acceptable to reduce females to their sexuality than to reduce males to their sexuality. The sexual double standard of music videos reflects the sexual double standard of the larger society. Ricky does not take his clothes off—not because he would not be even more sexually alluring if he did, but because he would never submit to the indignity of being depicted as a sexual object. For women, however, such indignity is expected to be a standard part of their gender role.

Although the depictions of sexuality in "La Vida Loca" are typical, music videos are diverse, and there are important exceptions. One of the most interesting of these exceptions is a recent video by TLC for their song "Unpretty." In contrast to most other videos, which implicitly confirm gender stereotypes, "Unpretty" directly challenges the cultural pressures that young women face with regard to sexuality. In the primary story line, a young woman considers breast enlargement at the urging of her boyfriend. She is shown going to a cosmetic surgery clinic and being prepared for surgery, but at the last minute she tears off the hospital gown and flees. Next she is shown with her boyfriend, angrily rejecting him for coercing her into the surgery. In a secondary story line, a plump adolescent girl is shown in her bedroom gazing at the thin magazine models she has pasted on her wall. She cuts out a picture of her own face and tapes it onto the body of one of the models, clearly aspiring to look like them. At the end of the video, however, she tears the models down off her walls as she decides to accept herself for what she is. Thus, in both story lines young women are shown rejecting the cultural influences that make them feel "so damned unpretty."

Another striking feature of music videos is that the visual images are often much sexier than the music. This is partly because visual depictions of sex are inherently more arousing than auditory depictions of sex, but also because the videos sometimes take a nonsexual song and make it highly sexual. One recent example of this is Lenny Kravitz's "Fly Away." The lyrics of the song have nothing to do with sex ("I want to get away/I want to fly away/Yeah, yeah, yeah."). The video, however, shows a club scene with Kravitz and his band playing the song as young people—especially the de rigueur scantily clad young women—dance lasciviously. At one point, one of the young women even takes her shirt off, although her bare breasts are censored by blurring them.

The reason for sexualizing music videos even when the topic of the song is nonsexual is not hard to discern: Sex sells, in music videos as elsewhere. Studies of college students have found that they tend to rate videos with sexual imagery higher than other videos (Hansen & Hansen, 1990; Zillmann & Mundorf, 1987). High school students, especially males, respond to sexually explicit videos even more favorably than do college students (Christenson & Roberts, 1998; Greeson, 1991).

TEENS' PERCEPTIONS OF SEXUALITY IN SONGS AND MUSIC VIDEOS

What do teens make of the sexual images in songs and music videos? To what extent do they perceive as sexual the themes and scenes that academics code as sexual in content analyses? Studies on this topic concur that young people interpret song lyrics and music video imagery differently, based on a variety of factors, including social class, ethnicity, gender, interests, and experiences (Christenson & Roberts, 1998). The most important factor influencing their interpretations is age (Strasburger, 1995). In particular, preadolescent and early adolescent children tend to be highly literal in their interpretations, so that they often miss the implied sexuality in the song. For example, Greenfield et al. (1987) examined responses to song lyrics and music videos among college students as well as children in the 4th, 8th, and 12th grades. The fourth and eighth graders often missed the meaning of the lyrics, especially when the lyrics involved sexuality. Reviewing studies of age differences in responses to song lyrics and music videos, Christenson and Roberts (1998) concluded that for children and early adolescents, "their ignorance helps preserve their innocence. ... it is not so much a case of 'you are what you hear' as 'you hear what you are' " (p. 179).

A THEORETICAL FRAMEWORK

Given that young people spend a great deal of their free time listening to music, that their music has a high degree of sexual content, and that sexuality is a key area of development during adolescence, it is surprising that there has not been more research devoted to the relation between music and sexuality in adolescence. Far more research has been conducted on adolescents and television (Strasburger, 1995), although adolescents spend more time listening to music than watching TV and they watch less TV than persons in any other stage of life (Arnett, 1995).

Furthermore, a substantial proportion of research on adolescents and music has been conducted using study designs of questionable validity. The most common design for studies in this area involves having college students respond to songs or music videos in a laboratory situation, in return for credit for a psychology course. The problems with this approach are many, including the facts that (a) college students are too different developmentally from adolescents for findings to be generalizable from one group to the other (Arnett, 2000); (b) college students are not representative even of their age-group; and (c) college students volunteering to take part in a study for course credit are not representative even of other college students. More importantly, the studies are frequently conducted in university classrooms or laboratories, and as a consequence may lack contextual validity. That is, it is difficult to assume that watching preselected music videos in a professor's lab or a university classroom is the same as watching music videos with friends, family, in the dorm, at a bar, or alone.

This design also ignores that adolescents make choices of which music and music videos to consume, based on their own preferences. A researcher might show music videos containing images of sexual violence to 20 subjects, and claim to find an effect of the music videos on the respondents' attitudes about violence toward women, when in reality only 2 of the 20 would ever watch such music videos of their own volition. The effects of the videos on those 2 respondents may be different from the effects on the other 18, yet this would not be apparent in the data analysis or the report of the results. The data from the only 2 individuals who would actually choose to watch these music videos would be lost in the noise from the 18 who would never be exposed to them in real life. This design treats people as blank slates, having no important differences among them that would lead them to make different choices about their music consumption or that would cause them to respond in different ways to the music and music videos that they do consume.

We believe that research on sex and teens' music would benefit from the application of a theoretical framework that focuses on what young people themselves say about the meanings of the music. Specifically, we propose a model based on the uses and gratifications approach to media research (Arnett, 1995; Rubin, 1994). At the heart of the this approach is the idea that people make choices about the media they consume, and that their choices are guided by the uses they believe they can make of media and the gratifications they gain from their media experiences. Rather than viewing people as passive and easily manipulated targets of media, the uses and gratifications approach views them as active agents who determine to a large extent the media to which they are exposed, through the choices they make in an environment in which a vast range of media content is available (Arnett, Larson, & Offer, 1995).

With respect to teens, music, and sex, the uses and gratifications approach suggests the questions: What uses do teens make of songs and music videos with sexual themes, and what gratifications do they gain from them? We address this question, using a framework that has been employed previously as a general framework for understanding adolescents' uses of media (Arnett, 1995). Here, we apply it specifically to adolescents' uses of songs and music videos with sexual themes, using current examples for illustration. The three uses considered are entertainment, identity formation, and coping. These three uses are not meant to be exhaustive, but to be considered examples of the uses that teens may make of sexually themed songs and music videos.

Entertainment

Adolescents use sexually themed songs and music videos as daily entertainment, as a way of pleasantly passing the time. Music provides an almost constant background to their activities outside of school, and most of the music they like best contains sexual themes (Christenson & Roberts, 1998). They listen to music while doing their homework, while driving a car, and while walking or jogging, but especially in contexts where the focus is on leisure; no teen party would be complete without music (Lull, 1987). For music videos, too, teens state that one of their top reasons for watching them is entertainment (Sun & Lull, 1986).

A substantial proportion of the songs and music videos that appeal to teens have entertainment as their evident aim. The songs and music videos of Madonna have provided good examples of this over the years. Neither the lyrics nor the music in her songs are very distinctive or original. The topics tend to be sexual—dancing, flirting, boys and girls meeting and pairing up and parting again—all long-standing, well-worn themes of popular music; the lyrics are also laden with clichés. But to teens, the appeal of the songs may be precisely the fact that they are so predictable and demand so little from the listener. They are like a tasty confection, easy to consume and quickly forgotten, but pleasant to experience for the moment—to dance to, to tap your foot to, to sing along with, to fantasize with.

Many music videos have elaborate dance routines that add to their entertainment value. Recent videos by Britney Spears, Jennifer Lopez, and Christina Aguilera are in this vein. For example, in "Baby One More Time" Britney Spears and her supporting cast engage in elaborate synchronized dance routines throughout the video. The setting is a high school, and they are shown dancing mainly in the hall and the gymnasium. The dancing is mildly provocative, and Britney is dressed in a revealing outfit. The lyrics of the song are actually rather somber and brooding, but the music and the dancing change the spirit of the video to pure entertainment, a celebration of youthful vigor and sexuality.

Identity Formation

Identity formation has long been viewed as one of the key developmental challenges of adolescence. It consists of gaining a clear sense of one's interests, needs, desires, and abilities with respect to love, work, and beliefs (Erikson, 1968). With respect to love, it includes both developing a sense of one's sexuality and developing a gender role identity, that is, a conception of oneself as a man or woman in relation to the gender role requirements of one's culture.

Music and music videos can play an important part in both love-related aspects of identity formation. The portrayal of sexuality offered in popular songs can best be described as recreational. Sex is often portrayed as light-hearted fun. A recent example is Lou Bega's "Mambo Number Five." This song consists mostly of Lou describing, or at least fantasizing about, his sexual adventures with a long list of women. He describes how he desires "a little bit" of each one of them—"a little bit of Sandra in the sun/A little bit of Mary all night long," and so on. In the video, Lou sings and dances in a snazzy suit and hat, while the women who are the objects of his desire dance around him, scantily clad. They all seem to be enjoying themselves immensely.

Thus, adolescents may learn from this that sex is a source of recreation, pure fun, not requiring commitment, not to be taken seriously. The sex of popular songs like "Mambo Number Five" is sex in a world without unwanted pregnancy, STDs, or even the complications of emotional relationships.

With regard to the gender role aspect of identity, songs and music videos often portray stereotyped gender roles, with males as aggressive and tough, females as vulnerable and needy or as seductresses. For example, in Limp Bizkit's recent "Nookie," the first part of the song is a hip-hop-style account of the singer's rejection by his girlfriend; this soon turns into an angry rant, as he shouts at her contemptuously, "I did it all for the nookie/The nookie/So you can take that cookie/And stick it up your (yeah!)." The male gender role, as portrayed in this song, means reacting to love-induced pain with anger.

Although analyses of songs and music videos indicate that most of them promote stereotypical gender roles, it is important not to stereotype the songs and videos themselves. They are diverse, and there are many exceptions to any generalization about them. The songs and videos of male performers like the Backstreet Boys are as emotionally vulnerable and needy as anything by female performers. As for aggressiveness, one of the most aggressive recent videos is by a female performer. In "Heartbreaker," Mariah Carey sings about her pain over her unfaithful boyfriend. In the video, Mariah and her friends trail the faithless boyfriend and his lover to a movie theater; Mariah then follows the lover to the ladies' room, where she physically assaults her! No protests were raised over the violence in this video—although it is more violent than anything that can be found in recent videos by male performers—perhaps because Mariah's violence is a violation of normative expectations for gender roles, and so is not taken seriously as promoting violence.

Coping

Another use of media common among adolescents is coping, especially in response to issues involving sexuality. Love and sex can result in frustration, disappointment, and pain, and the songs and videos popular among teens portray this side of sexuality as well. There are songs about unrequited love, songs about unfaithful lovers, songs about being lonely and wishing for a lover. All of these themes have long been staples of popular songs. Why would adolescents want to listen to songs about the unhappy side of sexual relationships? Because they know this side of sexuality all too well from their own lives, and listening to the sad songs consoles them, expresses what they have difficulty expressing themselves, and makes them feel that someone else has experienced what they are experiencing and understands how they feel (Arnett, 1996).

In studies using the "beeper" method, Larson (1995) has found that adolescents spend a considerable amount of time in their rooms alone, listening to music. When they are beeped during these times, their moods are often low; they frequently report being lonely or sad. Afterward, however, they feel revived and strengthened. They use the music as a way of coping with and working through painful emotions and difficult relationship issues, often related to sexuality. Even though the music is often sad, listening to sad music in a state of sadness has the paradoxical effect of making them feel better.

WHERE TO NOW? TOWARD AN EMIC APPROACH

What can we conclude about music, sex, and adolescents on the basis of the research that has been conducted so far? First, we know that music is an important part of teens' daily lives, and that most of the music they listen to has sexuality as its theme. Second, we know that many of the songs and music videos most popular among teens portray gender roles in a stereotyped way, although there are notable exceptions to this rule. Third, we know that teens make use of sexually themed songs and music videos for a variety of purposes in their lives, most notably entertainment, identity formation, and coping.

These conclusions represent a solid foundation for future research on music, sex, and adolescents. Where should research be focused now, given this foundation? We would argue that more attention should be directed toward what teens themselves say about the songs and music videos that appeal to them. What we know at this point is based mostly on the judgments of scholars. It is scholars who have asserted that the songs and videos promote stereotyped gender roles. It is scholars who have made most of the judgments about the uses that teens make of songs and videos. Now we should turn our attention to what teens themselves say about why they listen to sexually themed songs and watch sexually themed videos. In anthropological terminology, we should move from an etic approach, in which outsiders make judgments about the meanings of symbols and rites and behavior in a culture, to an emic approach, in which interpretations of these meanings come from the members of the culture themselves.

Here are some of the questions that could be addressed:

- Which sexually themed songs and videos do they like most? Are there sexually themed songs and videos that they dislike or reject? If so, why?
- To what extent are they conscious of the gender stereotyping in songs and videos? Do they respond to this stereotyping positively, negatively, or with mixed feelings?

- To what extent do they believe that the portrayals of sexuality in songs and videos reflect real-life sexuality?
- Do they believe they are influenced in their sexuality by the songs and videos they listen to and watch? In what ways?

One good model of how to proceed with this line of research can be found in the work of Steele and Brown (1995). They used several methods to explore teens' views of sexuality in the media. In one method, girls were asked to record in journals whatever they witnessed in the media about "love, sex and relationships." After a month of journal keeping, each girl was interviewed about her media uses. Another method, called "auto-driving," was also used, in which each teen took an interviewer on a tour of his or her bedroom, describing into a tape recorder everything in the room that held special meaning or significance. Many of these special items were media related—posters, magazine photos, concert tickets. The focus of Steele and Brown's (1995) research was on media use generally, but these and other similar methods could easily be applied specifically to the topic of sexuality and music. Through such methods, we are likely to gain new insights into the uses that teens make of sexually themed songs and music videos.

ACKNOWLEDGMENT

I wish to thank Jo-Ann Amadeo for her assistance with background research for this chapter.

REFERENCES

Arnett, J. J. (1995). Adolescents' uses of media for self-socialization. *Journal of Youth & Adolescence, 24,* 519–534.

Arnett, J. J. (1996). *Metalheads: Heavy metal music and adolescent alienation.* Boulder, CO: Westview Press.

Arnett, J. J. (2000). Emerging adulthood: A conception of development from the late teens through the twenties. *American Psychologist, 55,* 469–480.

Arnett, J. J., Larson, R., & Offer, D. (1995). Beyond effects: Adolescents as active media users. *Journal of Youth & Adolescence, 24,* 511–518.

Chadwick, B. A., & Heaton, T. B. (1996). *Statistical handbook of adolescents in America.* New York: Oryx Press.

Christenson, P. G., & Roberts, D. F. (1998). *It's not only rock & roll: Popular music in the lives of adolescents.* Cresskill, NJ: Hampton Press.

Cooper, V. (1985). Women in popular music: A quantitative analysis of feminine images over time. *Sex Roles, 13,* 499–506.

Edwards, E. D. (1994). Does love really stink? The "Mean World" of love and sex in popular music of the 1980s. In J. S. Epstein (Ed.), *Adolescents and their music: If it's too loud, you're too old* (pp. 225–249). New York: Garland.

Erikson, E. H. (1968). *Identity: Youth and crisis*. New York: Norton.

Greenfield, P. M., Bruzzone, L., Koyamatsu, K., Satuloff, W., Nixon, K., Brodie, M., & Kingsdale, D. (1987). What is rock music doing to the minds of our youth? A first experimental look at the effects of rock music lyrics and music videos. *Journal of Early Adolescence, 7*, 315–329.

Greeson, L. (1991). Recognition and ratings of television music videos: Age, gender, and sociocultural effects. *Journal of Applied Psychology, 21*, 1908–1920.

Hansen, C. H., & Hansen, R. D. (1990). The influence of sex and violence on the appeal of rock music videos. *Communication Research, 17*, 212–234.

Horatio Alger Foundation (1996). *The mood of American youth*. Alexandria, VA: Horatio Alger Foundation of Distinguished Americans.

Larson, R. (1995). Secrets in the bedroom: Adolescents' private use of media. *Journal of Youth & Adolescence, 24*, 535–550.

Leming, J. (1987). Rock music and the socialization of moral values in early adolescence. *Youth & Society, 18*, 363–383.

Lull, J. (1987). Listeners' communicative uses of popular music. In J. Lull (Ed.), *Popular music and communication* (2nd ed., pp. 1–32). Newbury Park, CA: Sage.

Roberts, D. F., & Hendricksen, L. (1990, June). *Music listening versus television watching among older adolescents*. Paper presented at the annual meeting of the International Communication Association, Dublin, Ireland.

Rubin, A. (1994). Media uses and effects: A uses-and-gratifications perspective. In J. Bryant & D. Zillmann (Eds.), *Media effects: Advances in theory and research* (pp. 417–436). Hillsdale, NJ: Lawrence Erlbaum Associates.

Seidman, S. (1992). An investigation of sex-role stereotyping in music videos. *Journal of Broadcasting and Electronic Media, 36*, 209–216.

Steele, J. R., & Brown, J. D. (1995). Adolescent room culture: Studying media in the context of everyday life. *Journal of Youth & Adolescence, 24*, 551–576.

Strasburger, V. C. (1995). *Adolescents and the media: Medical and psychological impact*. Thousand Oaks, CA: Sage.

Sun, S., & Lull, J. (1986). The adolescent audience for music videos and why they watch. *Journal of Communication, 36*, 115–125.

Tapper, J., Thorson, E., & Black, D. (1994). Variations in music videos as a function of their musical genre. *Journal of Broadcasting and Electronic Media, 38*, 103–113.

Utterback, E., Ljungdahl, E., Storm, N., Williams, M., & Kreutter, J. (1995). *Image and sound: A comparative analysis of gender roles in music videos*. Unpublished manuscript.

Zillmann, D., & Mundorf, N. (1987). Image effects in the appreciation of video rock. *Communication Research, 14*, 316–334.

13

Sexual Selves on the World Wide Web: Adolescent Girls' Home Pages as Sites for Sexual Self-Expression

Susannah Stern
University of North Carolina–Chapel Hill

Reprinted with special permission King Features Syndicate

It's 9:10 p.m. Anastasia, a high school senior, just concluded her daily journal entry. Tonight she narrated, in great detail, her most recent sexual encounter with her high school boyfriend. Anastasia described how they "rented a hotel room," "made love" using a condom ("We may be teenagers with raging hormones, but we're not stupid"), and afterward stopped at Wal-Mart to "buy a brush so I could fix my hair" before going home. She expressed how wonderful she felt and how she thought her boyfriend loved her, "even though he hasn't said it yet." She marveled, "If this is as close to being high as I get, I hope I never come down."

Remarkably, when Anastasia finished her intimate entry, she did not hurriedly shut her diary, lock it with a key, and hide it under her pillow. Rather, she clicked twice on her computer mouse and immediately uploaded her journal entry onto one of the most public and far-reaching media in existence: the World Wide Web (WWW).

Like countless other girls across the globe, Anastasia is the architect of her own WWW home page. Communicating not just with words, but also with images, sounds, and hypertext,[1] she posts her page to a geographically removed yet potentially global public. Personal home pages have been considered "people's self-created windows on themselves" (Wynn & Katz, 1997, p. 318), and girls like Anastasia display the selves they think they are, the selves they wish to become, and the selves they wish others to see (Markus & Nurius, 1986). They represent their multiple selves in diverse ways and with varying degrees of security (Stern, in press). Some engineer intricate sites that carry their visitors through detailed writings, photo galleries, and personal histories; others compose uncomplicated sites devoted to unusual hobbies and favorite musicians. And, as Anastasia's sexually candid entry illustrates, many girls' home pages also feature themes rarely spoken about, as the girls say, IRL ("In Real Life").

Sexual discussions and representations on adolescent girls' home pages are especially intriguing because the amalgam of private authorship and anonymous global readership offered by the WWW enables girls to speak both confidentially and publicly about a conventionally taboo topic. Adolescence in particular is frequently recognized as a life stage during which individuals actively and consciously begin to engage in identity construction. Sexuality is an important part of this burgeoning identity (Steinberg, 1993) and one with which adolescent girls are likely to be preoccupied. Adolescent girls with WWW access and expertise can take advantage of an assortment of technical features (aural, visual, textual, and hypertextual) to express their evolving sexual selves. Considering the unique intersection of

---

[1]Hypertext is a special feature made possible by HTML (Hyper Text Markup Language). Hypertext allows Web users to move between various locations on the Web by clicking on highlighted text and/or images.

these phenomena, I endeavored to learn more about the nature of adolescent girls' sexual self-expression on their home pages.

HOME PAGE ARCHITECTS: WHO ARE THEY?

In light of the mutable and disorganized nature of the WWW (home pages appear and disappear literally every day), no master index of sites exists to clarify exactly how many girls have created home pages or who they are. Moreover, relatively little attention has been paid to girls as home-page creators, or even as new media producers in general. Within the academic community, the focus has been predominantly on Web offerings either for girls or about girls, rather than those by girls. Manufacturers and market research companies (i.e., *Smartgirl Internette, GirlGames*) seem to be making the greatest effort to identify and communicate with girls online in their efforts to capitalize on the "new" teen girl market (Horovitz, 1999).

Despite the current lack of information about girls who create home pages, it is reasonable to conclude that they comprise an extremely small portion of the American adolescent girl population at large. Considering that WWW home-page construction necessitates repeated access to a computer, an Internet connection, space on a server, familiarity (if not dexterity) with Web navigation and site publication, at least elementary Web design skills, and ample time for building and publishing the page, the likelihood of any adolescent maintaining a home page is presumably quite small. Teens who have computers and access to the Internet at home (in slightly more than one third of households with children aged 8 to 17, as of 1998) are most likely to maintain WWW home pages (Turow, 1999); most teens are not granted sufficient time or guidance in school to develop computer and Web navigation skills, let alone Web design capabilities. Because they lack the most basic requirement, ready access to a computer, it is difficult for almost one third of *all* American teens to maintain WWW home pages; and one third of those with computers at home are also hindered because they lack an Internet connection (Turow, 1999). Notably, even of those with Internet access (8.4 million teens aged 13 to 17), far fewer girls than boys spend time online (National Science Foundation, 1997).

Not surprisingly, teens with Internet access at home usually are privileged socioeconomically. A 1997 study found that teens from families that earned more than $50,000 per year were much more likely than those from middle- or low-income families to have computers and Internet access at home (National Science Foundation, 1997). A 1999 study by the Annenberg Public Policy Center concluded that parents' experience with the Web outside the home was the primary predictor of an online connection in a household (Turow, 1999). Income disparities also tend to correlate highly with race, suggesting that girls who currently create home pages are most likely White.

Altogether, we can assume that the girls who create home pages are, at least currently, an elite group. Their privileged socioeconomic status and race are noteworthy in light of this study's focus on sexual expression. Girls from different classes often harbor differing values, worries, and expectations concerning sexuality. For instance, body image concerns have (at least until recently) largely been the preoccupation of upper-middle- and upper-class White girls (Brumberg, 1997; Phillips, 1998). Musings on girls' home pages about their "fat thighs" or their "need to lose weight" signal as much about their specific culture's emphasis on physical perfection as they do about individual girls' idiosyncrasies or about adolescent girl culture more broadly. White bourgeois culture has also historically emphasized self-development, and girls of this class commonly have been encouraged to document their self-evolution in such works as diaries and journals (Brumberg, 1997). Even for economically privileged girls who never kept a diary, their familiarity with the custom of journal keeping presumably makes them more familiar with and accepting of self-reflection and projection. In this context, self-expression might reasonably be seen as a legitimate, if not customary, undertaking for the girls who currently create home pages. Sexual self-expression seems an obvious natural outgrowth of self-reflection, particularly for girls during adolescence.

A Closer Look

Despite the current inability of most girls to create home pages, it is important to explore how those with means and interest choose to represent themselves. Not only can we learn more about how a select group of girls represent sexuality in a public forum, but we can also gain a better understanding of how the WWW might facilitate certain forms of self-expression.

To begin this exploration, I systematically analyzed 10 WWW home pages created by girls who were 13 to 18 years old in spring 1999.[2] The term *personal home page*[3] is used to refer to not-for-profit Web sites with a personal focus constructed by individuals. Despite the name, a home page usually actually consists of multiple "pages," or screens, within a Web site. Thus, a home page could comprise, for example, 60 pages (screens). I se-

---

[2]I included only home pages on which age and gender were either implicitly or explicitly identified. An explicit reference to gender, for example, included a picture of the female author of the site. An example of an implicit reference to age was a reference to the high school prom. Girls who were 18 were only considered for inclusion in the study if they indicated they were still in high school.

[3]Hereafter, the term *personal home page* is referred to only as *home page*.

lected the home pages for this study randomly from a list of more than 100 that was compiled by conducting key-word searches[4] in prominent WWW search engines[5] and following appropriate links. Only those home pages were included that addressed sexuality, broadly defined as "an integral part of development through the life span, involving gender roles, self-concept, body image, emotions, relationships, societal mores, as well as intercourse and other sexual behaviors" (Koch, 1993, p. 293).[6]

Qualitative content analysis (Altheide, 1996) was used to analyze the home pages. Many researchers have endorsed qualitative analysis of material culture (Ball & Smith, 1992; Berger, 1991). A qualitative approach seemed most appropriate at this point particularly because the subject is so new and unexplored. Qualitative analysis also allowed greater room for description and analysis of both manifest and latent content, and permitted significant themes to emerge (Altheide, 1996).

The girls' home pages were analyzed following a basic protocol (Altheide, 1996) that focused primarily on substantive features (content)) and formal features (style of writing, images, and links). Analysis began by compiling a descriptive summary sheet for each home page, and then these summaries were read and reread. The original home pages were visited multiple times. The constant comparison method was used to help organize and re-organize data on dimensions that emerged as distinctive and significant (Strauss & Corbin, 1994).

Although it is impossible to know girls' intentions or motivations when creating their home pages, I assumed that girls create their web pages intentionally and strategically. Girls who design home pages make decisions about how their page will look and what their audience will learn about them (Lindsay, 1996). This interpretation of girls' home pages is also grounded in studies of material culture that attest to the ability of artifacts to speak about the people who produced them (Altheide, 1996; Hodder, 1994). Conclusions for this study were drawn from the home pages themselves, based wholly on the selves the girls portrayed.

---

[4]Key words included: "girl home pages," "high school and girl," "teen girl." These terms elicited the 100 home pages included in the constructed universe. It is not known what proportion of the entire population of girls' pages online these 100 pages represent. Based purely on personal experience navigating the WWW, I would estimate that there are well over 500 girls' pages on the WWW and likely as many as several thousand.

[5]Search engines included: *Yahoo!* (http://www.yahoo.com/), *excite* (http://www.excite.com/), and AltaVista (http://www.altavista.com/).

[6]A random purposeful sampling technique was used to draw a sample of 10 pages. The first 10 randomly drawn sites that were deemed "information-rich" were included in the sample (Patton, 1990). One randomly selected home page was excluded from the sample because it was not deemed information-rich. This page focused entirely on a science project conducted by the author. Another home page was randomly selected in its place.

PARTITIONING THE SEXUAL SELF

Despite the variety of substantive and stylistic differences in the girls' home pages, striking similarities in their structure suggested the presence of already well-established home-page conventions. The 10 sites all began with an entry page that announced either the title of the site (for example, *A Keen City*) or the author's real or assumed name (for example, Caitlin, Diva, Misanthrope). Initial entry pages usually led to a directory where most girls had organized their sites into category-specific pages. With considerable creativity and varying degrees of self-evaluation, the girls intertwined representations of their sexual selves into each of the sections. The most common sections included:

- biography ("All About Me")
- online journal
- original writings (editorials, poetry, essays)
- photo gallery (pictures of self, friends, favorite media stars)
- music archives (favorite songs, lyrics, and performers; listings of acquired CDs)
- guest book
- listing of favorite links on the WWW and web ring memberships[7]

Although I initially tried to analyze the girls' home pages as whole bodies of work, it slowly became clear that the girls did not present a coherent, uniform sexual self throughout their home pages. On the contrary, the girls appeared to use the various sections of their home pages to speak in different ways about a variety of subjects. Overall, the girls' home pages suggested that certain types of expression belonged in particular provinces within the site, and such apportionment gave girls the opportunity to be inconsistent without being inauthentic.

Not only did the different sections of girls' home pages contain distinct genres of writing, but each also seemed to offer girls disparate opportunities for self-definition. In some areas of their home pages, girls overtly referenced their sexuality (such as self-concept and body image). In others, girls more vaguely represented their sexuality (such as physical pleasure and desire). Moreover, it seems that the girls used the various formats of each section either to affiliate themselves with or distance themselves from cer-

---

[7]Web rings interlink a series of individual Web sites to one another. Visitors who happen onto a site in a web ring need only click on the ring's icon to be carried to a site similar to its predecessor (Basch, 1998).

tain public identities. These self-presentation tactics suggested that the girls were still grappling with how they wished others to view them.

Biographies

The biography sections of girls' home pages communicated with the most deliberate and lucid voice. Because the fundamental aim of biography is self-explication, the girls willingly defined themselves in their own words. Girls have less control over the impression they create in the other sections of their home pages because their self-focus is less apparent and anticipated. Self-concept is a key sexuality element addressed in a definitive manner in biography sections. For example, on her "me" page, Katie elaborately explained herself in terms of her age (14, although "I don't look my age"), hobbies (reading, writing, watching "teevee," surfing the net), and psychology ("weird," "antisocial"). She even offered a character summary: "I'm a typical freshman. I have erratic mood swings, and can go from mild-mannered bookworm to psychotic mad-girl on a rampage in less than 5 seconds." Not only does Katie's self-synopsis suggest that she has likely bought into the "temperamental teen" stereotype, but it also allowed her to present herself—on her own terms—as a complex and changeable individual. In other sections of Katie's site (e.g., her poem "Overcoming the Jabberwock" or her short story "Destiny of Darkness"), her home-page visitors must draw their own conclusions about Katie (e.g., "she seems angry" or "she sounds imaginative"). By offering self-selected descriptors, girls more easily create the selves they want others to perceive.

The biography sections of girls' home pages tend to be the simplest in terms of length and structure (usually only one screen, often written in list form). For the most part, they tend to have few links, if any, and are heavily text-based with little or no images or music. In addition to the types of information the girls would likely supply in any autobiographical statement (age, hobbies, etc.), they also include statements about their personality types ("I'm Dana and I'm the type of girl your mother warned you about") and idiosyncracies. Katie, for example, explained, "I don't like animals, including small children that stare at me. I don't like the concept of being abandoned. Money frightens me, and I have trouble buying things. I aspire to be geekier than I already am."

Interestingly, but perhaps not surprisingly for girls in adolescence, relationships also emerged frequently in their biography sections as a component of girls' self-descriptions. For example, after identifying her year of birth (1982), car model (gray 1989 Dodge Omni), nicknames ("farmer bitch", "happy," "hey you"), and zodiac sign (Aries), Katie documented her "status" as "single." Katie apparently viewed her dating situation as a central part of her current identity. Leigh Ann's "About Me!" page approached dating status from another angle. Rather than emphasizing being single, Leigh Ann relayed her "CRUSH AT SCHOOL: C ... he knows who he is" as well as her obsession with various media celebrities such as the musical group the Moffatt Brothers. Dana also posted her personal profile ("My Red Self") in a series of phrases that describe who she thinks she is:

> Dana
> 15 years old
> American Egyptian
> Not a very happy person although I try and pretend to be ...
> Very passionate about things I love
> A Riot Grrl
> In love with a guy, Jafry ...

Like the other girls, Dana implied that her romantic interest in Jafry is as central to her current sense of self as her personality ("not a very happy person", "very passionate") and ethnic background (American Egyptian.)

Farther down her autobiographical list, Dana included: "Attracted to older guys (When I say older I mean 17, 18)." Such statements about romantic preferences were a frequent part of biographies. Katey, for example, listed what she "looks for in a guy": "Nice smile smart good looking, funny, athletic, ... i used to only like guys with blonde hair but for some reason now i like guys with dark hair, esp. ... WALTER!!) ..."[8] Articulating romantic ideals in an online biography is a noncommittal task, considering that preferences may be modified and updated as they change (as Katey indicated her recent interest in dark-haired boys.) Jocelyn, an eloquent 16-year-old from the Boston suburbs, explained on her home page: "I feel an almost constant need to change my web page to reflect who I am all the time." Comments like Jocelyn's imply that home pages probably are no more stable than the developing identities of the girls who create them.

Online Journals

Sexual behavior is most explicitly and saliently addressed in the online journals girls post on their WWW home pages. The online journals use the same spontaneous, stream-of-consciousness form that is the hallmark of most off-line journals. They also follow conventional journal formats by including the date at the beginning; using the first-person voice; and giving an almost ritualistic coverage of recent events, and a detailed description and analysis of feelings. Jocelyn explained:

---

[8] Original language, spelling, and punctuation are retained in all direct quotes throughout this chapter.

... I use [my online journal] as an outlet and as a way to express my feelings. My journal helps me to organize my thoughts into some form of coherence, to look back and see how much I've changed over the past few months, and has added a dimension of self-examination to my thinking.

Journals seem to be the preferred location within girls' home pages to ponder the morality of engaging in sexual activities. The girls' entries reflect their confusion about when and for whom it is "right" to "go all the way." Anastasia, who described an evening with her boyfriend, quoted at the beginning of this chapter, used her journal entry as a place to evaluate and assuage her worries about the progress of her relationship:

We haven't had sex yet, but we have talked about it. We parked in a secluded spot last night, but we got run off by some guy before we could actually do more than kiss. And his sister wouldn't let us use her house for a little while. I have been thinking a lot about sleeping with him. I love him, I really do, though I haven't told him.... I'm nervous about saying it.

Anastasia did decide to sleep with her boyfriend, just days after she wrote the words above. Both before and after, she voiced concern that she had not yet told her boyfriend that she loved him, and she worried that he also had not yet articulated his love for her. Anastasia's preoccupation with actually verbalizing their love seems reflective of a belief that sex should occur only in loving relationships. Thompson (1995) explained how the notion that love justifies sexual intimacy is supported both by mass culture and by sex education in schools. Tolman and Higgins (1996) also described how we have a "cultural story that girls' sexuality is about relationships and not desire" (p. 215). Anastasia used her journal to announce the love for her boyfriend that she could not yet admit face to face. Perhaps knowing that her journal was accessible to the general public made her statements of love feel more authentic, and thus her actions more legitimate.

Anastasia's conviction that her own sexual experiences are an acceptable part of a loving relationship corresponds closely with what Orenstein (1994) termed girls' "fear of falling." Orenstein conducted interviews with and observed eighth-grade girls and concluded

There is only one label worse than "schoolgirl" at Weston, and that's her inverse, the fallen girl, or in student parlance, the slut. A "slut" is not merely a girl who "does it," but any girl who—through her clothes, her makeup, her hairstyle, or her speech—seems as if she *might*. (p. 51)

Anastasia is quick to form such judgments about her peers:

I found out something today that made me kind of glad that Brian and I didn't go to Derrick's party Saturday night. Kim Hunter, a sophomore, had a little too much to drink that night. She sucked two guys' dicks at the same time at the party. She didn't even know one of the guys. Then she stood in the middle of the room and pulled up her shirt and bra and let the guys do whatever they wanted to her boobs. Maybe it was a good thing we went to the movies instead. That girl is turning into a little slut. And she wonders why I never talk to her. I told her I talk when I have something to say and left her standing there.

Anastasia's fear not only of being perceived as a slut but of even associating with one testifies to the seriousness with which the girls regard their perceived sexual identity. Anastasia shrewdly took advantage of the situation she described above to provide her online readers with a point of comparison: She is chaste when contrasted with the likes of Kim Hunter.

Kate, an Illinois high school junior, similarly fretted about the slut identity in her online journal and pondered the possibility that her closest friend, Anna, may have "fallen":

I don't fucking believe it. Anna is such a slut I could barf. I was talking to her at work and she was talking about her going to see her little Argentine friends last night. She goes, "I did what Amy did" aka she gave some guy she doesn't even know a blowjob. She gives someone a blowjob who she doesn't even KNOW, and who calls her a whore, and she thinks she's all better than me or something now. She didn't come right out and say it, but I could just tell by the way she was acting.

She said something like, "I guess I'm like Amy now" or some shit. The girl LIKES being a slut. She fucking LIKES being a fucking slut? What the hell?

Is this the fucking twilight zone?

Ok, when school starts, I'm on the fucking lookout for a new friend[s].

Kate's entry signals her own sexual standards. How can a girl—indeed, her friend—willingly participate in sexual activities in a noncommitted relationship? Like Anastasia, she seems unsure what the precise conditions are that make a girl a slut, but she uses her journal to hash them out. She also is concerned that Anna "thinks she's all better than me or something now." If being a slut is bad, Kate seems to be deliberating, why would Anna be proud of it? Kate's confused and hostile feelings toward her friend reflect a culture that has provided mixed messages about sex from all sectors, including families, religion, school, and the mass media. Especially in television and film, the line between what makes one woman a slut and another simply a beautiful, sensual woman is often difficult to distinguish. Perhaps Kate's words waver between disgust and uncertain envy because she is loathe to become a slut herself but scared of being left out or behind. Indeed, later in her journal, Kate posits that she is "the only fucking virgin left on the face of the earth, and the only person fucking proud of it and the only person who won't fucking degrade herself for sex from some fucking ass I don't even know!" Kate's profane language suggests she may be as angry and afraid as she is confident with her sexual standards.

Original Writings

The original writings the girls posted on their home pages ranged from poetry to short stories to essays. In each, the girls seemed to relinquish the deliberateness of their biographies and the conjecture of their journals in exchange for a more creative, mysterious, and theoretical voice. In these original writings, girls appeared to tackle the biggest issues in their lives—the issues that resurface often enough that the girls have devised multiple styles to express their complexity and consequences.

In their content, creativity, and candor, girls' original writings on their home pages resemble the type of expression commonly represented in zines, another late-20th-century mode of self-expression. Zines have been defined in numerous ways, but essentially the term (derived from *fanzine*) refers to nonprofit works usually self-published by those without access to mainstream communication resources. Zine producers often type or handwrite their pieces; photocopy them at a local copy shop; and distribute them by hand, by mail, and at local book and music shops. Recently, there has been a dramatic increase in the number of "personal, confessional" zines by teenage girls (Chu, 1997, p. 73). "Girl zines" (publications by and for girls and women) have emerged as a distinct genre—and one that allows girls to represent themselves and their thoughts in a variety of ways. Alternative communities such as lesbians and bisexuals, teenage mothers, and abused daughters publish their own zines to share and reflect on their stories of sexuality.

As in zines, the original writings girls post on their home pages also frequently detail matters of sexuality, especially love, sex, and heartbreak. The girls editorialize about such topics as homophobia, feminism, and bisexuality. Caitlin, for example, wrote a lengthy three-screen essay entitled "Yes, I Am Bi-sexual." She began:

> At first I was debating whether to broadcast my sexual orientation to the whole world wide web. I decided not to, because i am pretty damn closed about it, at least in the high school world. After some thought i decided to put up my views, because they should be heard (or maybe i just think so) . . . and because this is who i am, and i can't hide from it.

Caitlin appeared to view her home page as an appropriate forum from which to test run her identity claims. Despite her concern about broaching such a personal topic, she apparently felt entitled to express herself. Like the girls who produce zines, she seemed eager to address topics frequently ignored by the mass media, and she anticipated mainstream reactions to her statements. She continued:

> First off—i know some of you are shaking your heads saying one of two things: either "she's a lesbian in denial," or "this is trendy, she likes ani difranco, its a trend." you are both wrong. i was very confused at first knowing i like (gasp!) men and women, how could i? Isn't it gay or straight? Then i was introduced to the idea of bi-sexuality, and it all made sense ... "this is me"....

It seems almost as though Caitlin were carrying on an imaginary conversation—or perhaps it is one that she has experienced in her past. She wrote as though presenting an argument, conceding her point so that she could gain credibility by anticipating her readers' doubts:

> Next, i would like to explain how i "know" for those who don't believe me. Yes, i am a virgin, no you don't need to have sex to know your sexuality!
>   So, just recently i was thinking about this bi verses lesbian buisness, and i was trying to figure out if i really did fall under the bi catagory. Then i thought—fuck it! why do i need to figure out who exactly i am at this point? Why can't i say i'm open to either sex at this point? (Because I am) I think I've been leaning towards girls more lately, which is fine with me. Although, I always have a guy or two in mind :) And come to think of it, of all people, my mom described it perfectly to me—she said—"You may not feel this way, but what i'm sensing is that you are attracted to a certain type of person, regaurdless of gender." And i couldn't have worded it better myself. Yeah Mom!

It is interesting that Caitlin referenced her erratic interest in each gender and that she gave her rationale as though it should make perfect sense. Of course you should like someone for who they are, not what they are, she seemed to intimate. In so stating, Caitlin resists cultural pressures that she must choose one sex (preferably male) over the other. It is also noteworthy that she acknowledges her lack of sexual experience. Perhaps Caitlin included this information to persuade her audience (and perhaps even herself) that her sexual orientation is inherent and self-evident. Her commentary seems the culmination of much thinking about who she is and who she wants to be, and her ability to publicly present her logic may reassure Caitlin that her argument is reasonable.

Jen likewise took advantage of her home page to editorialize about sexuality, even titling one of her essays "Sexuality." Her statement was less organized and defiant than Caitlin's, perhaps because Jen was not defending herself, but a lifestyle she finds acceptable for others. Jen outlined the conflicting ideas she encounters in her real life regarding sexual orientation. She wrote:

> It's really stupid, the things people say. The stupidest of them all must be that "if you're not homophobic, you must be gay". . . . So I'm not gay. I don't fit into the ideal riot grrl picture, but whatever. I don't really go for cliches anyways. The guys I hang out with try to get a rise out of me by calling me a lesbian, but I could really care less, I just agree with them and let them figure it out for themselves. . . . I'm not homophobic. I don't see why I should be. It would really suck if I was, considering that enough of my friends are gay or bi. I just don't see why anyone cares.

Jen identified just one of the many contradictions she is likely to observe between accepted societal norms (homosexuality is something to be made fun of) and her own lived experience (some of her own friends are homosexual). She explained she "could really care less" about sexual orientation, yet her designation of an entire page in her Web site about the topic suggests otherwise.

Jen's and Caitlin's original writings imply that they are beginning to establish personal beliefs based on real-life experience (e.g., bisexuality is fine), and yet they find it difficult to completely discard the more mainstream expectations they have likely encountered their whole lives (girls should like boys). They effectively distance themselves by placing these essays in a distinct section of their home page that is clearly separated from such autobiographical writing as the biography and journal. They seem prepared to state their opinions in the relative "safety" of the WWW, where their real identities are somewhat protected. For example, Jen concluded her essay with a weak call to arms: "I wish I could change the world and get rid of homophobia, because it is stupid. Get over it. But I can't change the world, although I can try. So here's my efforts: if you're homophobic, stop that!"

Poetry was another frequent component of the original writing sections of girls' home pages. Like their essays, poetry allowed the girls to address serious and intimate matters without claiming personal authenticity. Although it seemed likely that much of the girls' poetry was based on personal experience, the genre provided a dimension of obscurity not possible in biographical and journal formats. That is, the scope of topics girls broached in their poetry may have been wider than in other forms of expression on their home pages because poetry is not intrinsically and expectedly self-descriptive. Indeed, it was in their poetry that girls addressed those ideas and feelings that American culture tends to teach them to repress or deny, such as sexual desire and physical pleasure. In their poetry, girls could express these "unladylike" feelings with the reassurance that, if necessary, they could deny their personal applicability. Amelia's poetry, for example, frequently referenced one of the least-discussed topics relevant to adolescent girls' sexuality: lesbian sexual pleasure. A final stanza of one of her poems read:

> violet on my bed
> arms and bras and sweaters
> and the glowing light
> of my phone off the hook
> she is under me
> at one a.m.
> in my room

Like Amelia's, most of the poems on the girls' home pages detailed sexual desire, pleasure, and confusion, topics less blatantly (if at all) approached in the other home page sections. Jen's poem, entitled "My Only," provided another example:

> at every minute
> you're always on my mind
> my longing
> not turned to despair
> like it was for him
> you're always in my heart
> you make me so . . .
> i know it's love because
> i thought i'd melt that night
> ready, waiting for you
> just to surround you
> to feel the thrust
> and the touch
> of your perfect lips
> soft fingertips
> blue eyes
> make me feel pretty
> maybe i'm not
> but you need me now
> i'll take your release.

Although girls have written about similar topics for decades (if not centuries; Brumberg, 1997; Thompson, 1995), their opportunity to showcase them before the public eye has been limited to such cloistered locations as bathroom stalls. Scholars have, indeed, developed a surprisingly large body of literature about such graffiti, coined *latrinalia*; and sexual expression has been identified as the most prominent of all topics addressed in girls' bathrooms (Anderson & Verplanck, 1983; Gadsby, 1996; Otta, 1993; Paretti, Carter, & McClinton, 1977; Schreer & Strichartz, 1997). Girl's home pages, although similar to graffiti in their potential anonymity, provide a potentially more diverse audience for them and also allow for more permanent and lengthy exhibitions.

Photo Galleries and Music Archives

The images and music the girls represented on their home pages reveal a great deal about how they would like to be seen (sometimes literally) and with whom they would like to be affiliated. Although a few of the girls posted "real-life" photographs of themselves or their friends, far more common was the appropriation of mass media representations, ranging from photographs of celebrities to song lyrics to "real audio" clips to scanned CD covers. Leigh Ann's "Moffatt Pics" section of her home page was scattered with images of her favorite music group, the Moffatt Brothers, a rock band of four brothers. Caitlin's page exhibited scanned photographs of all her favorite musicians, ranging from Bob Marley and Tori Amos to Bob Dylan and Dar Williams. Dana portrayed a large image of Courtney Love from the band Hole. Some of the girls included captions for the images ("Scott was born on March 30 and he's 15 yrs. old! He's the oldest Moffatt and he is the leader in a way"), although others merely posted images without commentary.

The photo galleries and musical archives provided a view of girls both as mass media users and mass media producers. Indeed, in these sections of their home pages, girls' roles intermingle; a girl can produce entire portions of her site by appropriating media materials that simultaneously document her use and her understanding of them. Steele and Brown (1995) suggested that media artifacts such as posters and pictures serve to ". . . remind teens of who they are, while at the same time telegraphing to parents and friends the selves they are constructing" (p. 567). Steele and Brown examined girls' bedrooms to learn how adolescent girls use media to construct their identities. Girls' home pages resemble bedrooms in that they frequently draw from media resources to construct a sense of who they are. Indeed, the WWW allows for greater physical appropriation of media materials than ever before. Adolescents who create their own home pages can present entire collages of media products merely by clicking on an image on another web page and saving it to a file, accumulating pictures of events, places, and personalities to paste onto their pages.

Not only do media representations on girls' home pages speak to their authors' media preferences, but they also allow the girls to communicate to their online audience how and with whom they would like to be identified. For example, Kate's references to Marilyn Manson (a heavy metal, self-described anti-Christian musician) helped distinguish her from Leigh Ann, an evident fan of the Backstreet Boys and Moffatt Brothers (clean-cut, all-boy, music groups). These diverse representations of taste help signal to other Web users girls' affiliation with particular subcultures (Larson, 1995).

Interestingly, not only did the home pages frequently reference a musical celebrity about whom their authors romanticized (i.e., Leigh-Ann's love for the Moffatt Brothers), but many of these pages also included images of women with whom the girls would like to be associated. Many of the women celebrities cited are well known for their free-spoken sexuality. Ani DiFranco, for example, is a celebrated bisexual musician whose song lyrics often address the difficulty of (as she writes in one song) being a member of "more than one club." Caitlin, who has recently discovered her own bisexuality, included representations of Ani DiFranco (photographs, song lyrics) intermittently throughout her site as well as in her "Music" and "Photos" sections. Her representations reflected her identification with DiFranco and her interest in connecting herself with a popular and accepted bisexual. For example, before she listed the lyrics for one of DiFranco's songs, Caitlin explained, "I like Ani DiFranco. No, I love Ani DiFranco. What can i say, i have an obsession." Her e-mail address is also a derivative of DiFranco's name (AniDchica@. . .).

Not all representations appropriated from the mass media by the girls in this study glamorized sexuality issues. Jen, for example, designed a game to provide commentary about impossible beauty standards. She called the game "Make Kate Fat," and it began with a picture of the famous "waif" model, Kate Moss. Visitors to Jen's site could decide what Kate Moss should eat (i.e., hamburger or hot dog), and each time they selected a food by clicking on it, Kate's image would be enhanced to make her look heavier. By the game's end, Kate Moss is an overweight woman. Although body image was addressed in many of the girls' sites (i.e., musings about weight loss in online journals), Jen's use of images to convey her frustration with unhealthy appearance ideals is simultaneously poignant and humorous. The game is also a fitting example of how Web technology allows for innovative, interactive, self-expression.

Guest Books

Girls' guest books on their home pages included the fewest sexual representations of any section in the home pages. This comes as little surprise, considering that most guest book commentary is written by home page visitors, rather than by the authors. What was interesting about the girls' guest books, however, was the degree to which most of the girls solicited feedback about their sites and the views espoused within them ("Please sign my guestbook!"). They seem eager for feedback and for a sense that the self they present on their home pages is both understood and appreciated.

Not only did the girls include guest books on their home pages for their visitors to sign, but many also posted their signed guest books for their visitors to peruse. In addition to leaving my own message, for example, I could visit Dana's signed guest book to see how others have responded to her home page. These responses provided a window on both the confirming and annoying responses girls with home pages received. Although many of the responses in girls' guest books were vague ("cool site") and kind ("you look nice and pretty. email me"), some responses were hostile and accusatory ("this page fucking sucks. . . . you are just a bitter little girl who is jealous of everyone who is better at the things you pretend to be good at . . ."). Some commentary, however, reacted directly to the content of girls' home pages and touched on issues relevant to girls' developing identity and their navigation through adolescence. Jen, for example, wrote at length in her home page about her disdain for people who discussed depression and suicide on their home pages, characterizing such people as sensationalistic and pathetic. Numerous girls responded to this commentary, and one outraged girl wrote:

> ok . . . i saw most of yer website. After the "depression" article, though, i lost interest. Since i myself have a website and on the website there is a page for my thoughts on my deppression, manic-deppression, drug use, suicide attempts, and self-mutilation yer comments were meant for me or someone like me. Do you really believe someone would "fake" attempting suicide just for attention? Yeah i guess your right. I LOVE looking at the scars from 8 stitches on my left wrist. I felt i needed something a little "extra" and just being sad is so pase'. C'mon kids lets all die! No honey . . . just because you don't understand the reasoning for broadcasting your pain (maybe you were looking for someone to say, it's ok. Maybe it might help someone to know that their not alone.)

Responses like these likely compel girls to reconsider the views they present on their home pages and perhaps even their understanding of their own emotions and experiences. They may also help girls gain a better understanding of the responsibility of public expression.

LINKS AND WEB RINGS

Links, a feature truly distinctive of the WWW, were present but not prevalent on girls' home pages. The most common type of links girls presented was to other girls' home pages. The girls seemed to seek to create a community of teens, and they promoted one another's pages in apparent understanding that the favor would be reciprocated. For most of the girls, merely linking to others' sites seemed insufficient because many belonged to multiple web rings as well. Web rings interlink a series of individual Web sites to one another. Visitors who happen onto a site in a web ring need only click on the ring's icon to be carried to a similar site. Web rings ensure that the girls will receive more visitors to their home pages because the number of gateways into their pages is boosted through their web ring memberships (Basch, 1998).

Most of the web rings to which the girls in this study belonged were specifically about adolescence or sexuality. Anastasia belonged to "Femme Fatales," a ring of "girls' diaries or real lives, real stories." Dana was a member of more than a dozen web rings, including "Eat my fuck," "I am Angry," "[gerl]," "Stronger girls" and "Revolution Grrl-Style." Each of these rings either explicitly or implicitly projected a self-identity, most often from an alternative, feminist, and/or liberal bent. As with their media appropriations in their photo galleries and music archives, it seems that the girls used their rings to ally themselves with a community of like-minded others. Much like wearing a particular brand of clothing or engaging in "alternative" behaviors (i.e., smoking, skateboarding, etc.), the girls signaled their subculture affiliations through their web ring memberships.

Despite the prominence of web rings and links to other home pages, many of the girls also linked to organizations that aim to improve, celebrate, or build awareness of issues concerning sexuality. Dana, for instance, linked to a site for rape abuse and incest; several of the other girls linked to alternative girl sites (i.e., ChickClick at http://www.chickclick.com) whose site creators aim to provide girls with information and entertainment rarely offered to them from mainstream media.

"WINDOWS ON THE AUTHOR'S FOREHEAD"

To conclude that girls are using their WWW home pages to explore and discuss sexuality (among other topics) is an understatement. In fact, the girls in this study clearly engage in web authorship to document an identity in which sexuality plays a major role. They even have established conventions for appropriate sexual expression in the various sections of their home pages. Biographies include reflective, explicit, descriptions of self, and original writings range from sensitive poetry to outspoken social critiques. Photo galleries depict snapshots of real-life sweethearts and adored celebrities, and music archives commemorate favorite performers with whom girls most identify, or whom they fancy. Guest books allow site visitors to comment on the girls' pages, encouraging girls to reflect on their expressive representations on their pages; links to various sites on the WWW suggest girls' affiliations with various sexual communities or subcultures that espouse particular identities. Web ring memberships imply girls' committed relationship to a cooperative of sites that share common themes or philosophies.

The girls seem to take strategic advantage of different expressive modes (e.g., poetry, journals, etc.) to define and/or distinguish their self-identities.

Indeed, in all facets of their pages, as perhaps in their lives, the girls who create home pages are broadcasting a sense of their developing selves—selves that inherently intersect with sexuality in adolescence. The WWW's ability to provide girls with an arena in which to document their passage through adolescence is even more extraordinary, given that home pages are living documents that can be updated as often as desired.

Overall, it appears that the girls use their home pages to say what they could have said before, indeed in the very ways they might have said it before, but with one distinct difference: Home pages grant them the potential for a large audience. The importance of speaking and being heard seems paramount for the girls who create home pages—as Jocelyn explained:

> You may want to ask me, "Why do you do this? Why do you share your inmost thoughts with the entire world?" Frankly, I think it's theraputic [sic]. It helps me to realize that I'm not the only one out there, that we're all connected through our experiences. It's great to meet someone, whether it be in real life or on the Internet, who has shared your experience, who *knows* how you feel and who can relate to you. Somehow the knowledge that there's someone else like you who shared how you feel, makes it a whole lot better.... [Home pages] ... are more like windows on the author's forehead, allowing you to look inside and see another person's thoughts.

Indeed, home pages offer a window-like view into a space we might otherwise be blocked from seeing. Girls' home pages, in particular, provide a look at many aspects of girls' lives that often go unseen, especially "inappropriate" aspects, such as sexuality. Their apparent willingness to design the very windows from which we can look inside their "forehead[s]" and hear their stories of sexuality suggests they are eager for an audience to see what they have to say about being female, adolescent, and sexual.

REFERENCES

Ahmed, S. (1981). Graffiti of Canadian high school students. *Psychological Reports, 49*, 559–562.

Altheide, D. (1996). Qualitative media analysis. *Qualitative research methods series, 38*. Newbury Park, CA: Sage.

Anderson, S., & Verplanck, W. (1983). When walls speak, what do they say? *The Psychological Record, 33*, 341–359.

Ball, M., & Smith, G. (1992). *Analyzing visual data*. Thousand Oaks, CA: Sage.

Bancroft, J., & Reinisch, J. (Eds.). (1990). *Adolescence and puberty*. New York: Oxford University Press.

Basch, R. (1998). Ring around the Web. *Computer Life, 4*(1), 62–64.

Berger, A. (1991). *Media analysis techniques*. Thousand Oaks, CA: Sage.

Brown, L. M., & Gilligan, C. (1992). *Meeting at the crossroads: Women's psychology development*. Cambridge, MA: Harvard University Press.

Brumberg, J. (1997). *The body project*. New York: Random House.

Card, J. (Ed.). (1993). *Handbook of adolescent sexuality and pregnancy: Research and evaluation instruments*. Newbury Park, CA: Sage.

Christensen, P. G., & Roberts, D. F. (1998). The nature of adolescence: Myths and realities. In P. G. Christensen & D. F. Roberts (Eds.), *It's not only rock & roll: Popular music in the lives of adolescents*. Cresskill, NJ: Hampton Press.

Chu, J. (1997). Navigating the media environment: How youth claim a place through zines. *Social Justice, 24*(3), 71–76.

Dorman, S. (1998). Technology and the gender gap. *Journal of School Health, 68*(4), p. 165(2).

Evard, M. (1996). "So please stop, thank you": Girls online. In L. Cherny & R. Weise (Eds.), *Wired women*. Seattle, WA: Seal Press.

Fine, M. (1988). Sexuality, schooling and adolescent females: The missing discourse of desire. *Harvard Educational Review, 58*(1), 29–53.

Furger, R. (1998). *Does Jane compute? Preserving our daughter's place in the cyber revolution*. New York: Warner Books.

Gadsby, J. (1996). Master's thesis. York University, Canada.

Gray, M. (1995). *Measuring the growth of the Web*. http://www.mit.edu/people/mkgraw/growth. Accessed May 3, 1999.

Green, K., & Taormino, T. (Eds.). (1997). *A girl's guide to taking over the world*. New York: St. Martin's Griffin.

Gross, D. (1994, September 5). Zine but not heard. *Time, 144*(10), 68–70.

Gunderloy, M. (1990). Zines. Where the action is: The very small press in America. *Whole Earth Review, 68*, 58–61.

Haffner, D. (1998). Facing facts: Sexual health for American adolescents. *Journal of Adolescent Health, 22*, 453–459.

Hodder, I. (1998). The interpretation of documents and material culture. In N. Denzin & Y. Lincoln (Eds.), *Collecting & interpreting qualitative materials* (pp. 110–129). Thousand Oaks, CA: Sage.

Horovitz, B. (1999, May 17). Marketing "where girls live." *USA Today*, pp. 1A, 2A.

Inness, S. (Ed.). (1998). *Delinquents & debutantes: Twentieth-century American girls' cultures*. New York: New York University Press.

Jupiter Communications (1999, June). *Kids and teens spend $1.3 billion online in 2002* [Press release]. Available: http://www.jupitercommunications.com/jupiter/press/releases/1999/0607.html

Koch, P. (1993). Promoting healthy sexual development during early adolescence. In R. Lerner (Ed.), *Early adolescence: Perspectives on research, policy and intervention* (pp. 293–307). Hillsdale, NJ: Lawrence Erlbaum Associates.

Larson, R. (1995). Secrets in the bedroom: Adolescents' private use of media. *Journal of Youth and Adolescence, 24*(5), 535–550.

Lindsay, L. (1996). *Web page design*. Electronic document. Accessed April 7, 1999. URL: http://gw3.epnet.com/fulltext.asp?...lyze%20or%20evaluate%29&fuzzyTerm=

Luna, C. (1987). Welcome to my nightmare. *Society, 24*, 73–79.

Markus, H., & Nurius, P. (1986). Possible selves. *American Psychology Society*, (24)7, 73–79.

Masserman, J., & Uribe, M. (1989). (Eds.), *Adolescent sexuality*. Springfield, IL: Thomas.

National Science Foundation. (1997). *U.S. teens and technology*. [Poll conducted by Gallup; executive summary by NSF in conjunction with CNN and *USA Today*]. Available: http://www.nsf.gov/od/lpa/nstw/teenov.htm

Orenstein, P. (1994). *School girls: Young women, self-esteem, and the confidence gap*. New York: Doubleday.

Otta, E. (1993). Graffiti in the 1990s: A study of inscriptions on restroom walls. *Journal of Social Psychology, 133*(4), 589–590.

Papert, S. (1996). *The connected family: Bridging the digital generation gap*. Atlanta, GA: Longstreet Press.

Paretti, P., Carter, R., & McClinton, B. (1977). Graffiti and adolescent personality. *Adolescence, 7*(45), 31–42.

Pastor, J., McCormick, J., & Fine, M. (1996). Makin' homes: An urban girl thing. In B. R. Leadbeater & N. Way (Eds.), *Urban girls: Resisting stereotypes, creating identities*. New York: New York University Press.

Patton, M. (1990). *Qualitative evaluation and research methods* (2nd ed.). Newbury Park, CA: Sage.

Phillips, L. (1998). *The girls report: What we know & need to know about growing up female*. New York: The National Council for Research on Women.

Pipher, M. (1994). *Reviving Ophelia: Saving the selves of adolescent girls*. New York: Ballantine.

Schreer, G., & Strichartz, J. (1997). Private restroom graffiti: An analysis of controversial social issues on two college campuses. *Psychological Reports, 81*, 1067–1074.

Sherman, A. (1998). *Cybergrrl: A woman's guide to the World Wide Web*. New York: Ballantine.

Steele, J., & Brown, J. (1995). Adolescent room culture: Studying media in the context of everyday life. *Journal of Youth and Adolescence, 24*(5), 551–576.

Steinberg, L. (1993). *Adolescence* (3rd ed.). New York: McGraw-Hill.

Stern, S. (in press). Adolescent girls' expression on WWW home pages: A qualitative analysis. *Convergence: The Journal of Research Into New Media Technologies*.

Strauss, A., & Corbin, J. (1994). Grounded theory methodology. In N. Denzin & Y. Lincoln (Eds.), *Handbook of qualitative research* (pp. 273–285). Thousand Oaks, CA: Sage.

Tapscott, D. (1998). *Growing up digital*. New York: McGraw-Hill.

Taylor, J., Gilligan, C., & Sullivan, A. (1995). *Between voice and silence: Women and girls, race and relationship*. Cambridge, MA: Harvard University Press.

Thompson, S. (1995). *Going all the way: Teenage girls' tales of sex, romance & pregnancy*. New York: Hill and Wang.

Tolman, D., & Higgins, T. (1996). How being a good girl can be bad for girls. In N. Maglin & D. Perry (Eds.), *"Bad girls," "good girls": Women, sex & power in the nineties*. New Brunswick, NJ: Rutgers University Press.

Turkle, S. (1995). *Life on the screen: Identity in the age of the Internet*. New York: Simon & Schuster.

Turow, J. (1999). *The Internet and the family: The view from parents, the view from the press* (Report Series No. 27). Philadelphia: The Annenberg Public Policy Center of the University of Pennsylvania.

Wagner, C. (January/February, 1998). Grrls' revolution: Young girls turn to self-publishing for self-expression. *The Futurist, 32*(1), 12.

Wynn, E., & Katz, J. (1997). Hyperbole over cyberspace. *The Information Society, 13*, 297–327.

Author Index

A

Abma, J., 5, 6, *22*
Abt, V., 87, *92*
Adivi, C., 35, 36, 44, 50, *54*
Aggleton, P., 35, *53*
Ahmed, S., *283*
AhYun, J., 82, 84, 86, 87, *93*
Allensworth, D. D., 183, *188*
Alterman, E., 184, *188*
Altheide, D., 269, *283*
Amonker, R. G., 27, 28*t*, 29, 30, *52*
Anderson, L., 244, *251*
Anderson, S., 278, *283*
Angell, E., 228, *251*
Antecol, M., 237, *251*
Appiah, O., 234, *251*
Arnett, J. J., 258, 259, 261, *263*
Arnould, E. J., 233, *252*
Austin, E., 21, *22*
Austin, L. J., 128, *149*

B

Babakus, E., 174, *188*
Bachen, C. M., 212, 213, 214, *224*
Baker, R., 185, *188*
Baldo, M., 35, *53*
Ball, M., 269, *283*
Ball-Rokeach, S. J., 131, *148*
Bancroft, J., *283*
Bandura, A., 16, *22*, 61, *76*, 97, *121*, 131, *147*
Bankole, A., 19, *24*
Baran, S. J., 61, *77*, 118, *121*
Barth, G. P., 39, *54*
Barth, R. P., 36, 42, *53*, *54*
Basch, R., 270, 282, *283*
Basil, M. D., 97, 98, 99, *121*

Batten, M., 168, *170*
Bauchner, H., 37, 38, 50, *54*
Becker, M. H., 186, *188*
Begun, B., 228, *251*
Bell, R. M., 49, *54*
Berger, A., 212, *224*, 269, *283*
Berger, J., 228, *251*
Berns, L. A., 35, *53*
Bhalla, S. K., 136, 137*f*, *148*
Bhapkar, G., 2, *23*
Biely, E., 60, 75, 77, 96, *122*
Biocca, F., 97, *121*, 129, *149*
Black, D., 256, *264*
Blackman, S. L., 174, *188*
Blouin, A. G., 131, *147*
Blum, R. W., 4, *22*
Blumenthal, E., 66, *78*
Boardman, B., 37, 38, 50, *54*
Bordony, M. V., 2, *23*
Brand, J. E., 235, *251*
Brigham, J., 99, 100, *121*
Brodie, M., 258, *264*
Brooks-Gunn, J., 126, *148*
Brown, B. B., 29, 38, 39, 49, 50, *53*
Brown, C., 199, *208*
Brown, J. D., 2, 15, 16, 17, *22*, 43, 44, 45, 50,
    52, *53*, 60, 61, *76*, 77, 97, 98, 99,
    100, 120, *121*, *123*, 156, 170, *171*,
    174, *188*, 214, *225*, 228, 229, 233,
    251, *252*, 263, *264*, 279, *285*
Brown, L. M., *283*
Brumberg, J. J., 126, 146, *148*, 268, 278, *283*
Bruzzone, L., 258, *264*
Bryant, J., 15, *24*, 61, 77
Bryant, W., 20, *22*
Buerkel-Rothfuss, N., 17, *24*, 43, 45, 50, *53*,
    61, *77*, 214, *225*
Bultman, L., 35, 49, *53*
Burggraf, K., 126, 129, *148*

287

Subject Index

A

AANCHOR (An Alternative National Curriculum on Responsibility), 35
ABC network, 11
Abortion
    female-oriented magazines, 160, 161*t*, 163, 165
    rates of, 7
Ace Ventura, 236
Adolescence
    cultural perceptions of, 2, 7–8
    overview, 2
    sexual activity and
        abortion, 7
        AIDS, 6, 155
        attractiveness, 4–5
        chlamydia, 6
        condoms, 6
        contraception, 6, 7
        cultural differences, 3, 7–8
        cultural norms, 3–4
        dating, 5
        gender differences, 3–4, 5–7, 154–155
        genital herpes, 7
        gonorrhea, 6, 7
        HIV, 6, 7, 155
        homosexuality, 5, 6
        intercourse, 5
        kissing, 5
        pregnancy rates, 7, 155
        racial differences, 7
        rape, 6
        sexually transmitted diseases (STDs), 6–7, 155
        touching, 5
    stages of

adulthood, 2–3
    early, 2
    gender differences, 2
    late, 2
    menarche, 2
    middle, 2
    "tween," 2
    summary, 21–22
Advocates for Youth, 51, 52
African Americans, *see also* Racial differences
    birth rates, 7
    music videos, 15
    television, 13
Age differences
    movies
        interaction with, 241
        selection of, 236–237
    music, 257–258
    music videos, 257–258
    Seventeen, 198–199
    television, 98, 99, 112
AIDS
    contraception and
        parents, 39, 41–42
        peers, 39
        school programs, 36, 37
    female-oriented magazines
        importance of, 157
        teen vs. women's, 160, 161*t*, 163, 166
    rates of, 6, 155
American Academy of Pediatricians (AAP), 21
American Social Health Association, 51
Anorexia nervosa, 4–5
Apollo 13, 15
Arguments, 217–218, 219, 221, 222
A River Runs Through It